Coping with Job Loss

Coping with Job Loss

How Individuals, Organizations, and Communities Respond to Layoffs

Carrie R. Leana
Daniel C. Feldman

Lexington Books

An Imprint of Macmillan, Inc.
NEW YORK
Maxwell Macmillan Canada
TORONTO
Maxwell Macmillan International
NEW YORK · OXFORD · SINGAPORE · SYDNEY

This book is part of the Lexington Book Issues in Organization and Management Series, Arthur P. Brief and Benjamin Schneider, general editors.

Library of Congress Cataloging-in-Publication Data

Leana, Carrie R.
  Coping with job loss : how individuals, organizations, and
communities respond to layoffs / Carrie R. Leana and Daniel C.
Feldman.

        p.   cm.—(Issues in organization and management series)
    Includes bibliographical references.
    ISBN 0-669-16569-7
    1. Unemployed—United States—Case studies.   2.   Employees—United
States—Dismissal of—Case studies.   3. Layoff systems—United
States—Case studies.   I. Feldman, Daniel C. II. Title.
III. Series
    HD5708.55.U6L43   1992
    331.13'7—dc20   91-39072
                                          CIP

Lexington Books
An Imprint of Macmillan, Inc.
866 Third Avenue, New York, N.Y. 10022

Maxwell Macmillan Canada, Inc.
1200 Eglinton Avenue East
Suite 200
Don Mills, Ontario M3C 3N1

Macmillan, Inc. is part of the Maxwell Communication Group of Companies.

Printed in the United States of America

printing number

1   2   3   4   5   6   7   8   9   10

For David Goldman and Shirley Feldman

Contents

List of Tables and Figures

TABLES

FIGURES

Foreword

Coping with Job Loss is a timely and important book. This book is timely because, as American industry changes, increasingly large numbers of workers will experience job loss due to plant closings, restructurings, mergers, geographical relocation, and so forth. Regardless of the cause of the job loss, workers will have to cope with the experience. This book is important because it documents the way workers *do* cope with job loss. Thus, the results of Carrie Leana and Daniel Feldman's research identify how management decisions and attributes of the workers themselves relate to the effectiveness with which workers cope with their job loss.

Leana and Feldman studied the job loss experiences of workers in two settings: the aerospace industry surrounding the Kennedy Space Center following the *Challenger* disaster and the steel industry in the Monongahela Valley of western Pennsylvania. For both sites, Leana and Feldman provide rich descriptions of the settings both before and after the immediate job loss experiences on which they focus and of the individual, family, and community reactions to the job loss.

Leana and Feldman provide great insight into the ways by which management decisions about handling the layoffs influence worker reactions to those layoffs. In addition, they document how different individuals really react quite differently to the job loss experience—some seeing it as a new challenge, others experiencing it as a damaging blow to their self-esteem; in short, how some rise to the challenge and others fail to.

This book is a wonderful example of how sensitive interviewers can make a painful experience come alive for readers without sacrificing objectivity. Indeed, by combining the interviews they conducted with the data they collected, they impart both a qualitative and quantitative understanding of the job loss experience.

Coping with Job Loss is both interesting and informative; it is both conceptually and practically useful; and it is timely and important. We welcome this book to our series and are glad to be able to present it to a wide readership.

Benjamin Schneider
Arthur P. Brief

1

Introduction

This book is about layoffs. It is about people who lose their jobs due to plant closings, work slowdowns, corporate downsizings, or mergers and acquisitions. It is about the institutions that play a major role in determining whether layoffs will occur and/or how they will be implemented—the corporations, the unions, state and federal unemployment agencies, and the legislatures. It is also, to some extent, about the people other than the laid-off workers who are affected by their unemployment—their spouses, children, parents, friends, co-workers and the members of their communities. In short, it is about what it means to lose a job because of factors outside one's personal control, and start life over again.

The Dimensions of the Problem

The recessions of the 1980s and early 1990s have focused attention once again on the problem of layoffs in the United States. Between 1980 and 1985, almost 2.5 million jobs were lost each year because of plant shutdowns, layoffs, and eliminations of positions.[1] In the first half of the 1980s, large numbers of these layoffs occurred in the so-called Rust Belt industries, such as steel and automobile manufacturing. Many of the corporations experiencing the largest layoffs—U.S. Steel, General Motors, Chrysler, Ford—cited competitive pressures from abroad, outdated technology, high labor costs, and shortsighted government policies as reasons for their downsizing programs. These layoffs were not widespread throughout the economy as a whole, but where they occurred, their effects were severe. It was not unusual for thousands of employees to be laid off at one time and entire communities rendered insolvent by a single plant closing.

The second half of the 1980s showed a somewhat different pattern. From 1985 to 1988, over a third of the Fortune 1,000 companies surveyed reduced their work forces 10 percent each year. Layoffs typically involved hundreds, rather than thousands, of workers at a time. Unlike the earlier downsizings, which were blamed on national or international business conditions, fewer than half of the personnel cuts in 1989 were attributed to a "business downturn." More and more companies were reducing their work forces, instead, to realize productivity gains or to save money by cutting personnel after a merger or acquisition.[2]

It is instructive, as well, to recognize who is most vulnerable to layoffs: hourly workers in large manufacturing firms. In the typical workforce reduction, 50 percent of those discharged are hourly employees; the remaining workers divide evenly among supervisory and middle management personnel, senior managers, technicians, and professionals. Twelve percent of the reported downsizings in 1989 affected only hourly employees; in a third of all downsizings, more than three-quarters of those discharged were hourly workers. Workers in large, manufacturing firms were more vulnerable than employees of smaller firms and employees in the service and not-for-profit sectors.[3]

What does the furture hold? First, downsizing will continue to be "an ongoing corporate activity, often practiced without regard to immediate profit performance."[4] In the American Management Association survey cited earlier, 30 percent of the firms that downsized planned to repeat the exercise. Reductions-in-force are no longer considered last-resort practices, but rather are ongoing corporate interventions designed to boost profitability.

Second, although blue-collar workers are still the most vulnerable to layoffs, their white-collar colleagues are catching up quickly. The merger mania of the mid-1980s focused top management's attention on middle- and upper-middle management as places to cut costs during restructuring and reorganization. AT&T cut its work force 10 percent (32,000 employees) to save $1 billion annually; twelve thousand of those laid off were managers. IT&T cut its workforce 44 percent (100,000 employees); headquarters staff was slashed from 850 to 350.[5] In the wake of the stock market crash of 1987, tens of thousands of stock brokers, investment counselors, and research analysts were laid off. Estimates suggest that about a quarter of a million managers with salaries over $40,000 lose their jobs each year.[6]

Third, unemployment as a fact of life will continue, if not worsen. Current statistics on unemployment and layoffs underestimate the dimensions of the problem. Even with unemployment of 6 percent, there would still be 7 million people out of work. Because government statistics do not include the discouraged job seekers (individuals who have stopped applying for new positions) and those who have joined the expanding ranks of the permanently unemployed, these figures vastly underrepresent the number of people actually out of work.[7] Furthermore, many of those who get new jobs are substantially underemployed (employed at jobs requiring significantly fewer skills and paying significantly lower wages than the jobs they lost). Many of these workers completely deplete their assets and never recover financially from their layoffs.[8] Thus, although layoffs during the 1990s may be done with "scalpels, not axes," it is clear the surgery will be performed regularly, even if not so dramatically as in the 1980s.[9]

Previous Research on Job Loss

Current research on layoffs and job loss is heavily influenced by research conducted during the Depression. Assumptions about the causes and consequences of job loss that inform much of the current research are grounded in the peculiar circumstances of the 1930s.

First, because unemployment was so widespread in the 1930s, much more attention was paid to aggregate differences between the employed and unemployed than to differences among the unemployed. Much of the research on job loss, for example, looked at differences in the psychological well-being of the employed and the unemployed to document the adverse effects of layoffs on workers; much less attention was paid to the differential impact of job loss on individuals depending on their own circumstances.

Second, unemployment in the Depression was recognized as a devastating blow to workers and their families. Thus, much of the research on job loss focused on documenting just how devastating job loss had been, rather than on explaining how and why unemployment causes the psychological distress that it does.

Third, because the Depression was a national economic disaster of unequaled proportions, much of the research on unemployment was conducted by labor economists. This research highlighted, for example, the relationship between national economic indicators and the incidence of admittances to mental hospitals,[10] the economic conditions under which job loss is most likely to occur,[11] and barriers to reemployment.[12] The links between macroeconomic factors and individual psychological factors were less extensively studied.

Fourth, because the Depression was so obviously the cause of unemployment in the 1930s, the unemployed were usually seen as passive victims of forces largely outside their own control; the psychological research focused largely on how individuals reacted to unemployment emotionally. Thus, we know relatively little about the types of initiatives individuals take to lessen the consequences of unemployment, and little about how effective these individual initiatives might be.

Fifth, to the extent that institutions were examined as sources of assistance to the unemployed, the research on unemployment looked at the federal government, particularly in the context of financial assistance programs. With the massive economic dislocations of the Depression, it is not surprising that researchers focused on that issue. It is only more recently that some attention has turned to the initiatives corporations, unions, and community political action groups can take to ameliorate some of the consequences of job loss. Similarly, it is only recently that the role of local and state governments has been fully explored, and that the role of the federal government in terms of providing non-welfare assistance (in the form of training incentives, corporate rehiring incentives, and plant closing disincentives) has been more thoroughly examined.

After a very long hiatus of extensive research on unemployment during the relatively high employment decades of the 1940s, 1950s and 1960s, the recessions of the 1970s and 1980s returned the topics of layoffs and job loss to the forefront. That research has focused on both: (1) the negative consequences of job loss for the psychological and physical well-being of the unemployed; and (2) the negative consequences of job loss for the spouse, children, friends, and co-workers of the laid-off employee. In addition, the more recent research examined the moderating effects of individual factors, (e.g., personality traits) and situational factors (e.g., outplacement assistance) that may ameliorate or worsen the effects of layoffs. The findings on each of these issues are briefly summarized below.

Negative Consequences of Layoffs for the Unemployed

On virtually every indicator of mental and physical health, job loss has a negative impact. People who have lost their jobs have been found to be more anxious, depressed, unhappy, and dissatisfied with life in general.[13] The unemployed have been found to have lowered self-esteem, to be more short-tempered, to be more fatalistic, and to be more pessimistic about the future.[14] In longitudinal studies of the unemployed, researchers have found that the unemployed have more psychological distress symptoms than those who have jobs, and that an individual's mental health worsens when he or she is laid off.[15] The evidence that unemployment has a substantial and negative impact on the psychological health of workers is consistent and convincing.

The research shows that layoffs may also negatively affect workers' physical well-being, although perhaps not so dramatically. Job loss seems to have the strongest effects on psychosomatic illnesses, such as sleeping disorders, eating disorders, overuse of sedatives, dermatitis, headaches, and listlessness.[16] Unemployment also has sizeable negative impacts on physical problems that contribute to more major illnesses, such as higher blood pressure, increased heart rate, palpitations, and ulcers.[17] Somewhat less pronounced links between unemployment and hospitalization rates, morbidity, and mortality have also been documented.[18] Thus, job loss is clearly not good for one's physical health, although people who are younger and healthier at the time of their layoff can be expected to weather their unemployment in somewhat better physical shape.

Impact on Family, Friends, and Co-workers

Over the last two decades increased attention has been paid to the impact of layoffs on those close to the unemployed. The research suggests that the negative consequences of job loss ripple outward to affect family, friends, and co-workers as well.

SPOUSES AND CHILDREN. As we discuss in more detail in Chapter 5, most of the research on unemployed workers has focused on males. Thus, the research on the impact of job loss on spouses has focused almost entirely on wives. Several consistent findings have emerged from this research.

First, wives of the unemployed suffer psychological problems similar to those of their husbands, albeit not with the same intensity or immediacy. Wives, too, often experience an increase in hostility, anxiety, depression, and psychosomatic illnesses. Thus, there is an indirect negative effect of unemployment on spouses.[19]

Second, job loss does seem to contribute to the rate of marital separation and divorce; some studies show that laid-off workers separate or divorce their spouses at three to four times the rate of employed workers. Although research samples in this area are generally too small to provide reliable estimates of the risk of marital breakdown, nonetheless, the research results conservatively interpreted suggest that unemployment can significantly threaten the marital relationship.[20]

Third, unemployment is associated with negative changes in the family climate. Husbands and wives faced with unemployment often report significantly less cohesiveness and supportiveness, and significantly more conflict in their families than do members of control group families.[21] There is also evidence that major changes take place in the actual division of labor between spouses in unemployed families. When men become unemployed, they may become significantly more active in the day-to-day tasks of running a family (feeding children, cleaning house, etc.); even when they become reemployed, the division of labor in the family may remain altered.[22] Ironically, spouses' beliefs about who should be the more dominant member of the marriage and about who should be responsible for child rearing and housework do not seem to change.[23]

There is less research on the impact of job loss on children. Anecdotal evidence suggests that children of the unemployed have more conflicts over authority with their fathers than do children of the employed, but there is no definitive data on this issue yet. Nevertheless, at the aggregate level, researchers have reported that "job loss is the environmental condition cited most often as placing a family at risk in terms of child abuse."[24]

FRIENDS AND CO-WORKERS. One of the problems unemployed workers find most troubling is the lack of companionship. The day-to-day interactions with co-workers are gone, and many laid-off workers become more withdrawn or reluctant to share their negative feelings with friends.[25]

Three patterns of relationships concerning friendship have emerged from the empirical research. First, the more time unemployed workers spend with friends, the less depressed and anxious they become. This friendship network not only mitigates psychological distress, but also provides stronger social pressure to get a job.[26] Second, the longer the period of unemployment, the more laid-off workers reduce the number of their social contacts. Their social network shrinks, and the unemployed rely increasingly on a few friends for support. Third, many acquaintanceships developed through shared activities seem to fall off over time as well, as unemployed workers cut out social entertainment requiring money.[27]

Very little research has been done on the impact of unemployed workers' moods and attitudes on the psychological well-being of their friends. The impact of layoffs on co-workers, however, has been much more systematically investigated. The results of several laboratory and field studies suggest that so-called survivors often lower their productivity, develop poorer job attitudes, and voluntarily leave their employers in the wake of layoffs of their co-workers.[28]

According to recent research, the rationale for this survivor reaction to layoffs is grounded in notions of equity and distributive justice. The results of these studies suggest that survivors' productivity and job attitudes are most adversely affected (1) when a layoff is seen as an unnecessary business decision; (2) when laid-off workers are informed of their terminations in a degrading or unfair way; (3) when the criteria used to select workers to be laid-off are seen as arbitrary, capricious, or politically motivated; and (4) when the laid-off workers were inadequately compensated.[29] Essentially, when survivors view the layoffs as unjust, they respond by distancing themselves from what they consider the source of the injustice, the organization which engaged in the unfair activity.

Moderating Variables in Job Loss

A third major line of research has examined those factors which ameliorate or worsen the impact of job loss. Researchers have examined both characteristics of the individual and characteristics of the situation to discover factors that might attenuate the consequences of layoffs.

PERSONALITY TRAITS. Empirical research on individual differences has looked at two sets of factors in particular: personality traits and demographic variables. Researchers have examined such personality traits as self-esteem and hardiness, flexibility and self-efficacy, and Type-A behavior pattern and internal locus of control.[30] There are some underlying reasons why these attributes, rather than others, have been studied.

Because job loss is such a negative event, social scientists have wanted to examine personality traits that might buffer individuals from feeling the full force of their loss. Qualities such as self-esteem and hardiness should help individuals be more resilient and self-reliant in the face of disappointment. Since the loss of a job strips away old routines and forces individuals to start "from scratch," psychologists have wanted to examine personality traits such as flexibility and self-efficacy because these predispositions might help individuals adapt more readily to novel situations. As we mentioned earlier, layoffs occur because of circumstances outside the personal control of the individual. Laid-off workers often feel apathetic and discouraged as a result of their terminations. Thus, it has been hypothesized that personality traits like internal locus of control and Type-A behavior pattern might predispose the unemployed to be more energetic and resourceful in trying to regain some semblance of normality in their lives. In general, the small amount of empirical research on personality traits has produced results in the predicted direction, but of relatively modest magnitude.

DEMOGRAPHIC FACTORS. The research on demographic factors has produced somewhat stronger results. Females and minorities are both more vulnerable to being laid off and to having difficulties becoming reemployed.[31] These results have to be interpreted with some caution, however, because of the small sample sizes of the studies in which these differences have been observed. Older blue-collar workers are somewhat less vulnerable to layoffs than their younger colleagues because of protections often provided by seniority, but have more difficulty finding reemployment when they are laid off.[32] More educated employees are less vulnerable to layoffs, although there do not seem to be major differences between highly and poorly educated workers in the amount of distress they suffer after a layoff.[33] Single persons seem to suffer less financial distress than laid-off workers with families, but have the disadvantage of receiving less social support.[34]

Overall, then, demographic factors have been shown to moderate the job loss phenomenon in two ways. First, they make certain classes of individuals more vulnerable to being laid-off; second, they make it harder for certain classes of individuals to become reemployed after they have been laid off.

SITUATIONAL FACTORS. A wide variety of situational factors have also been investigated as potential moderators of the impact of job loss. We will focus on three broad sets of situational moderators: economic conditions, government policies, and corporate interventions.

The set of moderating factors that has been studied the longest and most extensively involves current economic conditions.[35] Recessions and high unemployment rates make layoffs more likely and reemployment more difficult; high levels of inventory on hand and corporate restructuring in progress have much the same effect. Research from the 1980s suggests that the manufacturing sector, especially in the Northeast and Midwest, was the hardest hit by layoffs.

A second series of studies has explored the role of government agencies in ameliorating the negative consequences of job loss. The policies that have received the most attention are advance notification provisions, extended unemployment benefits, and initiatives to retrain workers.[36] Each of these policies is viewed as having a somewhat different impact on the unemployment experience. Advance notification of layoffs is seen as giving workers more time to find new employment, thereby decreasing both the length of time people are unemployed and the amount of psychological distress they experience. Extended unemployment benefits are viewed as effective means of keeping workers out of poverty, buffering them from financial disaster, and decreasing the amount of distress experienced by their spouses and children. Initiatives to retrain workers are perceived to be successful in helping the unemployed find new jobs, especially when layoffs have occurred in declining industries.

A third, and smaller, set of studies has examined corporate interventions, such as outplacement programs.[37] These studies, largely anecdotal or descriptive in nature, suggest that such programs can improve workers' job search skills and provide the unemployed with some companionship and some structure to the day.

In sum, the findings of the research studies on situational differences suggest that there are contextual factors that influence how much people suffer as a result of job loss. The results from the labor economic studies have generally been larger and have shown more statistically significant relationships than those on government and corporate interventions; whether this is due to widely different sample sizes or real differences is hard to determine.

Theoretical Perspectives on Job Loss

In a recent critical review of the job loss literature, Hartley and Fryer suggested that "the present state of psychological knowledge concerning unemployment is barely more insightful than a lay person's understanding, being essentially a redescription using the specialized jargon of social science."[38] They attribute this to a variety of problems, most notably, the lack of coherent theoretical underpinnings to the research that has been conducted, the insistence on the part of most researchers of treating the laid-off as entirely passive victims of economic forces, and the relative paucity of empirical job loss research conducted after the 1930s. The theory and research presented in the following chapters is an attempt to correct these shortcomings.

Job Loss and Theories of Stress

Independent of the level of analysis and research approach, the theoretical construct behind much of what we know about job loss is stress. Job loss can be seen as a stressful life event because it places individuals in situations that are uncertain, potentially theatening, and definitely disruptive to their day-to-day routines.[39]

Indeed, the concept of stress pervades the research conducted on job loss. For instance, in the economic research on the relationship between national economic indices and overall mental health in the population, the unstated—but presumed—intervening variable is stress: changes in the economy are assumed to bring to the surface latent emotional problems or generate new psychological problems for large numbers of citizens. In the research on job loss and physical and psychological well-being, the concept of stress also plays an important explanatory role. The continuous stress created by job loss is seen as the agent that causes deteriorating psychological health and induces stress-related illnesses such as heart disease and ulcers. In the research on the impact of job loss on an individual's family, friends, and co-workers, the concept of stress is also prominent. Because the individual is torn from existing routines and forced to establish new behavior patterns, people in the individual's social support system may also feel anxiety and be forced to change their routines and behavior patterns.

Thus, one of the goals of this book is to present an integrated theoretical framework for understanding job loss that is heavily based in the research on stress.

Job Loss, Deprivation, and Personal Control

Hartley and Fryer correctly observe that most of the research on job loss assumes that the unemployed are simply reactive in the face of their difficulties.[40] In most research studies, laid-off workers are assumed to be relatively passive agents who merely experience unemployment and its effects rather than as active agents who may respond in ways to circumvent or ameliorate these effects. In large part this is because the theoretical approach that underlies much of the job loss literature is a deprivation model: Job loss deprives individuals of desired activities, structures, and meanings to their lives, and once unemployed, individuals are assumed to be inactive, unstructured, and passive.[41] Thus, the issue of what steps individuals take to cope with job loss is seldom raised or addressed. Instead, individuals are typically asked only to report what happens to them as a result of losing their jobs (e.g., health problems) or the circumstances they find themselves in when the job loss occurs (e.g., social support networks).

Consequently, we know little about the prevalence or utility of individual coping strategies either in attaining new employment or in reestablishing a reasonable quality of life after a job loss. A second goal of the book, then, is to explore how individuals cope with job loss, what energizes unemployed workers to try to solve their problems on their own, and how effective those efforts turn out to be.

Empirical Data and Job Loss Research

Most of the labor economic research studies of job loss have been empirical in nature and have used large samples. This is not true of the social science research on job loss. With the exception of some of the research projects on worker health, much of what we know about the psychology and sociology of layoffs and job loss comes from descriptive or prescriptive qualitative studies done with relatively small data sets.

We tested our ideas on job loss against the data we collected from some one thousand laid-off workers at two research sites: the Space Coast in Florida in the wake of the *Challenger* disaster, and the Pittsburgh Steel Mills during the rapid decline of the "Rust Belt" industries. We surveyed and/or interviewed these laid-off workers about their work experiences before their layoffs, how the layoffs were implemented, the level and usefulness of any corporate assistance they received, how they coped with unemployment, how successful they have been in finding new employment, and how they—as well as their spouses and children—have adjusted to life without work. Although the work forces at these two sites stand in sharp contrast to each other—Northern, blue-collar workers versus Southern, white-collar workers—the similar experiences and reactions of these people are as instructive as the differences between them.

Thus, as we explored and refined our ideas about job loss, we drew heavily on a very rich and heterogeneous data set. In addition, we integrated our findings on layoffs with what research was available on other kinds of job loss (e.g., firings) and the experiences of the unemployed in general.

We conducted our research project guided by a set of premises somewhat different from those underlying most of the past research on layoffs. We view individuals as active rather than passive agents who behave in ways that affect how long they are unemployed and how unpleasant that period of unemployment is. Although we recognize that getting laid off is an involuntary act initiated by organizations rather than by individuals, we thereafter assume that individuals can make choices regarding how they will cope with job loss, and that the types of coping undertaken by individuals will affect the types and intensity of negative outcomes associated with job loss. Finally, we propose that much of the disparate literature on reactions to job loss, individual differences, and institutional interventions can best be understood within a theoretical framework suggested by the literature on stress.

A General Theory for Understanding Reactions to Layoffs

In Figure 1–1, we present the framework of our model. In this research, we explored seven general factors: (1) the context or situation of the layoff, (2) individual reactions to layoffs, (3) individual coping strategies, (4) outcomes of coping efforts, (5) personality traits, (6) demographic variables, and (7) company interventions. For introductory purposes, we will briefly discuss our framework below; more detailed theoretical propositions and data on those propositions will be provided in the chapters to follow.

Individual Reactions to Job Loss

The research on stress suggests that when individuals are faced with uncertain, threatening, and disruptive changes in their lives—such as job loss—they react in three ways.[42] First, they try to cognitively assess just how threatening the stressful event is: How severe is this problem? How reversible is it? Can I control it personally or is it caused by external forces? Second, they react emotionally to the stressful event. They can, for example, be depressed and feel passive about their problems, or they can feel challenged and energized to change their situation. Third, they can suffer physiological problems, ranging from eating and sleeping disorders to drug and alcohol

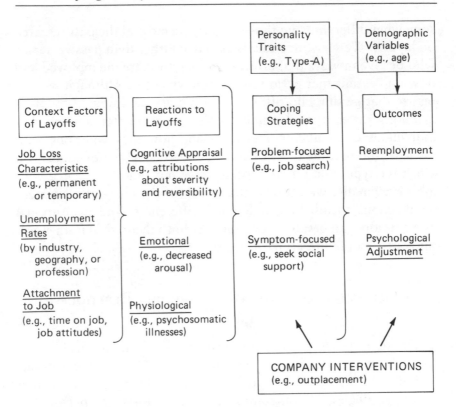

FIGURE 1-1
A General Model for Understanding Layoffs

abuse. Some of these physiological reactions might be expected to decrease their ability to handle their problems with unemployment successfully.

Our framework suggests that these stress reactions play two critical roles in helping us understand how people respond to job loss. First, the model suggests that the context of layoffs can be best understood in terms of how much stress is created for unemployed workers. Second, the model suggests that whether individuals' reactions to layoffs *activate* or enervate them will largely determine how much, and what type, of coping activity they engage in.

Context Factors of Layoffs

Many situational factors influence how an individual initially reacts to a stressful life event such as losing a job, but three context factors in particular—characteristics of the job loss itself, perceptions of unemployment levels, and attachment to the job—are expected to have the most substantial influences on the stress reactions of those laid-off.

Previous research suggests that the longer an individual has been out of work, the more adversely he or she will react to being jobless. Financial difficulties will increase, and it is likely social support will decrease. Similarly, individuals who are being laid off permanently will have more negative reactions to layoffs. These people are more likely to consider the layoff situation as hopeless and may be more likely to respond with depression, physical distress, and lethargy.[43]

Perceptions of unemployment levels should also play a role in influencing individual reactions. The higher workers perceive the unemployment rates in their communities and/or professions to be, the more pessimistic they will be about their prospects for finding new jobs, especially ones at equal pay. Thus, laid-off workers may experience the job loss as more intense, may be more likely to appraise it as irreversible, and may exhibit more emotional and physical distress symptoms as a result.[44] Consequently, they may be less likely to actively seek new employment.

Previous research also suggests that individuals who are most attached to their previous employers and professions respond most negatively to being laid off. For them losing a job means more than just losing money; it means losing a source of internal satisfaction and long-held social networks and structures to their lives. Moreover, the longer a person has held employment in one firm, the more likely he or she is to have firm-specific talents that may not be valued by other potential employers.[45]

Coping Strategies

Our model suggests that laid-off workers' perceptions, emotional reactions, and physiological reactions to job loss all influence how they cope with unemployment. We make an important distinction here between problem-focused and symptom-focused coping.[46] Problem-focused coping behaviors are attempts to change the environment by eliminating the source of stress itself. Examples of problem-focused coping related to job loss are seeking a new job or getting retraining in a new occupation. Symptom-focused coping behaviors are efforts to decrease the depression or loneliness often associated with job loss. Examples of symptom-focused coping strategies are joining social support groups or community groups.

In general, our model suggests that the less negatively a person reacts to job loss, the more likely he/she will be to use problem-focused coping. People who are more optimistic about their future prospects will be more likely to exert substantial efforts toward ending their own unemployment. In contrast, the more negatively the job loss is perceived and felt, the more individuals will use symptom-focused coping. The unemployed who view their job loss as irreversible, who feel apathetic and depressed, or who are drinking and sleeping too much are unlikely to be out actively seeking new jobs. Instead, they may take actions to decrease the intensity of their negative feelings.

Personality Factors

Personality traits predispose individuals to behave in consistent ways when faced with similar circumstances. Therefore, we would expect people who are faced with stressful events like layoffs to react as they react to other stressful work events in their lives.

Our model suggests, then, that there may be consistent coping styles that people use when faced with stressful events like job loss; these individual styles, as well as situation-specific reactions, will influence how much and what type of coping activities the unemployed engage in.

The three personality traits which we have included in this study are Type-A personality,[47] internal locus of control,[48] and self-esteem.[49] As we discussed earlier in the chapter, these personality traits may buffer laid-off workers from feeling the full brunt of a depression, sustain their spirits during unemployment, and predispose them toward trying to regain some control over their lives.

Outcome Variables

The literature on job loss suggests four outcomes should be assessed in determining long-term adjustment to unemployment: job reattainment, perceived prospects for reemployment, psychological distress, and overall satisfaction.[50] The first two of these factors concern the person's employment status. Is he or she currently employed? Is he or she employed at a job requiring the same skill levels and paying comparable wages, or is he or she underemployed? If a person is unemployed, how favorable are prospects for reemployment in the near future? The second set of factors concern workers' psychological adjustment to unemployment. Are they able to function adequately in day-to-day activities? How adversely has the layoff affected their quality of life? Have they been able to retain some semblance of normality during unemployment?

The model presented in Figure 1–1 proposes that the type and amount of coping people engage in will influence whether they get satisfactorily reemployed or adjust to life without work. More specifically, we propose that problem-focused coping should be more successful in helping people find new jobs because problem-focused coping most directly attacks the root cause of the stress and alleviates it most concretely. There are also some secondary benefits to using problem-focused coping in terms of psychological adjustment. Problem-focused coping can structure the individual's time and provide an environment with more social interaction as well. Furthermore, the more successfully individuals search for new jobs or retrain, the more positive spin-off effects there will be on their attitudes toward life in general.

Demographic Variables

The labor economic research, as well as the sociological literature, makes clear that individuals' demographic characteristics—independent of how much or how little they actively cope—can predict their chances for reemployment. Therefore, we have also collected data on age, education level, gender, and race. Consistent with prior research, we expected that older employees, those with less education, females, and minorities would feel more distress upon being laid-off, and would also face greater barriers to finding satisfactory reemployment.[51]

Corporate Interventions

While there have been numerous case studies done of the impact of corporate assistance programs, careful empirical assessments have lagged behind prescriptive writings on those interventions. Four company interventions have been cited as being particularly beneficial to the unemployed: advance notification, outplacement services, severance pay, and extended benefits.[52] In our studies, we collected data on whether laid-off workers received any of these forms of corporate assistance, and if so, how helpful they were.

Our model (see fig. 1–1) suggests that corporate interventions can play two roles in the job loss/job hunt process. First, these corporate interventions can directly help laid-off employees find new jobs. For instance, the most vocal advocates of outplacement services claim that these programs do exactly that. Second, we propose that these corporate interventions may also influence the amount and type of coping laid-off employees engage in. For example, advance notice, severance pay, and extended benefits may not directly affect whether people get rehired or are generally up-beat while they are unemployed. However, these policies may give the laid-off needed time and additional money to retrain or to relocate, which in turn influences their chances of getting satisfactorily reemployed and reestablished. Thus, corporate interventions may play an indirect, as well as a direct, role in what happens to the unemployed after layoffs.

Organization of the Book

The book is organized into seven chapters and an appendix. The chapters generally are sequenced to correspond to different segments of our model.

Chapter 2, along with the Appendix, describes our research sites, study participants, and research methods. Chapter 3 describes our research findings concerning the context of layoffs and individual reactions to unemployment. Here we look at just how adversely people react to job loss, and how different situational factors exacerbate, or soften, the effects of layoffs.

Chapter 4 presents our findings on coping strategies. In this chapter we look at the types of coping behaviors laid-off employees engage in and how effective those coping strategies are. Chapter 4 also includes a discussion of the impact of personality traits on individuals' coping strategies.

In Chapter 5, we turn our attention to corporate assistance programs. Here we show data on how much corporate assistance laid-off workers received, and how helpful those corporate assistance programs turned out to be. As noted earlier, we examine both the direct impact of corporate assistance programs on reemployment status and psychological adjustment and their indirect effects on individuals' coping strategies. Chapter 5 also includes a discussion of the impact that demographic factors have on outcomes.

Chapter 6 looks at institutional programs aimed at helping the unemployed, but from a different perspective. In this chapter we look at the role of unions and community groups in halting the number and severity of layoffs, in providing financial support and retraining for workers, and in monitoring the impact of widescale layoffs on communities and municipalities.

Chapter 7 summarizes and reflects on the results of our research, and offers suggestions for future theorizing and research on job loss. This chapter also includes some of our speculations about the roles that corporations, unions, and governmental agencies can play in helping the unemployed.

Throughout the book, we have tried to integrate our empirical findings with the theoretical writings of other scholars in the field as well as with illustrative quotes from the participants in our study. Because the mathematical backgrounds of our readers may vary, we have chosen to present the empirical data in the chapters in as accessible a way as possible. We have included a detailed appendix at the back of the book, however, for readers who are interested in more specifics on our measures and our statistical findings.

Notes

1. T. F. Buss and F. S. Redburn, *Mass Unemployment: Plant Closings and Community Mental Health* (Beverly Hills, Calif.: Sage, 1983).
2. E. R. Greenberg, "The latest AMA Survey on Downsizing," *Personnel* (October 1989): 38–44.
3. Ibid.
4. Ibid.
5. G. Russell, "Rebuilding to Survive," *Time*, 16 February 1987, pp. 44–45.

6. Ibid.
7. Buss and Redburn, *Mass Unemployment.*
8. D. O. Love and W. D. Torrence, "The Value of Advance Notice of Worker Displacement," *Southern Economic Journal* (1989): 626–43; M. Podgursky, and P. Swaim, "Job Displacement and Earnings Loss: Evidence from the Displaced Worker Survey," *Industrial and Labor Relations Review*, 41, (1987): 17–29.
9. Greenberg, "Latest AMA Survey."
10. M. H. Brenner, *Mental Illness and the Economy* (Cambridge: Harvard University Press, 1973).
11. R. J. Barro, "Unanticipated Money Growth and Unemployment in the United States," *American Economic Review* 67 (1977): 101–15.
12. R. Topel, "Inventories, Layoffs, and Short-Run Demand for Labor," *American Economic Review* 72 (1982): 769–87.
13. P. Warr, P. Jackson, and M. Banks, "Unemployment and Mental Health: Some British Studies," *Journal of Social Issues* 44 (1988): 47–48; R. C. Kessler, J. B. Turner, and J. S. House, "Effects of Unemployment on Health in a Community Survey: Main, Modifying, and Mediating Effects," *Journal of Social Issues* 44 (1988): 69–85.
14. C. Layton, "Externality and Unemployment: Change Score Analyses on Rotter's Locus of Control Scale for Male School-Leavers and Men Facing Redundancy," *Personality and Individual Differences* 8 (1987): 149–52; R. M. Cohn, "The Effect of Employment Status Change on Self Attitudes," *Social Psychology* 41 (1978): 81–93.
15. R. Payne and J. Hartley, "A Test of a Model for Explaining the Affective Experience of Unemployed Men," *Journal of Occupational Psychology* 60 (1987): 31–47; S. Cobb and S. V. Kasl, *Termination: The Consequences of Job Loss* (Washington, D.C.: National Institute for Occupational Safety and Health, Report No. 76–1261, 1977).
16. Kessler, Turner, and House, "Effects of Unemployment"; J. P. Grayson, "The Closure of a Factory and Its Impact on Health," *International Journal of Health Services* 15 (1985): 69–93.
17. M. W. Linn, R. Sandifer, and S. Stein, "Effects of Unemployment on Mental and Physical Health," *American Journal of Public Health* 75 (1985): 502–6.
18. M. Lajer, "Unemployment and Hospitalization among Bricklayers," *Scandinavian Journal of Social Medicine* 10 (1982): 3–10; P. R. Jackson and P. B. Warr, "Unemployment and Psychological Ill-Health: The Moderating Role of Duration and Age," *Psychological Medicine* 14 (1984): 605–14.
19. M. A. Dew, E. J. Bromet, and H. C. Schulberg, "A Comparative Analysis of Two Community Stressors' Long-Term Mental Health Effects," *American Journal of Community Psychology* 15 (1987): 167–84.
20. R. Liem and J. H. Liem, "Psychological Effects of Unemployment on Workers and Their Families," *Journal of Social Issues* 44 (1988): 87–105; Dew, Bromet, and Schulberg, "Comparative Analysis."
21. R. Liem and J. H. Liem, "Social Support and Stress: Some General Issues and

Their Application to the Problem of Unemployment," in L. Ferman and J. P. Gordus, eds., *Mental Health and the Economy*, 347–78 (Kalamazoo, Mich.: W. F. Upjohn Institute for Employment Research, 1979).

22. S. McElfresh, "Conjugal Power in Legitimating Norms: A New Perspective on Resource Theory" (Ph.D. diss., Boston College, 1983).
23. Ibid.
24. B. Justice and R. Justice, *The Abusing Family* (New York: Human Services Press, 1976).
25. C. R. Leana and D. C. Feldman, "Individual Responses to Job Loss: Perceptions, Reactions, and Coping Behaviors," *Journal of Management* 14 (1988): 375–89.
26. Warr, Jackson, and Banks, "Unemployment and Mental Health"; P. Ullah, M. H. Banks, and P. B. Warr, "Social Support, Social Pressures, and Psychological Distress during Unemployment," *Psychological Medicine* 15 (1985): 283–95.
27. P. B. Warr, "Reported Behavior Changes after Job Loss," *British Journal of Social Psychology* 23 (1984): 271–75; P. R. Jackson, "Personal Networks, Support Mobilization, and Unemployment," *Psychological Medicine* 18 (1988): 397–404.
28. L. Greenhalgh, "Maintaining Organizational Effectiveness during Organizational Retrenchment," *Journal of Applied Behavioral Science* 18 (1982): 155–70; J. Brockner, J. Davy, and C. Carter, "Layoffs, Self-Esteem, and Survivor Guilt: Motivational, Affective, and Attitudinal Consequences," *Organizational Behavior and Human Decision Processes* 36 (1985): 229–44.
29. J. Brockner, S. Grover, T. Reed, R. DeWitt, and M. O'Malley, "Survivors' Reactions to Layoffs: We Get By with a Little Help from Our Friends," *Administrative Science Quarterly* 32 (1987): 526–41; J. Greenberg, "A Taxonomy of Organizational Justice Theories," *Academy of Management Review* 12 (1987): 9–22; R. J. Bies, "The Predicament of Injustice: The Management of Moral Outrage," in L. L. Cummings and and B. M. Staw, eds., *Research in Organizational Behavior* 9: 289–319 (Greenwich, Conn.: JAI Press, 1987).
30. Cohn, "The Effect of Employment Status Change"; Leana and Feldman, "Individual Responses to Job Loss"; S. C. Kobasa, "Stressful Life Events, Personality, and Health: An Inquiry into Hardiness," *Journal of Personality and Social Psychology* 37 (1979): 1–11; M. Friedman and R. H. Rosenman, *Type A Behavior and Your Heart* (New York: Knopf, 1974); J. B. Rotter, "Some problems and misconceptions related to the construct of internal vs. external control of reinforcement." *Journal of Consulting and Clinical Psychology* 43 (1975): 56–67.
31. T. C. Nowak and K. A. Snyder, "Women's Struggle to Survive a Plant Shutdown," *Journal of Intergroup Relations* 11 (1983): 25–44; R. A. Aronson and R. B. McKersie, *Economic Consequences of Plant Shutdowns in New York State* (Ithaca, N.Y.: Cornell University, New York State School of Industrial and Labor Relations, 1980).
32. J. D. Mooney, "An Analysis of Unemployment among Professional Engineers

and Scientists," *Industrial and Labor Relations Review* 19 (1966): 517–28; L. F. Dunn, "Measuring the Value of Community," *Journal of Urban Economics* 6 (1979): 371–82.

33. H. G. Kaufman, *Factors Related to the Utilization and Career Development of Scientists and Engineers: A Longitudinal Study of Involuntary Termination* (Washington, D.C.: National Science Foundation, Technical Report No. SRS 77-20737, 1980).

34. C. R. Leana and D. C. Feldman, "Gender Differences in Responses to Job Loss," *Journal of Vocational Behavior* 38 (1990): 65–77.

35. Brenner, *Mental Illness*; Barro, "Unanticipated Money Growth and Unemployment"; Topel, "Inventories."

36. D. C. Feldman and C. R. Leana, "Managing Layoffs: Experiences at the Challenger Disaster Site and the Pittsburgh Steel Mills," *Organizational Dynamics* 18 (1989): 52–64; and "Job Loss and Retraining Programs: Joint Union and Management Efforts to Help Displaced Workers," in M. London, E. Bassman, and J. P. Fernandez, eds., *Human Resource Forecasting and Planning for the Twenty-First Century* (Westport, Conn.: Greenwood Press, 1990), 127–140.

37. J. Scherba, "Outplacement as a Personnel Responsibility," *Personnel* 50 (1973): 40–44; J. C. Latack and J. B. Dozier, "After the Ax Falls: Job Loss as a Career Transition," *Academy of Management Review* 11 (1986): 375–92.

38. J. Hartley and D. Fryer, "The Psychology of Unemployment: A Critical Appraisal," in G. Stephenson and J. Davis, eds., *Progress in Applied Social Psychology*, 2: (Chichester, England: Wiley, 1984), 186.

39. J. E. McGrath, "Stress and Behavior in Organizations," in M. D. Dunnette, ed., *Handbook of Industrial and Organizational Psychology*, 1351–96 (Chicago: Rand McNally, 1976); A. P. Brief, R. S. Schuler, and M. A. Van Sell, *Managing Job Stress* (Boston: Little, Brown, 1981); D. C. Feldman and J. M. Brett, "Coping with New Jobs: A Comparative Study of New Hires and Job Changers," *Academy of Management Journal* 26 (1983): 258–72.

40. Hartley and Fryer, "The Psychology of Unemployment."

41. M. Jahoda, *Employment and Unemployment* (London: Cambridge University Press, 1982).

42. S. Folkman and R. S. Lazarus, "An Analysis of Coping in a Middle-Aged Community Sample," *Journal of Health and Social Behavior* 21 (1980): 219–39.

43. H. G. Kaufman, *Professionals in Search of Work* (New York: John Wiley and Sons, 1982); D. Fryer, "Stages in the Psychological Response to Unemployment: A Disintegrative Review," *Current Psychological Research and Reviews* (1985): 257–73.

44. Barro, "Unanticipated Money Growth and Unemployment."

45. Dunn, "Measuring the Value of Community"; Folkman and Lazarus, "An Analysis of Coping."

46. L. I. Pearlin and C. Schooler, "The Structure of Coping," *Journal of Health and Social Behavior* 19 (1978): 2–21.
47. Friedman and Rosenman, *Type A Behavior*.
48. Rotter, "Generalized Expectancies."
49. Cohn, "The Effect of Employment Status Change."
50. C. R. Leana and J. M. Ivancevich, "Addressing the Problem of Involuntary Job Loss: Institutional Interventions and a Research Agenda," *Academy of Management Review* 12 (1987): 301–12.
51. Novak and Snyder, "Women's Struggle"; Aronson and McKersie, "Economic Consequences."
52. Leana and Ivancevich, "Addressing the Problem of Involuntary Job Loss."

The Participants and Their Communities

No matter how clinically or objectively one considers the issue of job loss, it is impossible to put completely out of mind the concrete, palpable disruption that layoffs cause for workers, their spouses and children, and the communities in which they live. In the next few chapters, we present a variety of theoretical perspectives and qualitative and quantitative data to explain how people react to job loss, why they respond as they do, how they cope with their predicament, and why some are more successful than others in becoming reemployed. To make those perspectives meaningful, though, we would first like to describe the participants in our studies, their former employers, their communities, and the changes that have occurred as a result of widespread layoffs. Although there are some similarities between the layoffs after the *Challenger* disaster and those in the steel mills of the Monongahela Valley, the contexts of these layoffs provide very different frames of reference for understanding and interpreting the participants' misfortunes.

The *Challenger* Disaster Site

The Community

When the space shuttle *Challenger* exploded on 28 January 1986, life along the "Space Coast" changed not only for NASA employees, but for the broader community as well.

The Space Coast in Florida (mainly Brevard County, population 275,000) is an area that relies heavily on the aerospace and the tourist industries. At peak employment levels, the Kennedy Space Center employs about 15,500 workers; engineering companies such as Harris and Lockheed Space Operations employ thousands more. Tourist-oriented businesses such as motels and restaurants, which cater to vacationers at Cocoa Beach and the Kennedy Space Center, are also major employers.

Within a month of the Challenger disaster, 1,100 people were laid off from Kennedy Space Center; in September 1986, another 1,400 were let go. Thus, employment at the Kennedy Space Center alone dropped 16 percent. It is estimated that another 3,500 workers were laid off by private engineering and manufacturing companies dependent on the aerospace industry.

The economic impact of the *Challenger* disaster was felt in other sectors of the Brevard County area as well. Many motels in the area reported occupancy rates of only 50 percent, down from 95 percent before the crash. Several motel operators, like Don Homol at the Sea Missile Hotel, took to dramatic advertising signs to attract business: "Stay Here. Help Me Pay My Bills." High profile, popular restaurants like Gatsby's reported business down 10 to 15 percent relative to the previous year.[1] Only the Visitor's Center (Spaceport USA) seemed to prosper, with visitors up 20 percent in 1987 to 1.6 million.

Especially hard hit was the real estate industry. Building permits for single-family homes fell 18 percent in 1986, from 3,502 units to 2,871. Overall construction contracts (both residential and commercial) were down 8 percent. The construction of a $6 million, 180-room Wilson World Hotel was postponed indefinitely. Vacancy rates in commercial buildings and industrial parks on NASA Causeway (the highway entrance to Kennedy Space Center) also climbed, as few investors looked to Brevard County as a place to establish themselves or to expand.

Even general retail business declined. The Brevard County Planning Department reported that gross sales declined 1.25 percent in 1986. Car dealers were particularly affected (although GM dealers were saved by GM's low interest rate promotions). The First Florida Bank of Merritt Island reported its consumer-loan delinquency rate was up 33 percent. Many so-called luxury services—such as pest control for lawns and houses—reported revenue drops as large as 20 percent.

For Brevard County residents, the *Challenger* disaster rekindled bad memories of earlier aerospace industry downturns. In 1967, a fire aboard the Apollo spacecraft killed astronauts Grissom, Chafee, and White. After that disaster, the space program virtually shut down for two years; almost sixteen thousand workers lost their jobs. Fortunately, after the *Challenger* disaster, the economic impact was not so strong. Fewer workers were laid off this time, the county's economic base was more diverse, and most people believed the space program would bounce back after one year instead of two.[2] Nevertheless, many employers were reluctant to hire laid-off aerospace workers. They believed the employees—especially those formerly with the Kennedy Space Center—would not remain on their jobs in the long run, since after the 1967 Apollo disaster aerospace workers quit their new jobs wholesale once "the Cape" started rehiring. As aerospace workers commented:

> The money is so much more at the Cape than at other businesses in the area. When you'd only make $6 an hour compared to $16 an hour, they kind of wonder where your allegiance lies."[3]

> The most difficult experiences I went through were when I went to apply for other jobs that had nothing to do with government work. They all had the same attitude: How do we know that you won't go back to that job if they have a recall?

Life at NASA and the Subcontractors

When most organizations that suffer financial reverses publicly announce their difficulties, it is generally only the business media that follow the story—and not for very long. The *Challenger* disaster, however, drew the attention of the world press to NASA and the subcontractors. The nationally-televised Rogers Commission hearings on the shuttle disaster kept the problems of NASA and the Kennedy Space Center in the public eye for months. When physicist Richard Feynman demonstrated the unreliability of the O-ring seals in cold weather merely by dropping a section of O-ring into his glass of ice water, the entire country began to question both the managerial and scientific competence of the space program.

Several important issues came out of the Rogers Commission that reflected negatively on the NASA scientists and administrators and on the manufacturers of component parts. First, the scheduling of the *Challenger* flight seemed rushed. As Robert Holtz (retired editor of *Aviation Week and Space Technology*) noted, "There is still a lot of schedule pressure driving NASA. . . . Their answer is always that [delays are] too expensive and wouldn't work anyway." Second, the quality assurance on "criticality 1 parts" (parts that, if defective, could lead to the loss of the orbiter or the crew) was insufficient. As Richard Feynman commented, "Everything in the shuttle was working on the edge, partially failing. The whole damn thing was in dangerous shape. What happened to be the thing that failed was a matter of chance."[4]

Third, serious questions were raised about the adequacy of the original design. Even after years of development, there are still substantial concerns about the ability of the O-rings, for instance, to withstand the pressures and temperatures to which they are exposed. Fourth, there were widely held perceptions that space flight was now safe for ordinary citizens—such as teacher Christa MacAuliffe— when, in fact, it was not. As astronaut Sally Ride noted: "I think that we may have been misleading people into thinking that this is a routine operation, that it's just like getting on an airline and going across the country. . . . It's not." Lastly, serious questions were raised about accountability in the process for making the final launch decision, both in terms of specific personnel responsible and in terms of relevant input from NASA operations not located at the Kennedy Space Center, such as the Marshall Space Center in Huntsville, Alabama. The Rogers Commission found that the decision-making process was disorganized, overly secretive, and often careless in its disregard of important administrative checks and balances.

As a result of these findings, both the employees who were laid off and the employees who remained had some feelings of guilt about the role they may have indirectly, or inadvertently, played in the disaster. One NASA employee noted, "A murder was committed, and I was an accessory to the fact." Another engineer commented: "As I see it, I am fortunate because all I lost was a job. . . . The crew lost their lives." Moreover, since the layoffs took place over several months, employees still remaining on their jobs were kept wondering when they would receive their pink slips. The Kennedy Space Center set up "KSC Carelines," a phone counseling service to deal with employees' feelings of guilt and remorse; at the height of the crisis, the KSC Carelines were getting two hundred calls a day.[5]

The Laid-Off Workers

The 163 participants in our Florida study were mainly employed in the aerospace industry, either as managers, engineers, or technical support staff. Our sample was largely under forty years old (average age of 38), Caucasian (90%), male (59%), married (75%) with one child. Most of the sample had spouses working full time (77%), and had lived in the Space Coast area over a decade (average residency of 13 years).

In terms of their careers, most of our participants had been working full time over fifteen years, and for their most recent employers (before layoffs) about four years. At the time they were laid off, most of our participants were making about $25,000 per year. At the time of the study, our sample had been unemployed an average of seventeen weeks; only 20 percent had found new jobs.

Over half of our sample had been laid off previously (52%). The layoffs were seen as permanent by 53 percent of our participants. Nevertheless, most of the Florida sample had high levels of commitment to their profession, and most (70%) were optimistic that they would soon find comparable new jobs. An *Orlando Sentinel* survey of laid-off workers conducted about the same time as our study reported very similar findings.

In addition to the variety of psychological, emotional, and physiological effects that job loss has on the unemployed—depression, fatigue, loneliness, loss of sleep, and so on—two particular issues appearing in the Florida sample are worth noting.

First, many of the Space Coast workers felt betrayed. They had worked hard for the Kennedy Space Center or other aerospace companies, and in return they felt they had received little reward for their loyalty. Their comments reflect that sense of anger and frustration:

I feel tossed aside, like an old shoe.

I feel betrayed. We were told about several big contracts, now there is nothing. I was lied to. I knocked myself out to help my company meet schedules that called for ridiculous overtime. Why?

I feel top management did not keep us informed enough about current conditions that might end up with a layoff.

In my case, I had just turned down a job offer from another job two weeks before my layoff. I had no indication it was coming.

The second issue to emerge was that of age bias, both in terms of the reasons behind their layoffs and in trying to find new jobs. Although we will take this issue up more fully in the chapters ahead, in profiling the participants here it is worth noting that those who were in late middle age expressed particular concern that their layoffs were arbitrary or motivated by company politics:

Age and salary had a great deal to do with my job loss. My job was not eliminated—myself, along with several others, were replaced by people half our age. Simple economics.

The layoffs were all intra-company politics.

Other laid-off employees commented more specifically on age discrimination:

In my case I'm up in age—I'm sixty-three—and I've tried for six months to find work. It makes you feel like less than nothing. You feel, I've hit the end of the world. There is no future.[6]

Old age is most definitely a drawback in seeking employment, no matter what the law says.

I feel I was laid off from a job I was very well-trained for, and satisfied in, due to discrimination.

Even after the recalls, the controversy over age bias did not subside. There were numerous court cases alleging that companies had hired new, younger, employees instead of recalling the older workers. As one respondent commented: "No matter whose fault it was that the *Challenger* exploded, it's a damn shame to lose seven lives. But it is affecting a lot more now."[7]

Spouses, Children, and Friends

Fortunately, these layoffs did not lead to a major increase in the divorce rate in this population. Approximately 7 percent of the Florida sample separated since the layoffs and 4 percent divorced, rates very close to those of the population as a whole.

However, financial matters were a source of great strain in the marriages of our study participants. Almost one quarter of our Florida respondents reported "severe" financial problems. That is not surprising considering that only 25 percent of these employees received more than one week's notice of the layoff; only a third received any outplacement assistance; less than a quarter received any extended benefits beyond severance pay.

Another source of stress for marriages was the need to move out of the current residence, or out of town altogether. The women in our study were particularly vocal in expressing these concerns, as evidenced by the comments of one respondent:

> Our marriage got pretty rocky when I got laid off. My husband quit his job and we moved. He thought we would be able to run from the things that had happened. I was offered my job back in December, but I turned it down to stay with my husband. That was the hardest thing to do. It still hurts. I am very homesick.

An unusual feature of the layoffs at the Space Coast is that most of the fifty thousand school-age children in Brevard County saw the *Challenger* disaster on television, especially because of the participation of Christa MacAuliffe, the first "Teacher in Space." In addition to the trauma of seeing the shuttle explode, children were faced with daily reminders associated with the layoffs: angry parents out of work and at home, fewer purchases of toys and clothes, fewer trips and vacations. One former Grumman computer operator commented: "I told them, 'Mommy's going to be spending more time with you.' When your kids say, 'Mommy you're getting mean,' it affects you."[8]

Another major negative consequence of losing a job was losing a social network of friends at work. Over half our participants reported feeling lonely. As one of the laid-off managers in Florida put it:

I was very pleased to have the (new) job but it proved to be very difficult to lose your job and your friends and your life as it had been. . . . I had moved and changed jobs before in my life. But it had always been my idea and this time it wasn't. . . . Even though it has been five months (since the move) I am still lonely.

Becoming Reemployed

As might be expected, those laid off on the Space Coast experienced terrible frustrations trying to become reemployed. As noted earlier, the local economy was poor, and yet large numbers of people were reentering the job market. Workers did not want to switch careers nor move out of Florida. Many believed their skills were so specialized that they could not be transferred to any other field. Others identified very strongly with the space program and its goals, and did not want to leave that type of work. Some simply viewed the layoffs as the normal employment cycle in the space industry.[9]

No matter their psychological outlook, Space Coast workers faced three particular difficulties. First, they had trouble even getting their foot in the door for interviews; laid-off employees contacted an average of thirty-five companies for an average of only three face-to-face interviews. Second, workers found themselves overqualified and overeducated for the jobs available; many people with college and graduate degrees could only find jobs in the fast food industry. Third, the few lucky ones who got new jobs generally had to take pay cuts of over 20 percent.

On a more positive note, one-sixth of the people we contacted were employed in better jobs than the ones from which they had been let go. Two participants, for instance, came out better for their experiences:

This was the push I needed to go back to school and work toward establishing (long-term) goals.

It took me only one month to find another job in the same field. In retrospect, this new job is more challenging, has better opportunity for career growth, and is with a more financially stable company.

For some, then, being laid off provided the stimulus they needed to get out of an old rut and try a new opportunity. As we will see next in the Pittsburgh studies, however, there are even fewer chances for laid-off employees to find better jobs when an entire industry and occupation collapses nationwide.

The Monongahela Valley Steel Mills

Although employment prospects were grim on the Florida Space Coast, Brevard County was a virtual land of opportunity compared to the Monongahela Valley outside of Pittsburgh. This is a region traditionally dominated by steel production economically and, in many ways, culturally as well. Moreover, in a region dominated by the steel industry, the industry itself was dominated by the U.S. Steel Corporation. In 1978, U.S. Steel had six operating facilities and employed 42,000 workers in the greater Pittsburgh area. By 1986, all but two of these plants were closed and employment was down to just over 6,700, a loss of over 35,000 jobs. Those eight years of plant closings and pink slips were described by one former steelworker as a "slow-motion holocaust."[10]

The Communities

The Monongahela Valley is nearly forty miles long and made up of over seventy communities and municipalities. The Monongahela River cuts through the area; on its banks are what remains of the massive steel mills that were once the economic center of these communities. Most of the mills are now rusting testimonies to industrial decline, idled by inefficient technology, an overvalued dollar through the 1980s, and shortsighted corporate investment practices.

With the decline of the steel industry came the decline of the communities that had so long depended on the mills for their livelihood. According to census figures, Allegheny County suffered the second-largest population loss in the country between 1980 and 1986. Over 76,000 people, or 5.3 percent of the total population, left during that period. Moreover, those people whom the county could least afford to lose—wage earners between the ages of eighteen and thirty-five—made up a disproportionate share of those leaving the area. Many of the communities were quickly becoming populated by the poor and the elderly.

The municipalities in the Monongahela Valley lost substantial tax revenue when the mills closed. Homestead lost 9.6 percent of its tax base between 1986 and 1987 alone, and neighboring Duquesne lost 6.3 percent in the same period. Local governments were forced to curtail police services and close schools. There was talk of municipal consolidation. Food banks, unemployment offices, and counseling services sprang up in storefronts once occupied by commercial enterprises.

The Homestead Mill Study

Our first study in the Pittsburgh area centered around one steel mill, U.S. Steel's Homestead Works. The original Homestead plant was built on the banks of the Monongahela River outside of Pittsburgh in 1879 as part of the Carnegie Steel Company. It is perhaps best known as the scene of a bloody labor clash in 1892 between workers and Pinkerton detectives hired by Carnegie.

In 1901, the Homestead works became part of the U.S. Steel Company, which at that time represented 65 percent of the steelmaking capacity in the United States. During World War II the plant expanded, displacing eight thousand homes along the river to make room for the facilities and equipment that would produce much of the armor plate for the U.S. Navy. Homestead also produced the structural steel used in the Empire State Building, the Sears Tower, and the U.S. Steel Building itself. At peak production during the war, Homestead employed nearly fifteen thousand workers.

By the 1970s, employment had been greatly reduced at Homestead but still there were approximately six thousand jobs. With mounting competition from more efficient steel producers in Japan, Korea, and other countries, U.S. Steel chose to diversify rather than modernize. Despite numerous federal tax incentives and loan programs designed to encourage reinvestment in steel production, U.S. Steel instead branched out into real estate, chemicals, and oil. By 1983 steel represented less than one-third of the company's total investments. At the same time, employment at the Homestead Works declined to fewer than four thousand in 1983, and to six hundred by the end of 1985. In 1986, the U.S. Steel Corporation removed the word steel from its name, changing it to the more generic USX Corporation. The last heat of steel was poured at the Homestead Works in 1986 when all but a handful of workers were permanently laid off.

THE STUDY PARTICIPANTS. In 1986, we surveyed 198 steelworkers from the U.S. Steel's Homestead plant. The participants in this study had lost their jobs over a twelve-month period. These employees were the last to be let go and had thus enjoyed substantial seniority and job stability. All were members of the United Steelworkers of America union. On the average, they had spent twenty-five years working full time, twenty-three of those years with U.S. Steel (now USX). At the time of our study, the Homestead group had been out of work an average of nine months; only 12 percent had found new jobs.

The average age of the participants in the Homestead sample was forty-seven. Ninety-seven percent were male, and ninety-four percent were Caucasian. Eighty-eight percent had completed high school, with one-third reporting some post-secondary education. Eighty percent were married, and sixty-four percent had at least one dependent child. Many of these steelworkers had spent their entire lives in the same community, as had their fathers and grandfathers before them. The average tenure in the community was over thirty years.

Less than one-third of the sample (31%) reported ever being laid off before. Unlike the Florida Space Coast workers, however, the vast majority of those from the Homestead plant understood that they would not be returning to work; 80 percent reported perceiving the layoff as permanent.

REPORTED PROBLEMS. The sense of hopelessness and abandonment was pervasive and severe among the Homestead steelworkers we surveyed. They reported that, on average, over five hundred others had been laid off at the same time that they were let go. Moreover, nearly 92 percent reported the unemployment levels in their communities as "high" or "very high," and 85 percent rated the overall unemployment levels among steelworkers to be "high" or "very high." There was a strong sense that, with the collapse of the steel industry in western Pennsylvania, their lives had also collapsed. Nearly one-third reported severe financial problems as a result of the layoff. Only 14 percent thought that they would find new jobs comparable to the ones they had lost in the mill.

Financial hardships led many workers to make drastic changes in lifestyles and, for the first time in their lives, turn to friends and extended family for help. Over half reported a significant decrease in their standards of living after losing their jobs; nearly a quarter reported asking friends and relatives for financial assistance. Five percent of the Homestead sample lost their houses to mortgage foreclosures, and another ten percent were forced to move because they could not pay their rent or mortgage. Some (7%) moved in with relatives because they could no longer afford housing on their own.

In addition to these immediate financial hardships, job loss also took its psychological toll. Among many, there was a strong sense of shock and disbelief. Life as they had known it—and as their fathers had known it before them—had suddenly changed. Where was a middle-aged man to go who had spent the better part of his life in a steel mill? In the words of some of the former steelworkers:

> After Vietnam I just wanted to make money and relax. I lived two blocks away from the mill. My father and his father worked there— the whole family. . . . I had everything I thought I wanted. . . . Who would have thought everything would fold up all of a sudden?

> What bothers me more than anything, when I was a kid growing up, times were happy. Mills were working good, the county and towns were alive. Now all around things are dying.[11]

The Economic Development Study

In 1989 we conducted a second study of former steelworkers in Pittsburgh. The participants in this study were drawn from six different steel plants that had either closed completely or severely cut back operations through the early and mid-1980s. Four of the six plants were owned by USX (Homestead, National, Clairton, and Duquesne), one was owned by the LTV Corporation (Pittsburgh Works), and one by the Wheeling-Pittsburgh Steel Corporation. Both LTV and Wheeling-Pittsburgh had filed for Chapter 11 bankruptcy. All were located in or near the Monongahela Valley outside of Pittsburgh.

The Economic Development study was conducted in conjunction with the United Steelworkers of America union, the Tri-State Conference on Steel (a community coalition), and the Steel Valley Authority (a state-chartered economic development authority in the Monongahela Valley founded by dislocated workers and community leaders). The primary objective of the study was to compile a data bank of skilled workers in the region who could be employed in potential new jobs created through public and private economic development projects. The secondary objective of the study was to gather demographic data and other information to profile the dislocated work force in the region. As part of the larger study, the participants were also asked to describe their present circumstances for us and to reflect on their layoff from the mills and its impact on their lives.

THE STUDY PARTICIPANTS. In total, 2,192 former steelworkers participated in the Economic Development study. The average age of the participants was fifty (age range 28 to 76 years). Like the Homestead study, nearly all of the participants were male (94%), Caucasian (90%), long-term residents of the region (average residency of 34 years), and high-school graduates (91%). Twenty-nine percent had some education beyond high school. Three-quarters of the participants were married. Of that number, 34 percent had spouses who worked full-time; 21 percent had spouses working part-time; and 44 percent reported that their spouses were not employed.

REPORTED PROBLEMS. The participants in the Economic Development study reported many of the same problems as those in the earlier Homestead study. Eight percent had to relocate because of financial problems, 22 percent had fallen behind on their mortgage payments, and 5 percent had lost their houses to mortgage foreclosure. Over half (53%) had gone without medical insurance since losing their jobs and, of those with insurance, 40 percent reported it was not adequate to meet their families' needs.

EMPLOYMENT. Unlike the participants in the earlier Homestead study, most of the participants in the Economic Development study were employed at the time they completed the survey (60%). Of those, two-thirds were employed full-time. These new jobs, however, were rated as vastly inferior to those they held in the steel mills. The average weekly wage reported in the new job was $285 or approximately $7 per hour in a forty-hour week. This is far less than what they reported they needed to support their families (average of $397 per week) and the amount that they had been making in their previous steel mill jobs. Eighty-five percent reported making over $8 per hour in their former jobs, with the most frequently reported earnings ranging between $10 and $12 per hour ($400 to $480 in a forty-hour week). This means that for most, their new jobs were paying 40 to 60 percent less than their former ones.

The new jobs were also reported to be inferior for a variety of other reasons. Seventy-six percent of the participants rated the new jobs worse on health and life insurance benefits. Seventy-eight percent rated them worse on benefits such as vacation and sick days. Sixty-nine percent felt their new jobs were worse in terms of career opportunities. Forty-seven percent rated them worse on health and safety concerns. Also, despite the fact that they had lost their steel jobs as a result of plant closings, 76 percent said their new jobs were no better in terms of job security, and 46 percent actually rated them worse.

Although all of the respondents were represented by a union in the previous jobs (the United Steelworkers), only 23 percent enjoyed union representation in their new ones. The participants who had reported working since the plant closings had held, on average, three different jobs. Not surprisingly, over 82 percent of all respondents who were currently working reported that they would like to find new jobs.

Of the forty percent of the sample who were currently unemployed, 79 percent were interested in working full time although half reported that they would accept part-time jobs. Fifty-eight percent had been actively looking for work in the previous month. Like the participants in the Florida study, nearly 60 percent felt that finding a new job was made more difficult because of their age. Over 60 percent felt that their having been steelworkers diminished their prospects for future employment.

Spouses, Children, and Friends

In both the Homestead and the Economic Development studies, the workers themselves were not, of course, the only ones affected by the plant closings. Spouses, children, and friends also had to adjust to the new circumstances. Just as in the Florida study, divorce rates did not rise sharply after layoffs for the Pittsburgh workers in either study; however, many reported increased marital friction brought about by financial problems and by the reversal of traditional gender roles when their spouses went to work. Many former workers also felt a diminishing of status with their children once they were no longer traditional breadwinners:

> My wife is self-employed, works very hard for her money. We make ends meet, but I feel I'm not pulling my share of the load. I apply for all types of jobs for which I feel I may be qualfied [but] nothing seems to work out. It hurts inside not to do my share.

> I have not yet gotten over the loss of my job or the loss of my wife and family through divorce. All followed the loss of my job and the hard time [I had] getting or holding a [new] job.

> My wife gets disgusted. I know, but she doesn't show it to me. I think my children look at me different than before. They wonder why I'm not working every day, why I'm not getting them what I should get them.

> My [thirteen-year-old] boy sympathizes more with me and what I'm going through. But he looks at me different. It's affected him more than the other kids. I'm not a man like I was before. He sees his mother coming home with the paycheck, sees me doing the house-work. I think he still loves me like he used to . . . but you just can't adjust to it.[12]

Other stories of husband-wife role reversal were a bit more hopeful:

> When I lost my job we had just had our third child so my wife and I talked it over and came up with the idea of me staying home and being Mr. Mom. She made more money than I did and the job I had was a job that was not going anywhere. Besides, with both of us working it was costing us an arm and a leg for child care. With me

staying home I have more time to look for a good job or go to school or retrain in a new job. I have been home since April but nothing has opened up yet. I'm still trying.

The impact of the mill closings may have more long-term effects on the children of the unemployed. Traditionally, sons followed their fathers into well-paying jobs in the steel mills and raised their own children in close proximity to where they had grown up. By the mid-1980s, however, all that had changed.

In a 1986 survey of graduating seniors from seven area high schools, 57 percent indicated that they would be leaving their hometowns after graduation, primarily to find a job. Over 48 percent indicated that there was no suitable work for them in the Pittsburgh region; of these, only half expected the job market to ever improve enough to permit them to return. In many communities, there were sharp increases in the number of students enlisting in the military after graduation. Among Duquesne High School seniors, for example, 25 percent planned to join the military after graduation, nearly three times as many as in 1981. Military service was seen by many students as a chance for job and financial stability no longer available at home. As one student planning to join the army put it: "You can feel so secure in the military. . . . The mill just shut down all of a sudden. I want to know that there's going to be something there for me. I don't want to worry about being poor."

Students' perceptions and plans were no doubt shaped by the experiences of their fathers. Twenty-three percent of the students' fathers were unemployed with another 9 percent working only part time. Nearly 36 percent indicated that their fathers had spent some time unemployed over the past five years. High school administrators and teachers also encouraged the students to leave. As one high school principal counseled, "Learn your lessons well and move on. There's nothing for you here."[13]

Reemployment, Retraining, and Relocation

The vast majority of the Pittsburgh steelworkers in our studies expended considerable effort looking for new jobs. In the Homestead study, over 85 percent followed up on "help wanted" advertisements, 48 percent tried to find work through a government employment agency, and nearly 24 percent utilized community job bank services. Much of this was to no avail, however, with 88 percent still unemployed at the time of the Homestead study in 1986 and 40 percent still unemployed in the Economic Development study three years later. Many went to great lengths to find new jobs, often for periods of time that stretched into months or years:

> I can't even get a $4 per hour job as a guard or a sewer cleaner because employers probably feel that as soon as a welding job opens up, I'll leave for it. I don't care if I ever weld again. I just want a decent job. Now I find I can't even acquire a bad job. Maybe it's because I'm forty-six [years old], too much experience, too little experience, bad attitude. I don't know. My hopes about obtaining employment have been built up and then dashed to the ground so many times it is a wonder I'm not in Mayview [State Mental Hospital].

> Since May 1986 I have been trying to get back into heavy industry to obtain proper employment. But it's the same story all over the region: nobody is hiring. In fact, most places were either cutting back their work force or were not hiring.

> I've sent resumes and gone to businesses that advertise job openings, but to no avail. Through my life I've picked up many skills not related to my job and I know that most of the jobs I've applied for could be done by me with a minimum amount of training time, but I've not been given the chance to show this. . . . After applying and being rejected for job opportunities, you get very depressed and discouraged.

> Security guard jobs are the only thing open to me. [They are] only part time, pay minimum wage, and no benefits. I have given out seventy resumes and have not even been called, let along considered for, any job. I am totally frustrated.

Like the Florida sample, the older workers in Pittsburgh also complained about age discrimination in attempting to find new jobs:

> I think the men in my age bracket have all but been forgotten about. Even if we were retrained in a different profession, we would find it very hard to find employment because of our age. I know there are laws to prevent age discrimination, but there are ways to get around the laws. . . . I am presently working as a security guard, five days a week, for $5.50 per hour, with no benefits and [it's] frowned upon

if I ask for a week's vacation. I cannot leave this job unless I am absolutely certain that I can quickly move to another one. I realize the younger generation must have somewhere to go, but you cannot sacrifice one generation for another. There has to be something for both. Where do we go from here?

At this point age discrimination is the biggest obstacle in finding a comparable paying job.

Although the government continues to put out untrue figures pertaining to employment in Pennsylvania, they refuse to address the real issues. Many former employees in the steel industry went from good-paying jobs to minimum- or a little above minimum-wage jobs. Most are underemployed, but have no choice and have to take what they can get. Very few are getting any kind of benefits. Certainly there is age discrimination. Just go [apply] for a job if you're in your fifties. No matter how good your health is or how young you look, there are just too many people looking and too few jobs to be had in this area.

Many who could not find jobs in the Pittsburgh area looked elsewhere for work. Fifty-eight percent of the Homestead workers reported looking for a job in a different community, and nearly 16 percent had made plans to move to a new area to look for work. Others enrolled in a variety of reeducation and retraining programs to prepare themselves for different careers. Nearly 43 percent reported taking some steps to learn a new skill or profession; 24 percent took courses at a college or university; 20 percent enrolled in technical retraining. These efforts were not without anxiety and hardship, however, particularly when they were not rewarded with comparable new jobs. A study done by the *Pittsburgh Post-Gazette*, for example, indicated that steelworkers who had gone through retraining were no better off financially than those who had not. In both cases, there was a substantial drop in both income and benefits in their new jobs: "Those who can be considered successes are still just approaching the wage they made in the mills."[14] As reported earlier, similar problems were reported by those responding to the Economic Development survey.

As in the Florida sample, however, there were a few success stories, people who emerged from the layoff experience feeling better off with their present circumstances and more optimistic about the future. Although in the minority, some were able to find new jobs that were more rewarding—both financially and psychologically—than their previous work. Former millworkers became electricians, accountants, nurses, or computer operators, and in the process, often gained new insights that extended well beyond the realm of blue-collar work.

> Blue collar is traditional. Things are planned out for you. Someone is taking care of you, rather than you taking care of yourself. Now it's more survival of the fittest.

> School got me back to reading. . . . It helped me open my eyes. I am not going to be a mill hunk.

> It was eighteen years before I went back to college, and that takes a lot of getting used to, a lot of rearranging yourself and rearranging your thoughts.

> Before I went to work eight hours and picked up my paycheck. Education tends to make you think more. I never knew the world ran like this.[15]

The issues of job search, retraining, and relocation will be discussed more thoroughly in Chapter 4 where we detail the variety of ways that dislocated workers try to cope with losing their jobs. Before turning to these issues, however, we will first explore more fully how people respond to job loss in terms of their perceptions, emotions, and behaviors.[16]

Notes

1. Much of this material was gathered from contemporary newspaper accounts. See especially C. Hinman, "Detour Takes Brevard Out of Fast Lane," *Orlando Sentinel*, Special Supplement, 25 January 1987, 1–16.
2. See J. Kelley, "Jobless Workers Feel Lost in Space," *USA Today*, 2 October 1986, p. 1.
3. Taken from J. J. Glisch, "Layoffs Hit KSC Workers in Wallet and Heart," *Orlando Sentinel*, Special Supplement, 25 January 1987, p. E9.
4. See J. Fisher and M. Thomas, "One Year Later: America and the *Challenger*," *Orlando Sentinel*, Special Supplement, 25 January 1987, pp. E1–E9.
5. See Kelley, "Jobless Workers"; L. McGinley, "NASA's Recovery from the *Challenger* Disaster Is Slow and Painful, and Far from Complete," *Wall Street Journal*, 26 January 1987, p. 50.
6. Glisch, "Layoffs Hit KSC Workers."
7. Kelley, "Jobless Workers."

8. Ibid.
9. See S. Holton, "Ex–Space Center Worker Launches Career in Earthbound High-Tech," *Orlando Sentinel*, Special Supplement, 25 January 1987, E9; D. Tracy, "He Built Rockets, Now Hunts for Job," *Orlando Sentinel*, Special Supplement, 25 January 1987, E8.
10. Mike Stout, former grievance chair, Local 1397, United Steelworkers of America, personal communication.
11. J. Blotzer, "When the Fire Dies: A Special Report on Pittsburgh's Laid-Off Workers," *Pittsburgh Post-Gazette*, Special Supplement, 30 December 1985.
12. Ibid.
13. J. Blotzer, "Leaving the Most Livable City: Graduates in Mon, Ohio Valleys Plan to Go Elsewhere for Jobs," *Pittsburgh Post-Gazette*, 18 June 1986, pp. 1, 6.
14. See Blotzer, "When the Fire Dies."
15. Ibid.
16. Readers who are interested in the more technical aspects of our studies may want to turn to the appendix. There we reprint our surveys and the statistics upon which the discussion in the next three chapters is based.

Reactions to Job Loss

One issue that has dominated both the scholarly research and the popular press coverage of job loss is the high degree of stress and disruption that laid-off workers and their families experience. The movie *Roger and Me* (1990) about the closing of General Motors plants in Flint, Michigan, captured many of the fears people have about layoffs—families were dispossessed from their homes, children were forced to adjust to vastly diminished standards of living, communities were devastated economically, institutions were rendered impotent, and anger and despair manifested themselves in crime, alcohol use, and the disintegration of both family and community. At the center of this turmoil are the dislocated workers themselves, struggling to make sense of their new lives.

In this chapter we focus on how people react when they experience layoffs and plant closings. We discuss how people perceive their worlds changing as a result of losing their jobs, how they react to it emotionally, and how they are affected physically.

First, we introduce the *stage models* of responses to unemployment. Much of the academic literature on job loss has suggested that people pass through identifiable and discrete phases in adapting to the stress of a layoff, from initial shock to later adjustment. We will discuss the different phases of adjustment after job loss, the evidence for these phase models of adjustment, and their utility in helping us understand the experience of unemployment.

Second, we discuss three different types of reactions to job loss: perceptual, emotional, and physiological. The perceptual reactions of individual workers to job loss include how the unemployed cognitively interpret what the job loss means for them in their lives: what caused the layoff, how much disruption they expect it will bring to their lives, and how likely they believe they will be to recover from their misfortunes. The emotional reactions of individual workers to a layoff include possible feelings of depression, anxiety, or discouragement in the wake of job loss. The physiological reactions of individual workers to job loss are the potentially negative impacts of unemployment on their health in terms of such factors as elevated blood pressure, sleeping difficulties, increased eating, and the abuse of alcohol and medication.

Third, we explore the situational and personal factors that determine how intensely unemployed workers react to job loss. In particular, we examine factors such as the person's financial circumstances, the feasibility of finding a new job, and how much the employee liked the job he or she lost. We offer here some empirical data as well as qualitative data from our study participants to illustrate the key findings.

Stage Models of Unemployment

Since the 1930s, a large body of the literature on job loss has focused on "stage models" of individual reactions to unemployment. These models suggest that people move through discrete stages of adjustment, typically beginning with feelings of shock, anger, and protest immediately following the job loss, then moving to a phase of optimism and active job search, and ending with pessimism, withdrawal, and passivity if the job search is unsuccessful. As Bakke noted over forty years ago, these stage models might explain how persons who are unemployed can, over time, become unemployable—mired in helplessness and resignation to their plight.[1]

The most influential of the stage-by-stage accounts of reactions to unemployment is Eisenberg and Lazarsfeld's model based on research conducted during the economic depression of the 1930s. In their words,

We find that all writers who have described the course of unemployment seem to agree on the following points: First, there is shock, which is followed by an active hunt for a job, during which the individual is still optimistic and unresigned; he still maintains an unbroken attitude. Second, when efforts fail, the individual becomes pessimistic, anxious, and suffers active distress; this is the most crucial state of all. And third, the individual becomes fatalistic and adapts himself to his new state but with narrower scope. He now has a broken attitude.[2]

More recently, Kaufman has described a four-stage model of response to unemployment based on his research with professionals who had lost their jobs. He describes the first stage as shock, relief, and relaxation, followed by the second stage in which the person makes a concerted effort to find a new job. If this search is unsuccessful, the person moves to the third stage in which he begins to feel vacillation, self-doubt, and anger, followed by the final stage, resignation and withdrawal. Kaufman's research suggests that professionals move from shock to resignation in a relatively short period of time, usually from five to seven months.[3] Newman describes a similar, but much slower, progression in her study of downward mobility among the middle class. She found that participants in her study took longer to spiral downward, with managers sometimes taking years after losing their jobs to accept their new, lower stations in life.[4]

Reports from Pittsburgh

Many of the industrial workers in our Pittsburgh studies described stages in their adjustments to the plant closings similar to those suggested by Kaufman. Following Newman, however, progress through these stages generally extended over long periods of time; often several years passed before resignation and withdrawal set in. In their narrative accounts, the participants in our studies described their initial shock and disorientation in the wake of the plant closings and their intensive searching and preparation for new jobs or new careers. Months and often years later, however, many had landed in jobs that were vastly inferior to their old ones in terms of pay, working conditions, and enjoyment. Worse yet, many found no jobs at all, despite long periods of unemployment. After continuous rejection and with diminishing expectations, their energy, self-confidence, and hope slowly eroded. These comments from our respondents illustrate their slide into despair:

> When I first lost my job, I thought I would have no problem finding a job for at least $7 per hour utilizing my seventeen years of experience. However, after sending out fifty to seventy-five resumes and receiving no response other than one phone call asking if I could run a machine I had no experience on and a failed interview for a management position in a small plant, my feelings of self-worth were shattered. In desperation I accepted a demeaning janitorial job for $4 per hour and later quit that job for a $5 per hour one [that] I was let go from in a month. I have worked less than four months in two years. I am now enrolled in Pittsburgh Technical Institute and I am the top student in the class. I can't understand why my considerable experience is of no use to anyone in the area. One of the reasons that I started school and do so well is that I was using it to give me some sense of value. However, I have extreme feelings of self-doubt whether I have chosen the right program. I long for the time when I knew I could do my job well and was a productive employee.

> Losing my job was hard. When I tried to get other jobs they always said no. I really just got tired of trying. No self-confidence left, I guess.

> After working in the same place for over half of your life you can never seem to realize that you are not going back. When I finally did, I found out most potential employers . . . were very prejudiced about age. . . . After this I was very upset and discouraged for a long time.

> At first you don't believe it. Next you get mad. After that you just don't give a damn.

Research on Stage Models

As noted by Fryer, the stage typology is a common one in the field of psychology and has been used to describe various phenomena ranging from child development to group dynamics. It has a particularly strong tradition in the literature on stress and responses to stressful life events. Selye's general adaptation syndrome, for example, suggests that the body adapts to stress in three distinct stages: alarm, resistance, and exhaustion. Stage models are also used to describe and explain bereavement processes commonly experienced after the death of a spouse or other close family member.[5]

Stage models of unemployment, then, have both intuitive appeal and follow easily from psychological theory. Fryer, however, is not convinced of their empirical support and, with others, has been quite critical of their wholesale application to research on job loss and in designing programs to counsel the unemployed. He notes that for stage-by-stage paradigms to be useful, one stage must, at a minimum, precede a second stage that is presumed to follow it in sequence. In reviewing fifty years of research, however, he concludes that "the evidence offered on behalf of stage/phase accounts of the experience of unemployment is meager in quantity and poor in quality." Moreover, "while it is possible that the response to unemployment may yet turn out to take the form of qualitatively discrete and distinct stages of psychological experience, this review of the current literature suggests no persuasive grounds for believing this is the case."[6]

While we share Fryer's skepticism regarding precise and predictable stages of adjustment, common experience does suggest that a person's reactions to losing a job—as with any stressful or involuntary loss—will change over time. Discouragement, financial pressures, and social isolation all affect feelings and behavior. At the same time, people should also respond differently to unemployment based on their idiosyncratic circumstances. These may range from the nature of the job loss in terms of its permanence or the feasibility of finding new employment, to financial considerations such as the extent of a person's obligations and savings.

In order to determine the validity of stage models of responses to job loss, we examined the data on how people react perceptually, emotionally, and physiologically at different stages or durations of unemployment. We consider these data in the next section.

Responses to Job Loss

Perceptual Changes

A person faced with the loss of a job has to make some sense out of its occurrence: Why did it happen? What does it say about my abilities, or my past career decisions, or my luck? How severe is my problem?

People faced with the uncertainty caused by job loss need to construct a new version of reality to explain the event. This sense-making reduces the uncertainty and lends meaning and structure to the unfamiliar. Once this new subjective reality is in place, the person can proceed as if it is objectively true. Lazarus and DeLongis define this process as cognitive appraisal; it refers to the way a person construes the significance of a stressful event in his or her life.[7]

Attribution theorists such as Kelly provide some clues to how people commonly make sense out of stressful events in their lives.[8] In terms of job loss, people make attributions about, or cognitively code, their terminations along at least three dimensions: (1) the *intensity* of the job loss in terms of the amount of stress, discomfort, or disruption it causes in their lives; (2) the *causality* of the job loss in terms of where they assign blame for losing their jobs; and (3) the *reversibility* of the job loss in terms of the probability of becoming reemployed. The participants in our studies in Florida and Pittsburgh commented extensively on all three dimensions of cognitive appraisal.

INTENSITY. For many people, the job loss was experienced as very intense, causing severe stress and disruption to their lives. Many described it in general terms as "the worse experience imaginable" or "the worst thing to ever happen to me." Many used metaphors of death or dying in their descriptions of the experience. Many, too, were quite graphic when describing the specific hardships it had caused in their lives:

> It has been the worst thing in thirty-eight years of my life to happen to me. It has caused many problems in my home, marriage, and everyday life. I will need a job to try to keep my home, car, food, etc. There is so much to say that words cannot explain.

> The feelings I have about losing my job in the steel mill would be the same feelings that hundreds and thousands of men (and women) have already expressed. My story is no different. It's the same story of another generation giving its life to the company but what's different now is my generation was not allowed to finish its career in the mills. I started out young and strong in the mill, bought a house, a car, raised a family and provided that family with everything it needed. But then it was all gone—my wife, the children, the house, then the car and everything else the mill helped to establish. Gone!

Today is May 22nd. I'm a thirty-six-year-old man who once had a wife, three young kids, a house, new car, and more. Today I'm back home living with my parents. I have a full-time job that grosses $200 a week. I pay child support, car payments, car insurance, some rent to my parents, and daily living expenses, and I am financially in a hole. Things just don't add up. I visit my children, whom I love dearly, every week and on weekends, but overall, life has been real hard these last four years. I can go on and on but, like I said in the beginning, my story is no different. It's all been said before hundreds of times by hundreds of men . . . (P.S. Some men did not survive! R.I.P.).

The sudden pressures that you experience are known only to those who have had this type of experience. You feel like you are being squeezed from all directions.

The shock of losing your job and starting [a new job] at $5 an hour or less is tremendous! I used to have a family life; now all I have is work, twelve hours a day, to meet my bills. The adjustment is unthinkable!

After becoming used to living like a decent human being, then losing your job, working six days a week just to make the house payment for two years before selling it at a loss, then losing your wife because of all the hardships that were not your fault, then looking endlessly for a decent job only to find jobs for $4 or $5 an hour [so that I] can't afford an apartment or any place to live so having to live out of a van for the past two-and-a-half years, *how should one feel?* Please, I'm a hard worker and did a good job. I always go to work—check my record! I want to be normal again, like a real human being with a house instead of a van.

Since losing my job, my life has changed completely. My wife now has to work and with both of us employed we don't earn the amount I did working for U.S. Steel. It's hard to make ends meet.

I never dreamed of the drastic changes that would occur: the money problems, arguing problems, tension between husband and wife, tension between parents and children, me working nights—my wife working days, constant strain on relationships, tears, my kids probably will not see college. I pray things get better.

Besides the death of a loved one, losing my job was one of the greatest hurts I have had in my life.

REVERSIBILITY. Many also commented on the hopelessness of their situation in terms of their perceived inability to reverse it. People commonly expressed discouragement, pessimism, and, in many cases, despair. Many saw themselves as never again being able to have the kinds of lives that they had once enjoyed, or never able to realize the lifestyles they felt they were building toward by their decades of labor. Many spoke of the future with worry, hopelessness, and a sense that their fates were out of their own control:

I once believed I had a future but the money people took it away.

I have tried many jobs since losing my job at [the mill]. There have not been any of these jobs to compare with the one [I had]. No benefits like I used to have. Wages are terrible on these jobs.

I always felt safe and secure in my job, was satisfied with my work and planned on being there until retirement. Now I'm not near as sure of myself.

At my age I should be living in what they call the "golden years." My home paid off, my children grown up and educated and gone on to their careers. Because I have five children, all college-educated, I was not able to save any money for the present. As a result life is now as big a burden as when I was raising children, especially economically. I cannot afford repairs to my home or new furniture, which both are over thirty years old, which I could do if I was gainfully employed.

What does a fifty-seven-year-old black woman have to look forward to? How can I survive on minimum wage?

There is no American dream anymore!

I'm the wife and I'd like to share some of the things that have happened to us because of the job [loss]. We moved in with my parents for five and a half years, causing severe strain on our family relationship. I wanted to be a full-time mother so we sacrificed. It almost cost us our marriage and our family relationship will never be the same. My husband just lost another job. Even if he gets called back he will always be the first laid off because he is low man. Most plants with shifts give the new man the second shift which ruins his time with our daughter during the week. One of the greatest accommodations that we made was the decision to have only one child, conceived when times were good. . . . We made accommodations alright. [We] gave up our dreams, learned to expect lean Christmases and birthdays, no vacations, ten-year-old cars, and worn clothing. These changes were the easiest. It's the loss of pride and the sinking feeling that no matter how hard you worked, it was all out of your control.

The mill had the three main opportunities you look for in a company: good wages, excellent medical coverage, and a pension. These three are impossible to find today.

First, you plan upon the basic areas, such as home and family. You save and wait for the appropriate time and the right home to purchase. Then, you begin to plan your family. After you're lucky enough to prove you are someone, you buy that home, you have children, plan on providing a solid future for them and yourself. Suddenly, all the dreams are shattered.

CAUSALITY. One of the most widely discussed issues regarding unemployment—particularly when it is associated with deindustrialization—is that of assigning cause or blame. Academic journals, as well as the popular business press, are filled with reports attempting to explain the reasons for economic restructuring in the United States. Explanations run the gamut from government policies on foreign trade, to the recent proliferation of corporate mergers and acquisitions, to changes in capital markets such as the appearance of "junk bonds" to fuel the acquisition frenzy. Organized labor has also weathered its share of finger pointing, with "big unionism" a common whipping boy for the decline of U.S. productivity in manufacturing.

Individual employees have not escaped blame by the experts. Beginning in the 1970s, books such as *Work in America* sounded the alarm on the decline of the American work ethic, particularly among younger, more educated employees. These reports chronicled the decline of the ethic of hard work and corporate loyalty and the rise in attitudes that instead emphasized individual fulfillment and monetary reward.[9]

The unemployed themselves are often described as also blaming themselves for losing their jobs. As described by Newman, this belief stems from the traditional American belief in individual control and self-reliance, and our unwillingness to question the "rightness" of our existing economic systems and assumptions:

American Puritan heritage, as embodied in the work ethic, sustains a steadfast belief in the ability of individuals to control the circumstances of their lives. When life does not proceed according to plan, Americans tend to assume that the fault lies within. We are far more likely to "blame the victim" than to assume that systemic economic conditions beyond the influence of any individual are responsible. This tendency is so pervasive that at times even the victims blame the victims, searching within to find the character flaw that has visited downward mobility upon them. Even they assume that economic dislocation is somehow uniquely their problem.[10]

Little such self-blame was found in our studies in Pittsburgh and Florida. Instead, people's assessments of the causes of their job loss were, almost without exception, external:

I feel as if I have been thrown out of a job for reasons I have no control over.

I had a job that I liked very much. I lost it through no fault of my own.

In terms of specific objects of external blame, the most common was the company that let them go. This was particularly pronounced among the laid-off steelworkers:

As far as I'm concerned, U.S. Steel ruined my life. They have caused a lot of heartache for me and my family.

I think most of the jobs in this area were lost due to the greed of the company. I don't think they realize or care about the damage they did to the people.

I feel that U.S. Steel lied to the union members in several areas: We took a pay cut to keep our jobs; we were told that if a profit was made, our jobs would be secure. This profit was made. Foreign steel was stockpiled at [the plant] and delivered as domestic steel. The plant was not kept up to date; the same conditions as in the 1930s were still there in the 1980s. I feel that [the plant] was mismanaged and overstaffed by management. There was no communication between workers and management. I feel I was a good worker: I completed an apprenticeship program; I took pride in my work. I gave my time and energy to U.S. Steel for half my life and was told I was no longer needed.

[I am] bitter, very bitter, to know that American business sold the American workers out for its greed, for money, and that the government did nothing about it and is still doing nothing about it. I was forced to live in poverty and it looks like that is the way I will be finishing up.

I feel U.S. Steel raped the employees it employed.

I feel betrayed by corporate greed and the American corporations' lack of concern [and failure to] reinvest money to modernize their [manufacturing] facilities.

I now work maintenance at a golf course for $4.30 per hour. I have one day off a week which is Sunday. There is no advancement; you work until you drop dead—whatever age you make it to. My wife works at a nursing home at minimum wage. I think it stinks, the closing of the mills. Yet you have people at the big office of U.S. Steel who give themselves a raise of $695,000 a year. There is no one— and I mean no one—who is worth that kind of money! I think those responsible for the shutdown [of the steel mill] should have to live the way we are living—the men who lost everything!

We took concessions, less benefits, and still they closed the mills, throwing thousands of workers to the dogs. We worked long and hard to make U.S. Steel the number one steelmaker in the country. I would compare the actions of the chairman of the board to that of Adolph Hitler. I would never want to work for U.S. Steel again, anywhere!

I think it is really wrong what the company did to me and my fellow workers. They put us out in the streets without any notice. They didn't give a damn about us. They caused families to break up and even suicides. I feel you have to be strong to live in today's society— mentally.

U.S. Steel used me until I was spent then cast me aside. . . . Now I know how a Vietnam Vet feels.

The laid-off employees in Florida also blamed their employers or other companies involved in the space program. Their comments are particularly critical of management competence and reflect a deep resentment of the perceived intra- and inter-company politics of government contract work.

I feel that I am, along with many others, having to pay for Morton Thiokol's mistakes in the *Challenger* disaster, as well as those of NASA Quality Control personnel.

The thing that upset me most about losing my job is that, in my opinion, it could have been avoided. My company gained another contract, but it took so long to do it that a layoff was unavoidable in their eyes. By the time they get the new contract geared up for production, I will be off work for twelve to fourteen months. My point is that if top management wouldn't have dragged their feet so long, the start-up of the new contract could have coincided more closely with the end of the old one. . . . In my opinion it was all company politics. The sad part is that there were a lot of good people used as the "playing pieces" in their little game.

Harris [a NASA subcontractor] is run by a country club of good old boys and their proteges—people who will not challenge them. They are not organized for success and do not want to take steps to do so. They are not interested in free-market challenge but instead live like parasites on the backs of taxpayers. . . . The layoff cost me $30,000 and I feel as though Harris reached into my pocket and took it from me.

The company did not exercise good judgment in laying off lower-paid employees while keeping an overabundance of much higher paid management and supervisory personnel.

Doing a good job doesn't matter at the Kennedy Space Center. Instead, it's whose butt you kiss and how good you do it.

The other common object of blame for the steelworkers was government, in particular its failure to stem the tide of foreign imports, which they saw as destroying American manufacturing industries such as steel. The steelworkers also criticized government's failure to offer adequate assistance when these industries declined.

I lost my job because of foreign imports. The Reagan Administration did not care about the American people.

It seems doing a good job does not count with the representatives that run the country. It is more important to assure the world that we are a free trade country. Unfortunately, this is done at the expense of the American worker. It is more important to keep the citizens of

Japan, Canada, and the European Common Market working. Our representatives say, "Don't worry, the Americans will survive." Of course, other officials snicker and agree. It is time for Americans to side with Americans!

As long as you have an actor like Ronald Reagan as President, you'll have this kind of situation. [He's a] union-busting friend of big business [with an] idiotic refusal to get tough with countries that dump their products here.

Why didn't the government do anything about unfair trade practices? Why has crime become our major industry?

Maybe President Bush should try supporting a family on minimum wage.

PERCEPTUAL CHANGES AND LEARNED HELPLESSNESS. A well-known theory in social psychology, that of learned helplessness, is a perspective that has been frequently utilized to explain how people ascribe meaning to, and make sense out of, stressful events in their lives. Learned helplessness theory suggests that when people are continually exposed to uncontrollable events—such as involuntary job loss and unsuccessful job search—they eventually come to believe that their current predicaments cannot be remedied by any actions on their part.[11] In effect, the unemployed may "learn" how to be helpless; they are conditioned to become depressed, apathetic, and unmotivated to find new jobs because their experience may have taught them that their efforts are of little consequence in improving their situation. They see their lives as out of their control; and, in this regard, their perceptions are remarkably similar to those described in the final phases of the stage models of unemployment.

Learned helplessness and its symptoms are affected by the attributions the person makes about the causes for an uncontrollable event such as losing one's job or failing to find a new one. The more severe people perceive the job loss, the lower their perceived likelihood of turning around their situation and getting reemployed; the more they see their unemployment as caused by others, the more passive they may become. Moreover, if the stage models of unemployment are correct, helpless feelings should escalate over time. The longer a person is out of work, the more intensely he or she will see the job loss as irreversible. These attributions should, in turn, color subsequent feelings and behavior.

STUDY FINDINGS. Our data from the Pittsburgh and Florida studies provided only modest support for stage models and learned helplessness theory. We looked at the relationship between how long people had been out of work and how they perceived the intensity, reversibility, and causality of the job loss. In analyses of variance (statistical tests used to examine differences among groups), the short-term unemployed and the long-term unemployed differed significantly only in their perceptions of the reversibility of their status (see fig. 3–1). The longer individuals were out of work, the less reversible they viewed their circumstances, i.e., the lower they perceived their ability to gain comparable reemployment. Neither perceived intensity nor causality varied significantly with length of unemployment. Thus, in our studies, increasing periods of unemployment were associated with increasing perceptions of hopelessness about finding a comparable new job. The objects of blame were consistently external, however, and the intensity of the experience did not significantly change over time.

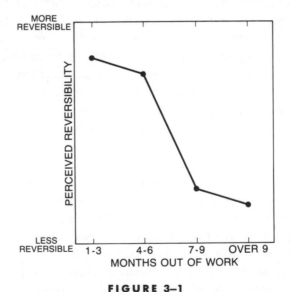

FIGURE 3–1

*Relationship of Length of Unemployment and Perceived
Reversibility of the Job Loss*

Emotional Distress

There is substantial evidence to suggest that job loss leads to a variety of negative changes in people's emotions. Various researchers have found that individuals who have lost their jobs report increased depression, increased boredom, decreased life satisfaction, increased loneliness and social isolation, a loss of sense of time and structure to the day, increased feelings of apathy, passivity, and resignation, and overwhelming pessimism and fatalism about life. These manifestations of decreased affect are commonly reported in studies of job loss.[12]

The participants in our studies also reported depression, social isolation, and loss of structure in their lives.

I feel very much degraded because all my life I had a good job.

Still depressed and sad about losing my job.

If I didn't have a strong mind, I think I would have jumped off the bridge like the other steelworkers did. It's really sad to work so hard and have nothing.

It's been difficult emotionally for me in the last eighteen months.

My house was saved by the Mon Valley Unemployed Committee but not without a $10,000 lien. [I] used charge cards for groceries and am still deeply in debt. [I] know personally of seven people who committed suicide directly related to the hardship of the layoff. I still suffer serious bouts of depression. It has been seven years since my layoff and I am still not financially or mentally recovered.

It was a very lonely and stressful time after being laid off from my old job.

I lost a lot of my self-confidence after being turned down for many jobs because I was a laid-off steelworker. I went through a bad case of depression trying to work at jobs that didn't pay much, worrying about paying my bills with what little I made and am still making.

The mental adjustment you must go through with so much time on your hands is very difficult.

My mental health has suffered much and sometimes I wonder what or if I have any worth. Slowly, I have been stripped of my dignity. . . . I really would like to get another chance at getting a better job for me and the sake of my family and my sanity.

These are quite common reactions to stressful events of any kind, particularly one such as job loss, which is so threatening to a person's sense of control. Not all emotional changes associated with layoffs, however, are associated with lack of energy or motivation. After a transition such as job loss, some people may also experience increased feelings of excitement, challenge, and aggression. Moreover, this anxiety can sometimes be more facilitative than debilitating—at least in the short run.

EMOTIONAL DISTRESS AND REACTANCE THEORY. Research on job loss has traditionally taken the perspective of the stress literature when investigating reactions to unemployment. Job loss is seen as a threatening event in a person's life, causing a great deal of uncertainty, and leading to the feelings of emotional distress described above. Not all people who experience a layoff exhibit this depressed affect, however; some may instead respond not with a lack of motivation or depression, but rather by becoming emotionally aroused and motivated to restore personal control in their lives. Reactance theory, most commonly associated with the work of Brehm, helps explain why some terminated employees become emotionally aroused and highly motivated to get back into the work force.

Brehm's work suggests that when an individual's personal control is threatened, he or she will become motivated to restore the lost control or freedom. According to the theory, the amount of reactance individuals will feel—that is, the amount of effort they will expend to restore their lost control or freedom—is a function of four factors: (1) the strength of the person's expectation of control or freedom to engage in a behavior, (2) the strength of the threat to the freedom, (3) the importance of the behavior, and (4) the implication that this loss of freedom has for other desired pursuits.[13]

In the case of job loss, the threatened behavior is, of course, the ability to work. We would expect that people would exhibit strong expectations that they will be able to work, feel threatened when this expectation is challenged, attach great importance to work, and feel that the loss of work has rather profound implications for other aspects of their lives. Thus, if Brehm's theory is correct, job loss should provoke strong reactance under most circumstances. This reactance should manifest itself through behaviors geared toward either restoring the person's sense of control (e.g., intensive job search) or, failing that, venting the frustration accompanying the loss of control (e.g., hostile and aggressive acts).

Indeed, reactance theory may help to explain some of the heightened behavior and emotions that may accompany the loss of a job—particularly in the initial and middle stages of unemployment. It does not, however, explain the more commonly-reported feelings of passivity and depression, and directly contradicts the learned helplessness model described previously.

Recent reconciliations of reactance and learned helplessness theories attempt to order the two in a temporal sequence that supports the stage models of reactions to unemployment. Wortman and Brehm, for example, have suggested that initial reactions to loss of control may take the form of reactance. After repeated failures to regain control over one's life (e.g., find a new job, retrain for a new profession), the person may learn to be helpless and exhibit the passivity and depressed affect so commonly reported in studies of job loss.[14]

STUDY FINDINGS. One might reasonably expect depressed affect to become more pronounced with the passage of time after a person loses his or her job. Data from the Pittsburgh and Florida studies, however, only partially support this proposition. In both studies, people showed the greatest levels of depression, apathy, etc., in the first six months of unemployment. Those out of work seven through nine months exhibited the lowest levels, while for those unemployed over nine months, depression once again rose (see fig. 3–2).

When interpreting these data, one should keep in mind that income through unemployment compensation (UC) benefits is available to people for the first six months after the job loss. After that time, the unemployed are often on their own. After this six-month period has elapsed, depression, apathy, and listlessness increase with time. Perhaps, as Brehm might suggest, once there is no income source (after six months), people respond first with reactance (seven to nine months) and only later (after nine months) sink into the depression and apathy that characterize helplessness.

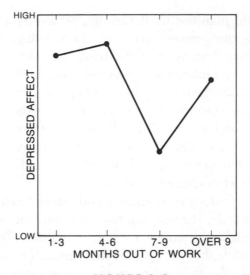

FIGURE 3–2

*Relationship of Length of Unemployment
and Level of Depressed Affect*

Physiological Distress

Seminal works by Cannon on homeostatis and Selye on the General Adaptation Syndrome have focused attention on the impact of stress on physiological health. This research, too, has taken a stage approach to individual reactions. According to Selye, during the initial stage following stress—the alarm stage—respiration, heart rates, and blood cholesterol increase. During the next stage, resistance, there is only a limited amount of adaptive energy left in the individual, and he or she becomes more prone to illness. In the third and final stage, the body becomes exhausted fighting the stressor. The person then becomes more susceptible to fatigue, disability, and (sometimes life-threatening) illnesses.[15]

JOB LOSS AND INDICATORS OF PHYSIOLOGICAL WELL-BEING. Several researchers have examined the relationship between job loss and indicators of physiological well-being. Kasl, Gore, and Cobb, for example, found that after losing their jobs, individuals reported a greater number of days not feeling well. Similarly, Payne, Warr, and Hartley found that over one fourth of the subjects in their study reported a deterioration in health since losing their jobs. Lajer reported that the annual hospitalization rates for workers only intermittently employed were double those of persons working steadily over the same period. Hill, Harrison, Sargeant, and Talbot found significant increases in self-reported disability. Cook, Cummings, Bartley, and Shaper also reported an increased frequency of doctor-diagnosed illness following unemployment.[16]

Several studies have examined specific aspects of physiological health, such as respiratory and gastrointestinal functioning, with equivocal results. For example, Cook et al. reported no greater frequency of bronchitis and lung disease in a sample of unemployed men, although O'Brian and Kabanoff did find increased self-reports of bronchial disorders and shortness of breath among their unemployed respondents. Research by Theorell, Lind, and Floderus reported no significant differences in the incidence of ulcers or gastritis among employed and unemployed respondents. Cobb and Kasl, however, reported a higher incidence of ulcers among terminated employees.[17]

Other studies have examined cardiovascular functioning. O'Brian and Kabanoff, for example, found a higher self-reported incidence of heart trouble among the unemployed. Similarly, Cook et al. reported a greater frequency of heart disease and hypertension in their unemployed sample.[18] Some of the participants in our studies associated their own layoffs with heart disease as well:

> I believe U.S. Steel knew when to lay me off so as to cause me to lose my early pension. Because of all the stress from this, I had a heart attack.

> I will always feel that my heart attack was a reaction to my job loss.

> After being on unemployment for five weeks, I had a massive heart attack which I think was partially caused by losing my job.

In addition to these signs of physiological distress, people may respond to job loss with behaviors detrimental to their physical health. Commonly reported responses to stress include increased smoking, drinking, and drug use, as well as changes in sleeping and eating patterns.[19] Such activities, although potentially harmful to the individual, may also deaden the intensity of the emotion associated with, or reduce the amount of conscious thought about, a stressful event such as job loss. Although these issues were not discussed as extensively as some others by the people in our studies, there were nonetheless some striking accounts of drinking, drug use, overeating, sleep disorders, and other behavioral manifestations of stress:

> I ran afoul of the law for marijuana possession in 1986. My usage was a result of avoiding dealing with the reality of a permanent plant closing. . . . I believe not enough emphasis is placed upon the psychological effects of plant closings on these people [who worked there]. While the hands of time have swung by, they have only succeeded in scarring these psychological wounds. These wounds are still in need of treatment.

> Once the personal pride is vanquished and a person goes down on his knees, he is praying or in deep depression or a combination of both. The following moments begin with bouts of weight gain, loss of faith, loss of friends, overwhelming changes in your children . . . and no one cares.

> [I] have had numerous people I worked with become drunks, divorced, drug addicts. Some of them have even been arrested a lot, lost everything they own. I also worked with one man who wiped out his entire family and himself.

> After being laid off I began to drink quite heavily and do drugs. I went to a number of rehabs and afterwards I felt like I really wasn't sure that starting over again at forty-four was worth it.

STUDY FINDINGS. Although many participants in our studies showed high levels of physiological and emotional distress, we did not find systematic differences in distress levels at different stages of unemployment. These findings are not at odds with those of other researchers, many of whom have also failed to find physiological distress increasing over time.[20]

Factors Influencing Reactions to Job Loss

Many factors may influence how a person reacts to losing a job. We have already discussed one of these—the length of time spent unemployed—and the descriptions of various reactions that are thought to accompany different stages of adjustment. Other idiosyncratic circumstances may also have a powerful influence on all three categories of reactions—perceptual, emotional, and physiological. Financial circumstances, the person's perceptions of the job market in his or her community, and the level of attachment he or she has to the lost job may all have even more profound effects on adjustment than does the "stage" of unemployment.

Financial Circumstances

PARTICIPANT REPORTS. Financial circumstances appeared to be a major factor in how the people in our studies perceived and responded to job loss. Person after person told of the hardships of a drastically reduced standard of living, often even after new jobs had been found:

> It is a shame [to] work all my life then at fifty-nine years old I wonder where my next meal is coming from.

> I was forced to give up a nice apartment because I could not afford the rent anymore. When my money ran out I had to get public assistance for one year. Then I got this job as a maid in a hotel. Work is not steady. When it is busy it's alright but when it's slow sometimes I get only three to four days a week. I worry. I had to move into a housing project. It is terrible here but I have no choice right now. Maybe someday . . .

> When I lost my job I was only fifty-four years old. I felt that I could have worked several more years. This would have helped me financially because my wife had lost her job because of serious illness, and I had a son die. The financial burden has been very high and my insurance benefits are very low and very costly. It was a struggle keeping my family, making house payments, paying utilities, buying food and other essentials.

> Our personal and financial situation is not adequate but we have to manage. We had to do housework for other people to make ends meet.

> What bothered me the most was that I couldn't meet my utility payments. The bill collectors would call and want payments and I had no money to make a payment. I am not able to pay my rent.

My parents are retired. They let me have four rooms and a bath free because I am not able to pay them.

Since my layoff three years ago, our life and financial situation have been very tough. . . . We've barely squeezed by with help from our family and lots of ingenuity. We've been living off of two jobs at minimum wage—one full time and one part time. I've finally worked my way up to $4.25 per hour after two and a half years at my current job [but] I've been told I won't get much more. We've been trying to start a family but were worried about affording kids until we finally decided it was now or never and now we are expecting in July. We're still wondering if we can afford a child but we want to take the chance before we get too old waiting for a decent paying job.

I feel pretty bad about losing my job [at the mill] but I am willing to work full time on something like janitorial work, grass-cutting jobs, painting jobs, etc. This would help us if I could get something like this. My wife works as a cashier at Giant Eagle [a large grocery chain]. We only clear around $185 per week, which isn't good in this day and age. I now work part time doing janitorial work.

My financial situation is public welfare.

Our financial income is not nearly enough to get us through. There are so many back bills that you just think will never go away and the money that is brought in is not even enough to pay all the utilities and the rent alone without help of cash assistance and food stamps. Without food stamps our kids would not be able to eat.

I am currently *very unhappy* with my job. I am a janitor at [a local hospital]. It is part time, no benefits, and no promise of it either in the future. There is no union so they push you with as much as they can get away with and maybe more. My wife is working part time also but only a couple of days a week at $4.25 per hour. We couldn't make it without the help of food stamps and welfare medical insurance.

Loss of medical insurance coverage was a particular concern for many of the people in our studies. In the second Pittsburgh survey, in fact, over half of the respondents (53%) had gone without health insurance of any sort at some time since the plant closing. Twenty-four percent still had no health insurance; of this number, over half were currently employed but without a medical benefits package. Even among those who were insured, over forty percent reported that their health insurance was not adequate to cover their families' needs. Those who purchased insurance on their own spoke of the financial hardships incurred by doing so:

> I miss medical coverage most of all. I have a family and the bulk of my income is for doctors and dentists and that just barely covers the barest of health needs of my family. I also miss the steady income that the mill produced. It bothers me to see my children growing and knowing I may never be able to take them on a vacation or give them any of the finer things in life.

> I haven't been able to afford health insurance since our coverage with the mill was stopped.

> Our financial situation is not good because we are unable to afford hospitalization [insurance] because of low wages. Companies don't seem to care if they carry it or not on their employees.

> My biggest problem is the cost of health insurance. From 1986 to 1989, [it] increased 52.9 percent!

> We have a son who is confined to a wheelchair with cerebral palsy. My dismissal was tragic for us because we lost all our [health] insurance and could not afford to pay for any. My wife had what they call a mini-stroke two years ago, and she had to have treatments and be hospitalized and is on medication every day. We are still paying these bills. We had to go to the food pantry for help [with groceries].

STUDY FINDINGS. According to the quantitative data, financial problems also influenced both how people perceived the job loss and how they reacted to it in terms of physiological and behavioral distress. In both the Pittsburgh and the Florida samples, the existence of financial problems after the job loss very strongly predicted the perceived intensity of the experience (see fig. 3–3). In addition, those reporting financial problems also reported more physiological and behavioral distress as well as depressed affect (see fig. 3–4). Thus, the quantitative data in our studies corroborate the importance of financial circumstances as reported by person after person in the written narratives and interviews.

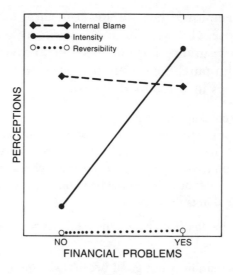

FIGURE 3–3

*Relationship of Financial Problems
and Perceptions of the Job Loss*

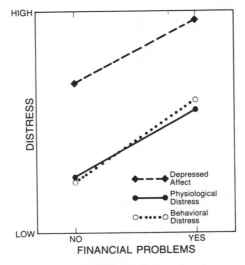

FIGURE 3–4

Relationship of Financial Problems and Distress

Perceptions of Labor Market Conditions

People's perceptions of the job market and their chances for reemployment in a similar job may also influence their reactions to job loss. The higher people view the unemployment rates in their communities, the more pessimistic they are likely to be about their prospects for finding a new job, especially one at comparable pay.[21] Thus, laid-off employees who consider the labor market poor and their chances for reemployment very low may cognitively appraise the job loss as more intense and less reversible and may exhibit more emotional and physical distress symptoms.

PARTICIPANT REPORTS. In both Pittsburgh and Florida, many of our study participants described weak labor markets, high unemployment rates, and little in the way of job opportunities. In Pittsburgh, many voiced concern that the only jobs available were those that paid at or near minimum wage. Many resented the decline in "official" unemployment rates in the latter part of the 1980s and insisted that these figures did not reflect reality as they knew it:

> This area is lacking in high-paying jobs. Most jobs in the area are very low paying and there still are hundreds of people applying for them, which should tell everyone that the government [unemployment] statistics are wrong.

> It stinks! Where did all the real jobs go?

> It is a pity that the dogs of American industry are taking full advantage of the poor economic conditions that presently exist in the Pittsburgh area.

> My new job is in auto sales. Auto sales in McKeesport [a mill town outside of Pittsburgh] is not an easy task so don't let any government officials bullshit you people. I see it first-hand. There are very few jobs that pay a decent wage.

> Since May 1986 I have been trying to get back into heavy industry to obtain proper employment. But it is the same story all over the region—nobody is hiring. In fact, most places were either cutting back their work force or were not hiring. I have a wife and two children to support and presently my wages are $3.85 per hour with no benefits. I receive food stamps from Welfare to subsidize my income at this time. I am also still looking for better work with higher

pay and benefits but apparently nobody wants a forty-six-year-old steelworker for employment.

Most jobs available pay the minimum wage with no benefits.

The laid-off aerospace workers in Florida also expressed pessimism regarding the local job market as well as cynicism over the perceived politics and cronyism in the world of government contract work. In addition, many reported their chances of reemployment were reduced because new employers felt they would leave if recalled to their former government positions:

> Most employers hesitate in hiring laid-off Space Center employees due to the possibility of recall and their inability to compete in wages and benefits.

> All the other current lay-offs in this community are a multiple strike against my chances of reemployment.

> A lot of companies, when placing ads in the newspaper, are falsely representing [themselves], especially companies dealing in government contracts. They will place these ads knowing that the openings will be filled by "who you know" personnel. It's frustrating!

> No one wanted to hire a space worker for fear that they would be called back, and private industry did not want to take a chance with them.

STUDY FINDINGS. To assess the effect of perceived labor market conditions on how people reacted to the job loss, we asked study participants to estimate how high they thought unemployment rates were in their communities. Analyses of variance showed that these estimates were significant predictors of both perceptions and distress reactions (see figs. 3–5 and 3–6). Perceptions of both intensity and reversibility were related to estimated unemployment rates. The higher people perceived unemployment rates to be, the more severe and the more irreversible they saw their plight. As these estimates increased, job losers tended to view their own job loss as more intense and less reversible. Both physiological and behavioral distress also increased with these estimates.

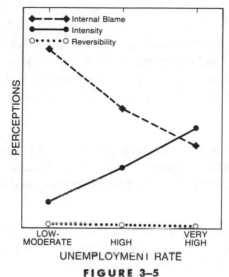

FIGURE 3–5

*Relationship of Reported Unemployment Rates
and Perceptions of the Job Loss*

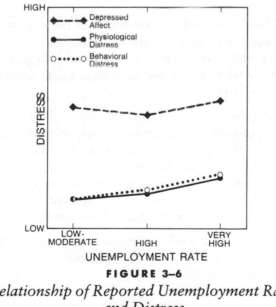

FIGURE 3–6

*Relationship of Reported Unemployment Rates
and Distress*

Job Attachment

People who are most attached to their previous employers and professions will likely respond more negatively to being laid off. For these employees, losing a job also means losing a source of internal satisfaction and long-held social networks and structures in their lives.[22]

PARTICIPANT REPORTS. Participants in studies in both Pittsburgh and Florida reflected the sense of loss they felt, not only for the job itself, but also for the friends, acquaintances, and way of life left behind:

> I gave U.S. Steel thirteen good, hard years. I miss it very much. I grew close to a lot of friends. Not seeing them or hearing their jokes and laughter hurts me inside. We all grew up inside those mills. Everyone knew everyone's family and kids. We were a close group, proud, and a satisfied group of mill workers. Financially, everyone will miss the good wages we had but it's the people, friends, that I miss more than anything.

> All I would like to say is that while I worked for [the mill], I really enjoyed my work. Wherever it would be, I ran the whole department and, on the second shift, myself. My bosses were the greatest. I had 23,000 parts to take care of and inventory. I sure do miss all the people I worked with.

> These people [who work with you] are more than just your co-workers. You've spent eight to ten hours a day with these guys. They see more of you than your family, and probably know more about your moods, attitudes, and ideas than anyone else you know. They laugh at your jokes, calm you when you're mad, and cheer you when you're down. If a personal crisis comes up, you know they'll be there for you—as you'd be for them. That's all over now.

> You'll never know how hard it is passing my plant in my car and knowing the memories I have and the lump that grows in my throat knowing I can never work there again.

STUDY FINDINGS. The quantitative data show how job attachment is related to reactions to the job loss. Those who reported greater job involvement in their previous jobs also viewed the job loss as a more intense and less reversible experience (see fig. 3–7). They

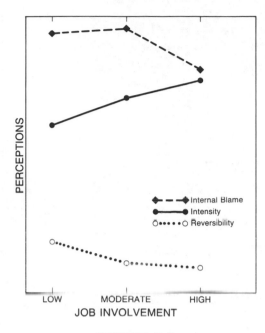

FIGURE 3–7
*Relationship of Job Involvement and Perceptions
of the Job Loss*

were, however, significantly more likely to blame external circumstances for the job loss, rather than to blame themselves. Job involvement was also significantly related to distress. Those who were
more involved with their previous jobs also reported more physiological distress, behavioral distress, and depressed affect (see fig.
3–8). Clearly, feeling more involvement in one's job is associated
with more negative reactions when that job is taken away. This
pattern held true for both the industrial workers in Pittsburgh and
the aerospace workers in Florida.

Summary of Findings

A critical issue in understanding the experience of job loss is the
relative power of different factors in predicting and explaining differences in individual reactions. Central to this issue is the question,
Which has a greater impact on how workers respond to layoffs—
the discrete stage of their adjustment to unemployment, or their

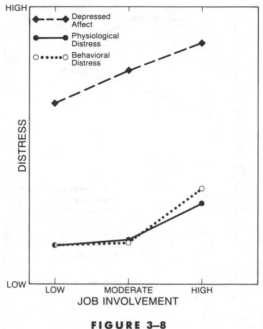

FIGURE 3–8

Relationship of Job Involvement and Distress

own idiosyncratic circumstances? There were some striking findings within both the Pittsburgh and Florida studies that address this question.

The existence of financial difficulties strongly affected the intensity of the job loss experience and was a strong predictor of distress reactions. These findings underscore Hartley and Fryer's contention that the effects of unemployment cannot be accurately assessed apart from the financial problems that often accompany job loss.[23] The level of involvement in the previous job also had significant effects on all three aspects of cognitive appraisal—intensity, reversibility, and causality—and on distress reactions for both samples. Collectively, these results suggest that the deprivation experienced by people as a result of job loss has both a financial component and a component more concerned with the meaning that work has in people's lives. The respondents' graphic narrative descriptions of the deprivation in their lives underscore and enrich these empirical findings.

An equally interesting similarity between the samples was the *lack* of consistent significant effects attributable to length of unemployment. Essentially, only perceived reversibility was consistently and linearly related to length of unemployment in our empirical analyses. The remaining nonsignificant results should, of course, be interpreted with caution, but it is of some interest that length of unemployment was not consistently related to other perceptions or distress responses in either sample—a finding at odds with the stage model theories of unemployment popular in the 1930s and, more recently, with Kaufman and others.[24]

These results suggest that idiosyncratic circumstances—financial distress, involvement with the previous job, and perceived labor-market conditions—are the more important influences on responses to job loss. These results offer no consistent support for the notion that extended unemployment is associated with more consistently negative (or, for that matter, positive) responses. Thus, we can offer no evidence in support of the stage models of unemployment but instead offer data that support the important effects of individual differences on responses to job loss.

The reasons for our interest in these differing responses to job loss is twofold. First, because people's general feelings about their lives are so intertwined with their experiences of work, their reactions to job loss signal disruptions reverberating not only to the quality of their own lives, but to their spouses' and childrens' lives as well. Second, we would expect that people's reactions to job loss would have a major impact on how they cope with unemployment, and ultimately on their long-term adjustment. Although the image of the unemployed portrayed in movies, television, and other venues of popular culture is almost exclusively that of passive victim, the unemployed are actually quite varied in how they cope with their new circumstances, and, as we see in the next chapter, sometimes very active in getting their lives back on track.

Notes

1. E. W. Bakke, *Citizens without Work* (New Haven: Yale University Press, 1949).
2. P. Eisenberg and P. E. Lazarsfeld, "The Psychological Effects of Unemployment," *Psychological Bulletin* 39 (1938): 358–90.
3. H. G. Kaufman, *Professionals in Search of Work* (New York: John Wiley and Sons, 1982).

4. K. S. Newman, *Falling from Grace: The Experience of Downward Mobility in the American Middle Class* (New York: Vintage Books, 1988).
5. See D. Fryer, "Stages in the Psychological Response to Unemployment: A Disintegrative Review," *Current Psychological Research & Reviews* (1985): 257–73, for a critique of stage models of unemployment. The general adaptation syndrome is described in H. Seyle, *The Stress of Life* (New York: McGraw Hill, 1976). A description of stages in bereavement is provided in C. Murray-Parkes, *Bereavement* (London: Tavistock, 1972).
6. See Fryer, "Stages."
7. R. S. Lazarus and A. DeLongis, "Psychological Stress and Coping in Aging," *American Psychologist* 38 (1983): 245–54.
8. H. H. Kelly, "The Process of Causal Attribution," *American Psychologist* 28 (1973): 107–8.
9. See, for example, *Work in America: Report of a Special Task Force to the Secretary of Health, Education, and Welfare* (Cambridge: MIT Press, 1973); and C. Lasch, *The Culture of Narcissism: American Life in an Age of Diminishing Expectations* (New York: W. W. Norton, 1978).
10. Newman, "Falling from Grace," p. 9.
11. A description of the revised learned helplessness model is provided in L. Y. Abramson, M. E. Eligman, and J. D. Teasdale, "Learned Helplessness in Humans: Critique and Reformulation," *Journal of Abnormal Psychology* 87 (1978): 49–74.
12. See, for example, J. M. Hill, "The Psychological Impact of Unemployment," *New Society* 43 (1978): 118–20; and R. M. Cohn, "The Effect of Employment Status Change on Self-Attitudes," *Social Psychology* 41 (1978): 81–93.
13. J. W. Brehm, *A Theory of Psychological Reactance* (New York: Academic Press, 1966); and S. S. Brehm and J. W. Brehm, *Psychological Reactance: A Theory of Freedom and Control* (New York: Academic Press, 1981).
14. C. B. Wortman and J. W. Brehm, "Responses to Uncontrollable Outcomes: An Integration of Reactance Theory and the Learned Helplessness Model," in L. Berkowitz, ed., *Advances in Experimental Social Psychology*, 8: 278–336 (New York: Academic Press, 1975).
15. See Selye, *The Stress of Life*; also W. B. Cannon, *The Wisdom of the Body* (New York: W. W. Norton, 1932).
16. S. V. Kasl, S. Gore, and S. Cobb, "The Experience of Losing a Job: Reported Changes in Health, Symptoms, and Illness Behavior," *Psychosomatic Medicine* 37 (1975): 106–22; R. L. Payne, P. Warr, and S. Hartley, *Social Class and the Experience of Unemployment*, MCR/SSRC SAPU memo 59, University of Sheffield, United Kingdom, (1983); M. Lajer, "Unemployment and Hospitalization among Bricklayers," *Scandinavian Journal of Social Medicine* 10 (1982): 3–10; J. M. Hill, R. M. Harrison, A. V. Sargeant, and V. Talbot, *Men Out of Work: A Study of Unemployment in Three English Towns* (Cambridge: Cambridge University Press, 1973); and D. G. Cook, R. O. Cummings, M. J. Bartley, and A. G. Shaper, "Health of the Unemployed Middle-Aged Men in Great Britain," *Lancet* 5 (1982): 1290–94.

17. Cook et al., "Health"; G. E. O'Brian and B. Kabanoff, "Comparisons of Unemployed and Employed Workers on Work Values, Locus of Control, and Health Variables," *Australian Psychologist* 14 (1979): 143–54; T. Theorell, E. Lind, and B. Floderus, "The Relationship of Disturbing Life Changes and Emotions to the Early Development of Myocardial Infarction and Other Serious Illness," *International Journal of Epidemiology* 4 (1975): 281–93; and S. Cobb and S. V. Kasl, *Termination: The Consequences of Job Loss* (Washington, D.C.: National Institute for Occupational Safety and Health, Report No. 76-1261, 1977).
18. Cook et al., "Health"; and O'Brian and Kabanoff, "Comparisons."
19. See A. P. Brief, R. S. Shuler, and M. VanSell, *Managing Job Stress* (Boston: Little, Brown, 1981).
20. See, for example, Cobb and Kasl, "Termination."
21. See R. J. Barro, "Unanticipated Money Growth and Unemployment in the United States," *American Economic Review* 67 (1977): 101–15.
22. See L. F. Dunn, "Measuring the Value of Community," *Journal of Urban Economics* 6 (1979): 371–82.
23. For a discussion of financial deprivation in job loss and a thorough critique of the job loss literature, see J. Hartley and D. Fryer, "The Psychology of Unemployment: A Critical Appraisal," in G. Stephenson and J. Davis, eds., *Progress in Applied Social Psychology*, 2: (Chichester, England: Wiley, 1986).
24. See, for example, Eisenberg and Lazarsfeld, "Psychological Effects"; and Kaufman, *Professionals*.

Coping with Job Loss

Traditionally, the research on job loss has treated the unemployed as relatively passive victims. Much of the research on laid-off workers has focused on documenting how depressed, or how anxious, or how physically or emotionally impaired the unemployed become. Indeed, underlying most of the job loss literature is the "deprivation model,"[1] which assumes that job loss makes workers more lethargic, inactive, and unanchored because it deprives them not only of financial security, but also of meaningful activity, companionship, and a structure to the day.

Our studies at the Pittsburgh steel mills and on the Florida Space Coast also documented these effects of unemployment. In addition, we sought to examine individual coping mechanisms. What do unemployed workers do to obtain new jobs? How do they achieve, maintain, or restore at least a semblance of normality to their lives? How successful are they?

In this chapter we examine how laid-off employees cope with job loss. First we discuss more fully the nature of coping behavior and how the negative reactions to job loss (described in Chapter 3) can motivate or energize laid-off workers to try to establish new routines after the shock of a layoff. We also look at the different types of coping behaviors used to reduce stress or to gain reemployment after job loss, and why some coping strategies are used more frequently than others.

Then we address the question: What causes some laid-off workers to be highly motivated and active in trying to get reemployed and regain some semblance of normalcy in their lives, while others remain relatively passive and apathetic? We look at how differing patterns of emotional and psychological reactions to job loss influence the ways in which people try to cope with unemployment.

Next we examine the consequences of coping behavior and the effectiveness of different coping strategies in gaining reemployment and reducing psychological distress. Here we also present data to illustrate the roles that personality traits (for example, the pattern of aggressiveness associated with Type-A behavior) and demographic characteristics (such as gender) play in how laid-off workers cope and adjust to job loss.

Finally we look at some important theoretical and practical implications our research findings have for how laid-off employees handle unemployment. Here we explore the most common patterns employees use to cope with layoffs, why these patterns emerge, and the differential effectiveness of various coping strategies in obtaining reemployment, both immediately after the job loss and later.

The Nature of Coping

By *coping*, we mean active attempts by individuals to establish new routines after they have experienced a stressful event. In the case of those who have lost their jobs, coping behaviors are attempts to gain reemployment and/or to regain some semblance of psychological well-being. In our study of the Pittsburgh steelworkers and the laid-off employees on the Space Coast, we looked at two broad classes of coping behaviors: problem-focused coping and symptom-focused coping.[2]

Problem-focused coping refers to behaviors a person engages in to control or eliminate the cause of the stress itself. In the context of job loss, examples of problem-focused coping might be getting training for a new occupation, searching for new jobs through newspaper ads, or attempting to relocate to an area with better employment prospects. These coping behaviors help laid-off workers directly eliminate the cause of the stress itself (i.e., getting a new job eliminates the period of unemployment).

Symptom-focused coping refers to behaviors a person engages in to alleviate the negative consequences of a stressful event. In the context of job loss, examples of symptom-focused coping might be applying for governmental financial assistance, seeking out social support or counseling, or becoming involved in community pro-grams to help the unemployed. These coping behaviors help dimin-ish the negative feelings of isolation, depression, or financial distress generated by job loss, but do nothing to change the person's em-ployment status.[3]

How the Unemployed Try to Cope

As we observed in the last chapter, people who have lost their jobs often experience depression, apathy, and anxiety and, for some, increased symptoms of physical illness as well. The research on job stress gives us a framework for understanding why the unemployed don't simply surrender to their distress.[4]

First, job loss forces individuals to change their lives, despite their initial unwillingness to do so. Certainly, the unemployed feel vulnerable, angry, and depressed; however, often job loss provides the needed incentive—although a harsh one—to change directions, to get out of a line of work in which they weren't very happy to begin with, or to move to a more economically viable community.[5] Some comments from our respondents support this point:

> I went back to school to obtain an associate's degree from the com munity college. Since then I've retrained myself through reading and learning on the job. . . . I'm moving to Tennessee because there is no work here.

> I may have been more fortunate than many others who worked at the mills. I could see the handwriting on the wall, and knew that jobs would soon be lost. With that in mind, I began classes for an associate degree at the junior college. . . . I am not sure that once I have my degree I will be able to work satisfactorily in my field, but I do know for a fact attending college certainly opens many doors that once were closed to someone with just a high school degree.

Second, coping can help eliminate the initial source of stress—unemployment. Many of our respondents came to realize that only by taking action could they eliminate their joblessness.[6] As some of the steelworkers in our study observed:

> I survived my unemployment and have started to put together my life. My retraining helped. Although I'm not working in the same

field, it gave me the electrical training to go along with my mechanical background to pass and score high enough to secure a maintenance position with the U.S. Postal Service.

I have found that I had no trouble getting a [new job]. When I worked at the mills, I worked in the machine shop. I was good at what I did. I ran as many machines as I could for variety and change. The people that had always stuck with one machine seem to have had quite a bit more difficulty getting decent jobs. . . . There seems to be a big shortage of manual machinists. I now do prototype work on laboratory equipment. While interviewing, I turned down nine out of fourteen jobs. You got to be good.

Third, even coping efforts not directly aimed at gaining new employment can alleviate some of the negative consequences of job loss by providing the unemployed with some structure to their day and chances for companionship. One of the biggest issues that unemployed workers face is that time hangs heavy on their hands. Days seem to stretch endlessly before them; there is no pressing reason to get up early, or to get out of the house, or to get to bed at a reasonable hour.[7] Moreover, many people we talked to noted how much they miss the friendship and support of their co-workers, who often acted as an extended family.

Thus, coping behaviors that get the unemployed out of the house and into contact with other people bring additional benefits over and above making progress towards finding new jobs. In fact, comments from many steelworkers who got additional training focused on these positive side effects:[8]

After a while, when people were getting into their courses, even their appearances changed. They dressed better and were clean shaven.

I could see a different attitude . . . self-respect and self-confidence.

School brought me out. It gave me something to do. . . . It gave me a lift. It gave me another outlook.

Coping, then, can help the unemployed reestablish some routines in their lives, reaffirm their sense of personal control, and regain their confidence about their competence.[9]

Frequency of Coping Behavior

In our surveys in Florida and Pittsburgh, we asked our respondents to indicate the extent to which they had engaged in active coping behaviors since being laid off. We focused on six distinct strategies for coping: (1) searching for a new job on their own initiative; (2) seeking education and/or training; (3) investigating geographical relocation; (4) getting involved in community activities; (5) applying for financial assistance beyond unemployment insurance; and (6) seeking social support.

Table 4–1 displays the behaviors we investigated within each coping strategy, as well as the percentage of respondents who reported engaging in each behavior. The table presents data for the Homestead and Florida samples separately, as well as for both groups combined.

JOB SEARCH ACTIVITY. As Table 4–1 suggests, some sort of self-initiated job search was pursued by nearly all our respondents, with following up on "help wanted" notices being the most frequent strategy. This is not surprising, given that many had obtained their original jobs through this method. In general, the local economies both on the Space Coast and in the Monongahela Valley were quite depressed prior and subsequent to the layoffs. Therefore, two active job search strategies—using governmental agencies and community job bank services—were viewed as less viable alternatives since the perception was that there were very few jobs available in the local area.

For example, at the Monongahela Valley Job Search Assistance Center, bulletin boards for displaced steelworkers listed jobs available nationwide, from health physics engineer to ditch digger. Each Monday morning, a "Network Meeting" convened among a dozen or so laid-off steelworkers, each of whom had signed a "contract" obliging him to spend twenty hours a week looking for work in return for the services provided by the center. These meetings began much like an Alcoholics Anonymous gathering. For instance, the first speaker at one such meeting stood up and announced: "My name is Joe. I was laid off in June 1984. I have a part-time cleaning job. It keeps me off welfare. We ain't giving up."[10]

This center provided laid-off steelworkers with workshops on job

TABLE 4–1

Frequency of the Use of Coping Strategies for Homestead, Florida, and Full Samples

	Homestead* (N=198)	Florida (N=163)	Full sample (N=361)
Job search activity	85.1%	83.8%	86.3%
1. Followed up on "help wanted" notices			
2. Tried to get a job through a government agency	48.2	69.3	59.8
3. Used community job bank services	23.7	23.1	25.4
Seeking retraining	24.5	38.2	26.7
1. Took courses at college or university			
2. Participated in technical retraining program	20.0	5.0	13.3
3. Took steps to learn new trade/ profession	42.9	37.8	41.1
Seeking to relocate	25.0	64.6	45.2
1. Looked for a job in a different city			
2. Made plans to move to a new community	15.7	30.8	23.7
3. Looked for job opportunities outside your community	58.6	76.9	67.3
Community activism	26.1	8.5	18.5
1. Became active in community effort to aid the unemployed			
2. Became active in community efforts to stop unemployment	26.2	1.4	13.7
3. Went to a support group for the unemployed	30.7	42.7	39.4
Seeking financial assistance	13.5	15.4	16.0
1. Asked for financial assistance from friends or relatives			
2. Applied for aid in utility payments	10.0	.7	7.0
3. Applied for food stamps	7.1	2.8	6.1

TABLE 4–1 (continued)

	Homestead* (N = 198)	Florida (N = 163)	Full sample (N = 361)
Seeking social support 1. Talked to your spouse about your feelings	78.7%	81.6%	79.1%
2. Kept in touch with people on the old job	86.2	88.0	85.9
3. Talked to friends about problems with being unemployed	80.6	79.3	78.9

*Data represent percent of total respondents in each study who reported using the coping strategy indicated.

search skills, resume preparation, interviewing, and job search contacts via correspondence and in person. However, with as many as 55 percent of the heads of household out of work at some time during the mid-1980s, many steelworkers had given up. Moreover, in the Pittsburgh–Beaver County area, there were 89,200 fewer jobs in 1985 than there were in 1979; even with new jobs in the service economy added, that meant a fifty thousand job shortfall.[11]

Many of our respondents commented extensively on how frustrating their job search efforts had been:

> I repeatedly applied for other jobs, never hearing from them. I even went to County Commissions, Veterans Outreach, and at no time did I ever get a response. And yes, I would keep calling places and renewing the applications and this too failed.

> It was very difficult to obtain employment. Employers thought they would lose you if the mills called back. . . . So many people in a small area were applying for the same jobs. . . . Most people didn't make the money we steelworkers made and disliked us for it.

> No one wants a fifty-four-year-old ex-steelworker who belonged to a union. We are thought to be overpaid and lazy with too many benefits and too much vacation.

> I have applied for numerous jobs in any field and never hear a word from any of them. This includes government job service, free-lance applications, anything I hear is available I apply for but to no avail.

> Schooling was available but the job opportunities were not.

I don't see how a retraining program would help me as I have thirty years work experience on about twenty different jobs. Inquiring about a higher college degree, I was told only bachelors degrees were available and I have a Business Administration and Psychology degree now that doesn't help in finding a job at my age. Retraining is fine if there is a job at the end of the tunnel, but in most documented cases it just leads to another dead end.

My husband graduated six months ago from business school with a 3.6 GPA and a two-year degree in accounting management, but where did that get him? Nowhere. . . . He enlisted the services of three temporary agencies and has worked in short-term positions for $5 per hour . . . but he can't convince them to hire him full time. He is not looking for an $18 an hour mill job. He is ready to start over again and make a go of it. The new prospective employers are too narrow-minded and think all you want is bucks.

I passed the civil service test and scored over 100 percent and I can't get a job! The government said unemployment was at an all time low! Ha!

RETRAINING. Relatively few employees were offered training opportunities by their companies, or sought out further education in local technical schools or colleges. Younger workers were generally more willing to get retrained, and generally reaped more benefits for their efforts. For instance, one twenty-six-year-old steelworker took out a $4,500 loan and enrolled in a one-year retail management course. Through a part-time internship while in school, he obtained a store management job upon graduation; while his starting pay was somewhat less than his peak pay as a steelworker, the future potential earnings are much stronger. A thirty-three-year-old steelworker returned to school to become a heating and air-conditioning technician; a thirty-year-old millworker returned to community college to study agriculture.[12]

One lucky young steelworker who did get company training benefitted greatly from it: "I took advantage of U.S. Steel's Industrial Studies Program in Electronics and Welding. I also attended Steel Center Vo-Tech for courses after my layoff. These courses dressed up my resume considerably and I feel they were largely responsible for my finding the job I now have."

There were two dominant reasons why many of the unemployed

did not choose to get more training. First, many of the older workers felt that getting more education at their stage in life would not be worthwhile. Second, financial difficulties or family concerns kept many out of the classroom.

> I graduated from my community college at the top of my class with a 99 average and no days missed. I paid for additional testing to become a master certified ASE Automotive Technician. No major auto dealership was interested in me due to my age.

> I didn't pursue schooling because I didn't think I could support my family and go to school.

> After four years of college, I make $1,000 less than I did at my old job. . . . I am much worse off now. These people that are going through retraining programs wearing rose-colored glasses are in for a rude awakening!

> I wouldn't complete retraining because I was denied benefits for the remainder of the 104 week allotment, and I have utilized only 46 weeks so far.

> I am now going to school to become an X-ray technician. The problem that I am having is that I will be out of government cash assistance a full year before I graduate. Also, most training programs that are worth attending start their programs once a year, usually in the fall. When a person loses their job and when training actually starts can be months apart. It takes time to assess what type of school you want to attend, too.

RELOCATION. Almost half of our respondents looked for job opportunities outside their home communities; however, fewer than a quarter of them actually made concrete plans to relocate.

In the Florida sample, many of the workers decided they would try to wait out the layoffs. Many figured they would be called back before the year was up and did not want to uproot. Moreover, the market for aerospace and computer personnel nationally was soft at the same time, so that relocating wouldn't solve the unemployment problem unless people were also prepared to change occupations as well. As one Florida employee noted, relocating could also be very disruptive. "When I lost my job, the company I worked for offered me a comparable job in another city. I took the job and therefore had to move. I was very pleased to have the job but it proved to be very difficult to lose your job and your friends and your life as it had been. The bad part of it all was that I felt not in control of my own life. I had moved and changed jobs before in my life. But it had always been my idea and this time it wasn't. Even though it has been five months (since the move) I am still lonely."

In the Homestead sample, many of the younger steelworkers saw no point in waiting for the situation to change, especially when they viewed the future of U.S. Steel as bleak in the long term. Some of the younger steelworkers moved to Connecticut to work at General Dynamics; others moved to Florida and Texas for construction jobs; still others entered military service. For many, relocating paid off. Forty-eight percent lined up new jobs before they left Pennsylvania, and of the others, 69 percent found a job in less than a month. The downside of the move was a cut in pay; the average pay of those who left was 34 percent less than the pay they were earning in the mills ($268/week vs. $408/week); however, over 80 percent of those who moved were much more satisfied with their new jobs and their new job security.[13]

For many of the older Pittsburgh respondents, though, relocating seemed much less desirable. First, many of these workers had very deep ties in the community which they were unwilling to sever; their fathers, brothers, and extended families had worked in the same mills and lived in the same towns. These individuals were especially reluctant to uproot. Second, housing prices had dropped so dramatically in the Monongahela Valley area that many workers would have been worse off financially selling at a loss than they would be staying in Pittsburgh:

> I probably would relocate to another area and make more money, but I was born here and my family is here and I intend to stay here. I've fallen behind on my bills, and have had to go without things, but with a lot of hard work, determination, and patience, I know definitely I'll make it.

> Trying to relocate to another area is very tough. I bought my home in 1978 for $30,000 and spent $10,000 over the years in home improvements and can't sell the home today for $20,000. I also went in the hole $10,000 in loans through the Home Mortgage Assistance Program. I cannot take that kind of loss.

COMMUNITY ACTIVISM. About a quarter of the respondents became active in community groups to aid the unemployed or to try to stop further unemployment. Community activism was greater in the Pittsburgh area than in Florida; chronic unemployment is greater in the Monongahela Valley, and there are more long-standing church, civic, and union organizations to serve laid-off workers.

One of the better known community groups in Pittsburgh is the Tri-State Conference, located in the Pennsylvania–West Virginia–Ohio steel-producing region. This community group joined forces with unions in an attempt to prevent closure of additional steel factories. It conducted economic impact studies to demonstrate that industrial parks proposed to replace steel facilities did not create many jobs for local residents. It aggressively lobbied with local and state politicians against the business decisions of U.S. Steel, and used the media to draw negative reactions to U.S. Steel's handling of the layoffs. The Tri-State Conference also promoted strategies for obtaining employee ownership of plants slated to be closed down.[14]

Another prominent community group in Pittsburgh was the Rainbow Kitchen and the Homestead Unemployed Center. The center was set up by former steelworkers to run support groups for the unemployed, to help with groceries and hot lunches for their children, and to provide laid-off workers with financial and psychological counseling.[15]

In Florida, the federal government set up an unemployed worker assistance center at Brevard Community College. Besides serving as a clearinghouse for placement opportunities and assisting the unemployed prepare resumes and practice interviewing, center directors ran several ongoing support groups for laid-off workers. When the Kennedy Space Center all but closed for two years in the 1970s after the Grissom-Chaffee-White launch fire, the Brevard County area experienced widespread, and deep, financial distress and community disintegration. In hopes of avoiding a repeat of the earlier disaster, the federal government provided nearly a million dollars to the Unemployed Worker Assistance Center at Brevard Community College.

SEEKING SOCIAL SUPPORT. Clearly the most frequently used symptom-focused coping strategy was seeking social support. Laid-off workers turned to spouses, friends, and former coworkers as outlets for their anxieties and apprehensions about unemployment.

As we noted in earlier chapters, two consistent themes emerged from our respondents about social support. First, many of the unemployed emphasized the depth of their sense of despair. Second, many workers felt that they were draining their friends' and families' patience; over time, the unemployed began to feel there were fewer and fewer supportive people left to turn to:

> I looked up the word "unemployment" in the dictionary. It means "without a job." I thought it was a social disease the way my friends and family—yes, even my family—avoid me for fear I might ask them for something.

> Losing my job at this mill was a devastating experience. I not only lost good wages, excellent benefits, and the security of belonging to a union but a lot of friends who are now scattered all over the country.

> The company that I worked for for almost twenty years seems to have abandoned me. Approaching the personnel office is a complete waste of time. And I'm wearing my friends' patience thin by contacting them all too often.

> Over a year ago my wife of 22 years divorced me. This is the only part of losing my job I can't figure out. How can a wife just throw you out like a bag of garbage when things get tough?

SEEKING FINANCIAL ASSISTANCE. Very few of our study participants reported that they applied for any kind of financial assistance other than basic unemployment benefits. They may have been reluctant to report receiving assistance. Part of the reluctance to apply for financial aid may also have stemmed from the embarrassment and humiliation they experienced at governmental agencies. As one of our respondents put it: "Government job service employees treat an older job seeker like he or she has AIDS. That goes for state unemployment offices."

Another issue raised by many was the frustration they faced when dealing with the government bureaucracy or the bureaucracy of their former employers.

I had to wait two years to collect my pension. In those two years it was a struggle keeping my family, making house payments, paying utilities, buying food, and other essentials.

My wife deserted me and our son before I got my pension in 1986. I was going to go to school for robotics but no agency would pay for schooling and let me work, too.

I am in the process or at least trying to start my own business. I have been to see, or called, or researched the information and guidance I need. I only needed a question answered. Neither the Small Business Administration, the Pennsylvania Job Service, the Federal Minority Department, the Pittsburgh Chamber of Commerce, nor the Carnegie Library would help me. If I were Donald Trump and needed ten million dollars it would be available immediately. I only need a little guidance and I'm not Trump so I am considered not worth helping.

I was treated very unfairly about my training benefits. They tell me one thing and do the complete opposite. They said I didn't sign up within the 210 day sign-up time, but then overruled and reversed in my favor. I am still waiting for word about my benefits, which I think is very unfair.

Applying for extended governmental benefits was more common in Pittsburgh than in Florida, in large part because the layoffs lasted longer there. In the Pittsburgh–Beaver County area, the number of people who qualified for food stamps nearly doubled between 1980 and 1985 (from 35,491 to 63,806). Food banks also proliferated; in Allegheny County alone, 230 agencies served 50,000 people every month. In the Pittsburgh metropolitan area, the number of people on welfare from two-parent families with strong work histories increased more than threefold between 1980 and 1985, from 5,496 to 17,073.[16]

Determinants of Coping Behavior

There was a good deal of variability in how our respondents in both the Pittsburgh and Florida studies coped with job loss. We looked at two sets of factors that influence how laid-off workers select different coping strategies: reactions to job loss and personality traits.

Reactions to Job Loss

Some people view getting reemployed as an insurmountable challenge; others consider it as much less threatening or accept it as an irreversible circumstance. Some become very upset, both emotionally and physically; others take it with equanimity. We had two hypotheses, in particular, about how reactions to job loss would influence coping behavior.

First, we proposed that the more negatively people reacted to job loss—emotionally, physically, and in terms of perceiving the job loss as severe and irreversible—the less problem-focused coping they would engage in. Our rationale was that the more anxious and upset unemployed workers are, the less energy and enthusiasm they would have to engage in constructive behaviors to get a new job.

Second, we proposed that the more negatively people reacted to job loss, the more symptom-focused coping they would engage in. Our rationale was that people who are highly anxious and upset will put more energy into reducing their stress levels by seeking more social support, for instance, to alleviate the intensity of their reactions to job loss.

Personality Traits

Previous research suggests that certain personality characteristics might also influence how people cope with job loss.[17] We extended this to propose that, in addition to the situational factors that influence how unemployed workers cope with job loss, there are also stable individual differences in how people try to handle adverse circumstance in their lives. In this study, we looked at three personality variables in particular: locus of control, Type-A personality, and self-esteem.

Internal locus of control refers to a predisposition to view important events in one's life as under one's own personal control. By contrast, individuals with an external locus of control tend to see what happens to them as largely out of their own hands; they believe that events in their lives are caused and directed by other people, chance events, luck, or random situational factors.[18] In the context of job loss, we expected that people with an internal locus of control would be more motivated to engage in active coping than those with an external locus of control.

The Type-A personality is aggressive, ambitious, and driven. Type-A personalities are willing to oppose others to get what they want. When placed in circumstances where there are many obstacles, they will keep plugging away rather than give up. By contrast, Type-B personalities feel less pressure, are more likely to let things "roll off their backs," and are less likely to fight every issue. Consequently, we expected that Type-A personalities will engage in more active coping than Type-B personalities.

Self-esteem refers to a personality predisposition to view oneself and one's abilities in a positive light. Individuals with high self-esteem have greater confidence in their ability to deal successfully with stress. Research suggests, too, that people with high self-esteem are better able to cope with extreme strain and stress and are less likely to be heart attack prone.[20] Consequently, we expected that individuals with high self-esteem should experience lower levels of stress when faced with job loss, and should be able to sustain more active coping in these threatening, uncertain circumstances.

Study Findings

In general, our results suggested that reactions to job loss have the most impact on four active coping strategies: job search, geographical relocation, seeking financial assistance, and retraining (see fig. 4–1).

The more intense employees considered the job loss, the less coping of any type they engaged in. It seems as if the intensity of the job loss created a sense of "learned helplessness" among the unemployed. The magnitude of the event, combined with feelings of lack of control, seemed to make the laid-off workers despair over obtaining new jobs. And, as we saw in the last chapter, the longer an employee is laid off, the more he or she will view the job loss as irreversible.

One steelworker who had trouble becoming reemployed, or even energized for further job hunting, made the following comments: "I feel adrift. I get depressed. You go from being on the job, to this. Sitting around and looking at the walls. It's terrible. You see other people going about their lives and accomplishing things and getting

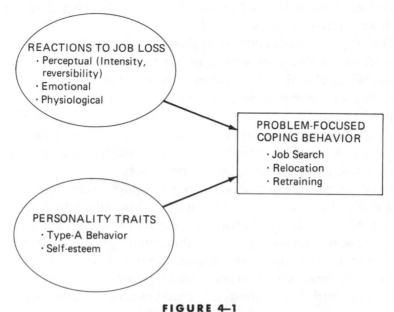

FIGURE 4–1

Determinants of Coping Behavior

more material possessions and you start to think you're not worthy. You feel inadequate, like a sponge, like I'm wasting time."[21]

In contrast, perceptions of reversibility were more likely to lead to some problem-focused coping, especially self-initiated job search, geographical relocation, and seeking retraining. When our respondents viewed the job loss as more readily remedied, they were more likely to spend the time and effort to get out of the unpleasant situations they found themselves in as a result of layoffs. Younger and better educated individuals, such as those in Florida, were more likely to see the layoff as reversible and to engage in active coping. Older workers in Pittsburgh, with almost thirty years in the system, often opted for early retirement instead:

> If I had not had the years needed for pension, I would probably have lost most of everything I own. I have been turned down for decent-paying jobs because of my age. I did not plan for early layoff or retirement but I know I'm a lot better off than most of the younger men with small children and big mortgages. I have no doubt I'll survive without too much problem, but this is not the end I hoped for.

I was only fifty-one years of age on my last day of work. Wished I could have worked a few more years but was grateful I had enough time to receive a pension. . . . It is only because of my age that I'm not interested in training.

Fortunately, I was out of debt when I lost my job at age fifty-four, but I was hoping to work a few years to build a savings account for our later years. Being unskilled and in my fifties, it was impossible to get employment that paid a decent living wage. I am very doubtful that any retraining or skills that I may acquire at my age would be very helpful in obtaining decent employment. Therefore, I will not waste my time and other people's time and money on retraining.

A married female professional in our Florida sample found herself in a similar bind. Unable to find new work, she unhappily resigned herself to being a homemaker again: "A lot of people say I should consider myself *lucky* for being able to stay home with my son, which I enjoy. But I didn't work for ten years at my career to become a homemaker, which I'm very poor at."

In general, perceptions of the layoff being externally caused did not influence coping behavior. This is most likely because almost all employees viewed their layoffs as caused by external business conditions; we simply did not have much variance in this perception so we could not compare the effects of internal versus external blame.

Consistent with our predictions, the less negative arousal and physiological distress the laid-off workers experienced, the more active coping they engaged in, especially in terms of job search and geographical relocation. Strongly adverse emotional and physical reactions to layoffs seemed to dampen active coping efforts; laid-off workers with these strongly negative stress reactions were simply too depleted to put much energy into looking for new jobs locally or in other parts of the country.

Our hypothesis that less negative reactions to job loss are associated with more problem-focused coping was generally upheld, but our hypothesis that more negative reactions to job loss are associated with more symptom-focusing coping was not. Almost all laid-off employees, independent of their reactions, engaged in some sort of symptom-focused coping, especially seeking social support.

In terms of personality characteristics, Type-A personality is the trait most closely associated with coping behavior. Type-A person-alities are more likely to actively search for new jobs, investigate geographical relocation, apply for financial aid, and become in-volved in community activities. Their predisposition to be active in dealing with their environments carries over even into negative sit-uations such as layoffs: Type-A's are more motivated to try to change the situation through problem-focused coping.

Locus of control played a much less significant role in influencing coping behavior. Most of our respondents viewed their layoffs as caused by such external factors as the balance of trade, budget deficits, accidents, poor business decisions, or governmental policy decisions; therefore, our respondents, independent of where their typical locus of control lay, did not take personal responsibility for their problems. This was equally true in the Florida and Pittsburgh samples.

The relationships between self-esteem and active coping were generally weak, but in the predicted direction. The lower an indi-vidual's self-esteem, the less likely he or she was to engage in active coping behavior, especially in terms of trying to find new jobs. Individuals with low self-esteem not only faced an objectively poor job market, but also had to overcome self-defeating perceptions that they were somehow unworthy of being rehired.

Summary

In general, reactions to job loss were better predictors of coping behaviors than were personality traits. Type A-personality and self-esteem did predict active coping; internal locus of control did not, largely because most laid-off workers accurately blamed their un-employment on external forces.

Consequences of Coping

In addition to the causes of coping behavior, we were also interested in exploring its consequences. Were people who used active coping strategies more successful in getting new jobs and in reestablishing some semblance of normality in their lives? To address these ques-tions, we first examined four outcome variables that represent the consequences of coping behavior.

Outcome Variables

The lay person may view employment as a dichotomous variable—one is either employed or not—but labor economists argue that job reattainment status should be categorized in at least three ways: (1) satisfactory reemployment (a new job at least as good as the lost one is obtained); (2) underemployment (a new job is obtained, but it is not as good as the one lost); and (3) continued unemployment (no new job is found).[22] Thus, in terms of examining consequences of coping behavior, we want to know not only whether workers became reemployed, but also whether they became reemployed in comparable jobs at comparable wages. At the times of our studies, over 80 percent of our respondents in the Florida and Homestead samples were unemployed. Moreover, even though 60 peprcent of those in the Economic Development study did report having jobs, most of those were considerably underemployed:

> When I first lost my job, I thought I would have no problem finding a job for at least $7 an hour utilizing my seventeen years experience. . . . In desperation I accepted a demeaning janitorial job for $4 an hour and later quit that job for a $5 an hour one and was let go within one month.

> When I lost my job I was very depressed. I was struggling to make ends meet. When I lost my job I didn't have much notice. I had to take a minimum wage job which was a big drop in my salary. My wife divorced me and I could not find a decent job.

> I am very unhappy with my job. I am a janitor at a local hospital. It is part time, no benefits, and no promise of either in the future.

> I am presently working through a temporary agency. My wages are low, benefits are none.

> I am currently working as a security guard for $4.75 per hour. Because of this substandard wage, I also drive a school bus for nine months out of the year to supplement my income. With both these incomes, I'm just able to make ends meet.

In the Florida and Homestead studies, we asked respondents who were still unemployed at the time of our study to indicate their perceived prospects for future employment. Possible responses were: (1) "In the near future I will obtain a job as good as the one I lost";

(2) "I will obtain a job as good as the one I lost, but it will take some time"; (3) "I will obtain another job but it won't be as good and it may take some time"; and (4) "There is no end in sight to my unemployment." Seventy percent of the Pittsburgh steelworkers were pessimistic about their ability to obtain satisfactory reemployment, as opposed to 14 percent of their Florida counterparts. Their comments reflect this pessimism:

> I lost a lot of my self-confidence, after being turned down for many jobs because I was a laid-off steelworker. I went through a bad case of depression trying to work at jobs that didn't pay much, worrying about paying my bills with what little I made and am still making.

> I will never find another job as good or one that pays as well as the one at the mill.

> I can't find a job that paid the same as I had, and I can't find a job that is related to what I did.

In addition to reemployment status we also used two global measures of emotional adjustment as outcome variables. First, we utilized a measure of employees' overall psychological health, which detects mild psychiatric disorders and has been validated with a variety of employed and unemployed samples.[23] Second, we used a measure of overall life satisfaction, which included questions concerning satisfaction with family, personal relations, standard of living, work accomplishments, and so forth.[24]

Our expectations were (1) that problem-focused coping would improve employment status and prospects for reemployment, and (2) that symptom-focused coping would improve psychological health and life satisfaction. Our rationale was that problem-focused coping would be effective in reducing the cause of the stress (i.e., unemployment), and that symptom-focused coping would be effective in reducing the adverse symptoms of the stress of unemployment (e.g., depression and anxiety).

Study Results

The results of the empirical research on coping strategies and their impact on outcome variables are shown in Figure 4–2. For each of the four outcome variables (reemployment status, prospects for

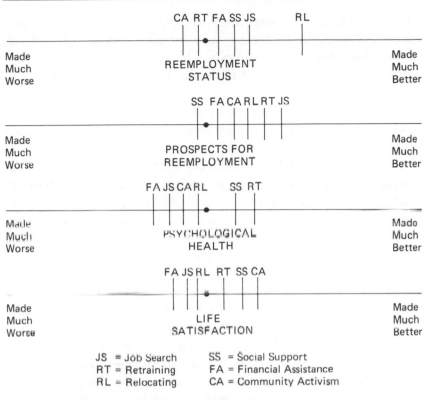

JS = Job Search   SS = Social Support
RT = Retraining   FA = Financial Assistance
RL = Relocating   CA = Community Activism

FIGURE 4–2

Coping Strategies and Outcome Variables

reemployment, psychological health, and life satisfaction), the six coping strategies are arranged from most helpful to least helpful.
In general, problem-focused coping strategies were associated with better reemployment. This was especially true for geographical relocation. The reason for this result is quite clear. Very often, plant closings and layoffs are not isolated events; they reflect poor economic conditions in an industry and/or in a geographical area. When the steel mills closed, it was not simply a matter of one or two mills closing; it was a matter of much of the steel industry going down at the same time. Similarly, when the Kennedy Space Center cut back operations, there were very few aerospace jobs elsewhere for these workers in the same geographical area, since all the subcontractors who depended on the Kennedy Space Center were also closing or cutting back. Thus, when there are widespread layoffs,

relocating is often the most effective reemployment strategy, despite the possible losses in housing investments. It is increasingly difficult to find jobs in the same geographical location at even roughly comparable wages when a poor labor market is flooded with excess workers.

Almost all the coping strategies we looked at had at least some modest positive effect on prospects for reemployment, especially the problem-focused strategies: job search, retraining, and relocation. In contrast, those individuals who engaged in the most community activism had the worst reemployment. Whether community activism was the *product* of a prolonged unsuccessful job search—or whether community activism was a *substitute* for active job search—cannot be determined without longitudinal data.

The slightly negative effect of social support on reemployment prospects is surprising, but is partially explained by differences between the Florida and Homestead samples. In the Florida sample, seeking social support was *positively* related to reemployment prospects. Most of the Florida employees hoped to ride out the present downturn and obtain their old jobs back, or at least similar aerospace jobs near Cape Canaveral. These employees used social support to bolster their feelings of optimism. In contrast, in the Homestead sample, seeking social support was *negatively* related to reemployment prospects (and since the Homestead sample was larger than the Florida sample, the overall result came out slightly negative). These steelworkers had been unemployed much longer than their Florida counterparts, and were much more pessimistic about getting reemployed in the near future. For them, conversations with other laid-off workers only served to reinforce their sense of hopelessness rather than to temper it.

The results for psychological health and life satisfaction are surprising and instructive in two regards. First, the symptom-focused coping strategies had very little positive impact on laid-off employees' feelings. Seeking financial assistance from government agencies, as we noted earlier in the chapter, was found to be very distasteful to the unemployed and certainly did nothing to boost their morale. Seeking social support and community activism for some respondents did fulfill their social needs and provided companionship, but, again, did not necessarily raise their spirits much. Getting reemployed *does* substantially lift workers' psychological health and life satisfaction; symptom-focused coping ameliorates it only very slightly.

Second, the results here suggest that active, problem-focused coping can actually *decrease* psychological health and life satisfaction. Although getting retraining provides workers with some structure to their day and some hope for the future, job search and relocation have at least short-run negative consequences for the psychological well-being of laid-off workers.

As we discovered in these studies, the act of problem-focused coping is itself unpleasant. The comments from our study participants reported earlier in the chapter illustrate how distasteful and frustrating laid-off workers found job hunting, and how unsettling the process of uprooting one's family and moving often proved to be. Thus, coping is itself stressful. Although it may help individuals extricate themselves from adverse situations in the long run, in the short run it often increases those aversive feelings.

Previous research on job change and job relocation also suggests that when individuals try to actively cope *too soon* after a stressful life event, they may actually hurt their employment prospects.[25] Laid-off workers may not be calm enough, or self-assured enough, soon after their job loss to handle the inevitable tension of searching for new jobs. They may present themselves as insecure, or nervous, or incapable. As a result, they may get quickly discouraged by their initial failures and stop their job hunting too soon. Similarly, under the immediate shock of job loss, laid-off employees may not be able to think clearly enough about important decisions such as changing careers or moving out of town. Their initial instinctive reaction—to ride out the storm, to hang on—may be less rational than more thoughtful considerations that might occur in the subsequent few weeks or months.

Thus, our original speculations about the positive benefits of problem-focused coping are generally supported by our study findings. However, our ideas are revised and tempered by our discovery that the benefits of problem-focused coping in theory are somewhat offset by the real difficulties active coping creates in practice. Moreover, symptom-focused coping may not be as salutary as we originally predicted.

Role of Demographic Variables

Previous research on job loss suggests that an employee's demographic characteristics influence his or her chances of obtaining employment independently of the amount of effort put into the job search or the type of coping strategies employed. In particular, age, education, race, gender, and marital status seem to be the important factors. Thus, in addition to looking at the impact of coping strategies on becoming reemployed and maintaining psychological well-being, we also considered the role these five demographic characteristics played in adjustment as well.

A G E. Several studies have documented the difficulties encountered by middle-aged and older workers seeking reemployment. Age has consistently been found to be a significant determinant of how long people stay unemployed, both for professional workers and for blue-collar workers. Moreover, middle-aged and older workers seem to have greater barriers to reentering the work force.[26] The older Florida participants felt that their employers had used age—rather than seniority—in determining who should be laid off. Moreover, in both Pittsburgh and Florida, respondents felt that when companies started to rehire, they rehired younger—rather than older—workers first:

> The salaried people were not laid off in order of seniority. It seemed the older people in age were first.
>
> I was not a victim of rust-belt-overpriced-labor syndrome. . . . Rather, I was the victim of some cleaning house of overpriced types who could be replaced by fresh-out-of-school workers at half the salary.
>
> At the present time I am fifty years of age. This makes finding an adequate line of work extremely difficult.
>
> I believe my employer discriminated against my age by taking younger workers to other facilities. I also believe all others, where I put applications in, discriminate against age. I feel I should be able to find some decent job without retraining, especially at my age. By the time I retrain I'll be too old to work.
>
> At fifty-nine it is harder to find employment again at a decent wage.

EDUCATION. Several researchers have reported that workers lacking a college education have more difficulty getting reemployed than college graduates.[27] Comments from participants in our studies also suggest this dynamic was at work here as well:

I feel all those who lost their jobs due to the layoff should have been prepared ahead of time by being told all about it. USX should have been responsible for placing all those who were laid off in retraining programs for those that needed more training and jobs for those who had the skills. . . . How do you go about retraining when you know nothing else but the mill? How do you prepare for another type of work, when this is something you have never thought about? Where do you go from here?

I haven't been able to get steady employment in this area since graduating high school.

I am now completing my last semester (in college) . . . I am not sure that once I have my degree I will be able to work in my field (journalism), but I do know for a fact, attending college certainly opens many doors that once were closed to someone with just a high school degree.

RACE. The national unemployment rate for black workers is consistently higher than that of white workers. Generally this is true regardless of industry, job classification, age, or gender. The current unemployment rate for black workers is over double that of white workers, and the average time spent before reemployment is also significantly greater.[28] Whether it is due to discrimination or lack of education, black workers seem to fare even worse than white workers after layoffs in terms of getting reemployed.

GENDER. Most studies of involuntary job loss have focused exclusively on males. This focus is typically justified using common stereotypes about the importance of work for women.

Women are frequently assumed to adjust more readily to job loss because work is seen as less central to women's identities than it is to men's. The traditional roles of wife and mother are still assumed to be at least as important—if not of primary importance—in women's lives.[29] Moreover, women as a group are disproportionately represented at the bottom of authority, reward, and status hierarchies at work. When women lose their jobs, the loss is not seen to be as important to them as it is to men since the jobs themselves are not seen to be as interesting or as lucrative as traditional male jobs.[30]

There is some research, however, that suggests that these traditional assumptions and stereotypes do not accurately represent many working women—those who are primary wage earners, those who are the sole support for dependent children, those who are recent entrants into nontraditional jobs, and those, for whatever reason, who value and enjoy their work. For these women job loss may be even more devastating than it is for their male counterparts, since women generally fare worse than men in terms of both their financial resources and their abilities to replace lost jobs.[31] Moreover, many recent research studies have reported that unemployed women generally have a more difficult time obtaining satisfactory reemployment than their male counterparts, and that females, once laid-off, are twice as likly as their male counterparts to be unemployed for longer than a year.[32]

MARITAL STATUS. Whether males or females fare worse during unemployment is highly intertwined with the issue of marital status. It has been fairly commonly assumed that unemployed married men are under more pressure than single men because they have more dependents to shelter, feed, clothe, and educate. Certainly, the comments of male heads of household illustrate the pressures they feel during unemployment:

> We bought our home (recently) and have four children at home. When I was let go I could not possibly make my bill payments the way I should and thus went to my credit cards where I ran my Mastercard and others sky high. I have put my house up for sale to pay off my debts and maybe buy a smaller place or rent. Hopefully things will turn around for my wife and I.

> I am having a hard time getting out of the poverty level and I'm getting older. I have three children and a wife to support for four years. I have only been able to make $10,000 to $12,000 a year. It's a hard struggle. . . . I am forced to accept many dead-end jobs because of my immediate needs to my family. . . . As it looks now, our future financially looks grim, we're still struggling to get off food stamps.

In contrast, much of the literature on job loss has implicitly or explicitly assumed that married women are more buffered from the negative effects of unemployment because of their spouses' income. However, given that over two-thirds of married women today are in the labor force, and that many two-career families depend heavily on both incomes to sustain their standards of living, the differences between married and single women may not be as pronounced as this literature seems to suggest.

STUDY RESULTS. The overall results of our studies confirm many of the anecdotal accounts of older workers. Our findings on age suggest that younger workers perceived themselves as having a better chance of becoming satisfactorily reemployed and/or having better prospects for reemployment (see fig. 4–3). Consistent with the comments from older workers cited above, older workers as a group perceived themselves as having greater difficulties becoming reemployed, in some cases because of age bias and in other cases because of their own unwillingness to retrain or relocate. Moreover, in Florida there are several lawsuits pending about age bias, involving not only the criteria used to lay off employees but also over whether younger workers were rehired preferentially when recalls began. Much the same is occurring in the Pittsburgh area as well, with several laid-off older workers alleging they were unfairly treated in the job market (see figure 4.3).

Surprisingly, however, older laid-off employees had more equa-

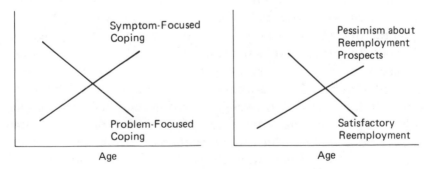

FIGURE 4–3

Age, Coping Behavior, and Employment Status

nimity about their lives, experiencing less psychological distress and more overall satisfaction. Comments from our participants suggest that many of the older workers, although frustrated by their layoffs, are past their highest expense years in terms of mortgage payments and child support, and can make it to retirement without equally high paying jobs:

> Was only fifty-one years of age on my last day of work. Wished I could have worked a few more years but was grateful that I had enough time to receive a pension.

> I liked the work I was doing. I worked forty-one and a half years in that mill. I miss most of the men that I worked with. I worked hard at my job but I made a good living while I was working. No regrets.

> At age fifty-nine and a half I collected (unemployment) benefits for six months. Grabbed my pension and ran. . . . Under the new U.S. Government tax set-up and between my wife's income, my pension, and social security benefits, any earned income (from) part-time employment could throw me into a different tax bracket, making part-time employment less than justified.

In the Florida sample, the younger, better educated workers were more optimistic about being recalled. They were paid less than their older counterparts, and their technical knowledge was more current; in their nonunionized environment, they felt the most confident about getting their old jobs back. The Pittsburgh sample was comprised of unionized workers, who were more likely to be recalled in order of age and seniority. Often it was the younger, better-educated workers who had taken mill jobs for lack of other job opportunities who were in the worst predicament. Their education did not help them find jobs outside the steel industry, and their age worked against them in terms of getting recalled to the mills. Thus, the more educated Florida workers also had a better psychological state of mind than did the well-educated in the Pittsburgh sample.

In terms of race, there were not many blacks who participated in any of our studies. Thus, we were unable to examine differences between blacks and whites in terms of coping, reemployment, or adjustment.

Although there were few women in the Pittsburgh studies, women represented over 40 percent of the Florida sample, so we were able to examine potential gender differences there. Contrary to gender stereotypes, women showed slightly *higher* levels of depressed affect and greater psychological, physiological, and emotional distress than men; these differences, however, were not statistically significant.

In terms of reemployment efforts, women appeared to cope with job loss differently from men. Those behaviors aimed most directly at rectifying the situation—e.g., job search, relocation—were used less by women than men. Instead, women seemed to rely more on symptom-focused coping—e.g., talking to friends, getting involved in group activities—that may alleviate stress but do little to solve the problem. If these findings can be generalized, they may account at least in part for women's traditional difficulty in securing suitable reemployment.

Whereas in the past this difference in coping may have been attributed—either explicitly or implicitly—to women's reduced trauma as a result of job loss and therefore reduced motivation to find reemployment, women may instead be more pessimistic about their opportunities. Both government unemployment statistics and previous research on women's success in gaining reemployment indicate that this pessimism may be warranted, and that special efforts may need to be made to facilitate women's reentry into the work force.[33]

In terms of marital status, our results are consistent with those of previous researchers. Married laid-off workers, because of the support of their spouses and families, have less psychological distress as a consequence of unemployment. However, single workers are more likely to relocate or retrain to get new jobs; they are less entwined in a network of family, friendship, and housing obligations that could impede their efforts to uproot and change directions in life.

SUMMARY. As predicted, younger workers were more optimistic about becoming satisfactorily reemployed. Older workers, however, were calmer about unemployment, largely because for many their expensive years were behind them and their pensions were in sight. The effects of education varied with the profession and the location—in Florida, the more educated workers were more optimistic and suffered less distress, but in Pittsburgh the reverse was true. In the Florida sample unemployed women showed higher levels of distress than men, but were also less active in seeking out new jobs. Married respondents reported less distress than single respondents—a finding consistent with research on the population as a whole.

Coping Reconsidered

The patterns of relationships described in this chapter have implications that are instructive for both our theoretical understanding of coping behavior and our practical understanding of how best to cope with the problems of job loss.

Theoretical Issues

The results of our research suggest that laid-off workers do make active attempts to address their unemployment problems, both through problem-focused coping aimed at securing new employment and through symptom-focused coping aimed at ameliorating the adverse consequences of job loss. Thus, in future studies of job loss, sole reliance on a deprivation model—which characterizes the unemployed as passive agents—is unwarranted. Instead, researchers must also focus on what individuals do to cope with job loss, rather than merely on what happens to them as a result of job loss. To fully understand what job loss means to a person, these results indicate that it is necessary to also understand what the person does about it.

The results presented in this chapter also suggest there are two common patterns of reactions to job loss. People who view their layoffs as severe, irreversible, and emotionally upsetting are the least likely to engage in problem-focused coping; these individuals are also the least optimistic about their future employment prospects. In contrast, people who view their layoffs as less severe, more readily reversible, and more challenging are more likely to engage in problem-focused coping and to perceive themselves as having higher prospects for reemployment.

These two different patterns of coping with job loss can be seen in the differences between laid-off workers in Pittsburgh and Florida. In Pittsburgh, layoffs were large scale, with little hope of recall, in areas with high unemployment. Workers there felt that their layoffs were severe and irreversible; hence, there was little point in even trying to get reemployed. In contrast, in Florida, layoffs were much smaller in scale, and with more hope of recalls. Here, laid-off workers viewed their layoffs as less severe and more reversible, and consequently engaged in more problem-focused coping.

The results on the relationships between demographic variables and coping behaviors can also be understood in the context of reactions to job loss. For instance, women viewed their layoffs as somewhat more severe, less reversible, and more negative emotionally, and consequently engaged in less problem-focused coping. Older workers were more tied to their communities and were more reluctant to move; they also tended to feel "too old" to learn a new trade, even when it was clear (in the case of the steelworkers, certainly) that their occupation and industry were declining. Many women were more pessimistic about their chances for reemployment, and were too tied down by spouses, children, and communities to drastically change career paths; hence, it is not surprising that they, too, engaged in less problem-focused coping. In Pittsburgh, the better-educated workers were demoralized about finding jobs that paid even $7 an hour, and over time even stopped looking; in Florida, the better-educated workers viewed their job loss as temporary and more readily reversible, and thus engaged in more problem-focused coping.

Practical Issues

The data we collected at the Pittsburgh steel mills and on the Space Coast suggest that different coping strategies are more effective than others in facilitating reemployment. Individuals who use problem-focused coping strategies are more optimistic about finding satisfactory reemployment and have more actual success to justify this optimism. Although job layoffs are beyond the control of the workers themselves, their individual efforts after the job loss may significantly influence the levels and types of outcomes they experience as a result of their terminations.

These results also suggest that the very act of coping may, in itself, be stressful and associated with adverse psychological and physiological reactions. While behaviors such as self-initiated job searching are certainly instrumental in obtaining a new job and structuring the day's routine, they are also activities filled with frustration and rejection. In the Florida sample, for instance, the average laid-off worker had to contact a dozen companies for every face-to-face interview. Similarly, geographic relocation facilitates reemployment but also causes discomfort and disruption to job seekers and their families.[34]

These data suggest the possibility that the newly unemployed may benefit from a short cooling-off period before they actively search for reemployment, or move, or make a decision to go back to school. With all the stress immediately following a termination, it is unlikely that individuals will make good decisions about their careers and jobs right away.[35] Moreover, initial attempts to job hunt may be more likely to fail because the job seekers are overwrought, less self-confident, less self-assured, and more likely to reveal embarrassing or potentially negative information about themselves. These findings support the need for financial assistance to make this cooling-off period feasible.

Perhaps the greatest irony is that the coping strategies that may be the most beneficial for laid-off workers may also be the most underutilized or the most misused because they are so stressful. This dilemma underscores the need for company-sponsored programs and policies designed to ease the transition for employees and point them in useful directions for obtaining reemployment.

Notes

1. M. Jahoda, *Employment and Unemployment* (London: Cambridge University Press, 1982).
2. S. Folkman and R. S. Lazarus, "An Analysis of Coping in a Middle-Aged Community Sample," *Journal of Health and Social Behavior* 21 (1980): 219–39.
3. J. M. Brett, D. C. Feldman, and L. R. Weingart, "Feedback-Seeking and Adjustment: An Empirical Comparison of New Hires and Job Changers," *Journal of Management* 16 (1990): 737–749.
4. A. P. Brief, R. S. Schuler, and M. Van Sell, *Managing Job Stress* (Boston: Little, Brown, 1981); J. E. McGrath, "Stress and Behavior in Organizations," in M. D. Dunnette, ed., *Handbook of Industrial and Organizational Psychology*, 2351–96 (Chicago: Rand McNally, 1976).
5. J. C. Latack and J. B. Dozier, "After the Ax Falls: Job Loss as a Career

Transition," *Academy of Management Review* 11 (1986): 375–92; C. R. Leana and D. C. Feldman, "Individual Responses to Job Loss: Perceptions, Reactions, and Coping Behaviors," *Journal of Management* 14 (1988): 375–89.

6. C. R. Leana and D. C. Feldman, "Individual Responses to Job Loss: Empirical Findings from Two Field Studies," *Human Relations*, 43(1990): 1155–1181; R. Gal and R. S. Lazarus, "The Role of Activity in Anticipating and Confronting Stressful Situations," *Journal of Human Stress* 1 (1975): 4–20; S. Roth and L. J. Cohen, "Approach, Avoidance, and Coping with Stress," *American Psychologist* 41 (1986): 813–19.

7. D. Dooley and R. Catalano, "Recent Research on the Psychological Effects of Unemployment," *Journal of Social Issues* 44 (1988): 1–12; P. Warr, P. Jackson, and M. Banks, "Unemployment and Mental Health: Some British Studies," *Journal of Social Issues* 44 (1988): 47–68.

8. E. Bergholz, "Some Retrain for New Careers," *Pittsburgh Post Gazette*, 30 December 1985, pp. 33–36.

9. D. C. Feldman and J. B. Brett, "Coping with New Jobs: A Comparative Study of New Hires and Job Changers," *Academy of Management Journal* 26 (1983): 258–79; L. I. Pearlin and C. Schooler, "The Structure of Coping," *Journal of Health and Social Behavior* 19 (1978): 2–21.

10. D. Corn, "Dreams Gone to Rust," *Harper's Magazine*, September 1985, pp. 56–64.

11. W. E. Deibler, "Many Hang In, But It's Not Easy," *Pittsburgh Post Gazette*, 30 December 1985, p. 11.

12. Bergholz, "Some Retrain."

13. J. Blotzer and E. Bergholz, "Moving On When Hope Runs Out," *Pittsburgh Post Gazette*, 30 December 1985, pp. 39–40.

14. J. Leff, "United States Steel Corporation and the Steel Valley Authority" (Cambridge: Harvard Business School Case No. 0-386-172, 1986).

15. W. Greider, "They Had an American Dream," *Rolling Stone*, 20 June 1985, pp. 47–49.

16. J. Blotzer, "Jobless Adrift, Cling to Hope," *Pittsburgh Post Gazette*, 30 December 1985, pp. 33–36.

17. R. M. Cohn, "The Effect of Employment Status Change on Self-Attitudes," *Social Psychology* 41 (1978): 81–93; Leana and Feldman, "Individual Responses to Job Loss: Perceptions, Reactions, and Coping Behavior."

18. J. B. Rotter, "Some problems and misconceptions related to the construct of internal vs. external control of reinforcement." *Journal of Consulting and Clinical Psychology* 43 (1975): 56–67; P. E. Spector, "Behavior in Organizations as a Function of Employees' Locus of Control," *Psychological Bulletin* 91 (1982): 482–97.

19. M. Friedman and R. H. Rosenman, *Type A Behavior and Your Heart* (New York: Knopf, 1974).

20. Bruno Bettleheim, "Individual and Mass Behavior in Extreme Situations," in E. E. Maccoby, ed., *Readings in Social Psychology* (New York: Holt, Rinehart,

and Winston, 1958); S. V. Kasl, S. Gore, and S. Cobb, "The Experience of Losing a Job: Reported Changes in Health, Symptoms, and Illness Behavior," *Psychosomatic Medicine* 37 (1975): 106–22.

21. Blotzer, "Jobless Adrift."
22. H. G. Kaufman, *Factors Related to the Utilization and Career Development of Scientists and Engineers: A Longitudinal Study of Involuntary Termination* (Washington, D.C.: National Science Foundation, Technical Report No. SRS 77-20737, 1980).
23. P. Goldberg, *The Detection of Psychiatric Illness by Questionnaire* (London: Oxford University Press, 1972).
24. M. H. Banks, C. W. Clegg, P. R. Jackson, N. J. Kemp, E. M. Stafford, and T. D. Wall, "The Use of the General Health Questionnaire as an Indication of Mental Health in an Occupational Setting," *Journal of Occupational Psychology* 53 (1980): 187–94; Leana and Feldman, "Individual Responses to Job Loss: Empirical Findings from Two Field Studies."
25. R. W. White, "Strategies of Adaptation: An Attempt at Systematic Description," in G. V. Coelho, D. A. Hamburg, and J. E. Adams, eds., *Coping and Adaptation*, (New York: Basic Books, 1974), 47–68; Gal and Lazarus, "The Role of Activity"; Pearlin and Schooler, "The Structure of Coping"; Brett, Feldman, and Weingart, "Feedback Seeking and Adjustment."
26. R. P. Loomba, *A Study of the Reemployment and Unemployment Experience of Scientists and Engineers Laid Off from 62 Aerospace and Electronic Firms in the San Francisco Bay Area during 1963–1965* (San Jose, Calif.: Manpower Research Group Technical Report, San Jose State College, 1987); J. D. Mooney, "An Analysis of Unemployment among Professional Engineers and Scientists," *Industrial and Labor Relations Review* 19 (1966): 517–28; Warr, Jackson, and Banks, "Unemployment and Mental Health."
27. Kaufman, *Factors*; Loomba, *A Study*; Mooney, *An Analysis*; Warr, Jackson, and Banks, "Unemployment and Mental Health"; R. L. Payne and J. G. Jones, "Social Class and Reemployment: Changes in Health and Perceived Financial Circumstances," *Journal of Occupational Behavior* 8 (1987): 175–84.
28. T. F. Buss and F. S. Redburn, *Mass Unemployment: Plant Closings and Community Mental Health* (Beverly Hills, Calif.: Sage, 1983); P. B. Warr and P. R. Jackson, "Factors Influencing the Psychological Impact of Prolonged Unemployment and Reemployment," *Psychological Medicine* 15 (1985): 795–807; P. Ullah, "Unemployed Black Youths in a Northern City," in D. Fryer and P. Ullah, eds., *Unemployed People*, 110–47 (Milton Keynes, U.K.: Open University Press, 1987).
29. M. M. Harris, T. Heller, and D. Braddock, "Sex Differences of Psychological Well-Being During a Facility Closure," *Journal of Management* 14 (1988): 391–402; S. V. Kasl and S. Cobb, "Some Mental Health Consequences of Plant Closing and Job Loss," in L. Ferman and J. Gordus, eds., *Mental Health and the Economy* (Kalamazoo, Mich.: Upjohn Institute for Employment Research, 1979), 255–300.
30. G. Marshall, "On the Sociology of Women's Unemployment, Its Neglect and

Significance," *Sociological Review* 32 (1984): 234–59; R. Donovan, N. Jaffe, and Y. N. Pirie, "Unemployment among Low-Income Women: An Exploratory Study," *Social Work*, 1987 (July–August): 301–5.

31. T. C. Nowak and K. A. Snyder, "Women's Struggle to Survive a Plant Shutdown," *Journal of Intergroup Relations* 11 (1983): 25–44.
32. M. A. Dew, E. J. Bromet and H. C. Schulberg, "A Comparative Analysis of Two Community Stressors' Long-Term Mental Health Effects," *American Journal of Community Psychology* 15 (1987): 167–84; R. Liem and J. H. Liem, "Psychological Effects of Unemployment on Workers and Their Families," *Journal of Social Issues* 44 (1988): 87–105; M. Bartell and R. Bartell, "An Integrative Perspective on the Psychological Response of Women and Men to Unemployment," *Journal of Economic Psychology* 6 (1985): 27–49.
33. Bartell and Bartell, "An Integrative Perspective"; Nowak and Snyder, "Women's Struggle."
34. Feldman and Brett, "Coping with New Jobs."
35. I. L. Janis and L. Mann, *Decision Making: A Psychological Analysis of Conflict, Choice, and Commitment* (New York: Free Press, 1977).

5

Corporate Interventions

In the waning days of the 1988 presidential election, one of the issues that captured the national spotlight was the then-proposed Worker Adjustment and Retraining Notification (WARN) Act, which required employers to notify workers sixty days in advance of a plant closing or large-scale layoff. This debate raised several important questions about the role of corporations in employee layoffs. Do corporations have any responsibilities or obligations to employees whom they lay off or to the communities in which they are located? What benefits might laid-off workers accrue from corporate assistance programs, and at what cost to organizations in terms of financial outlays and loss of management discretion? How successful have various corporate assistance programs been in helping laid-off workers find re-employment or adjust to job loss, and why have some corporations' programs been more successful than others?

A recent survey of chief executive officers (CEO's) of Fortune 500 companies suggests that, independent of their legal obligations, corporate officers generally believed that companies should take concrete actions to help displaced employees.[1] These actions include providing counseling services to laid-off workers and their families, providing in-house job transfers, conducting seminars on what problems to expect after plant closings and how community agencies can help, teaching job search skills and contacting employment agencies, providing severance benefits and continued health benefits, and allowing employees or their communities the opportunity to either buy out the plant or redevelop the facility economically.

Four corporate interventions have been most frequently used to soften the effects of layoffs: advance notification, severance pay and extended benefits, retraining programs, and outplacement programs. In this chapter we discuss why, and how, each intervention can help laid-off employees, and give some examples from corporations that have implemented each type of assistance program. We also look at the effect of these four interventions on the Space Coast and at the Pittsburgh steel mills and discuss the impact these programs have on how employees cope with job loss and on how successful they are in becoming satisfactorily reemployed. Important differences between the technical workers in Florida and the steelworkers in Pittsburgh are highlighted here as well.

Next we explore another sensitive aspect of the role of the corporation in plant closings and widespread layoffs. Do corporations implement the layoffs in such a way as to leave departing employees a sense of dignity and remaining employees the impression that layoffs were handled fairly and honorably? As we saw in earlier chapters, many of the laid-off workers felt that the layoffs were announced to them in a cavalier manner, that the criteria for the layoffs were arbitrary, that the layoffs were implemented without respect or consideration for affected workers, and that layoff procedures disrupted the morale and productivity of "surviving" employees. Thus, we explore policies and procedures for implementing layoffs that are both more humane and create conditions for continued productivity within the organization. Examples from corporations that have handled layoffs particularly effectively (or ineffectively) are highlighted as well.

We conclude with a discussion of alternatives to layoffs corporations should consider when faced with adverse business conditions. Changes in internal staffing practices, compensation policies, labor-management relationships, and company-community relationships are strategies that could reduce or render unnecessary massive layoffs. Given the long-term negative consequences layoffs can have both for employers and their employees, carefully considering possible alternatives to layoffs is in itself an important corporate intervention.

Corporate Assistance Programs

Over the past twenty years, four corporate interventions have gained particular currency as means of aiding employees after layoffs: advance notification; severance pay and extended benefits; retraining programs; and outplacement programs. Each of these interventions, in its own way, can help laid-off workers better cope with job loss and/or more successfully find satisfactory reemployment.

Advance Notification

Of all the corporate programs, none has received as much recent attention as advance notification. When we review the research on advance notification, we can see clearly that (1) traditionally workers have seldom received advance notice of layoffs,[2] and (2) management has consistently opposed providing such notice.[3] Estimates from the early 1980s (before the passage of the WARN Act) suggest that 80 percent of the corporations that laid off workers provided less than four weeks' notice of impending terminations and many gave *less than a few hours' notice* even to professional employees.[4]

The WARN Act of 1988 is federal legislation that generally requires employers to give at least sixty-days notice when a plant closing or downsizing will result in laying off at least fifty employees or one-third of the work force. The legislation provides for an exception, however, if "unforeseeable business circumstances" prevent the employer from meeting the requirement. Moreover, although the law asks employers to consult in good faith with employees for a "mutually satisfactory alternative" to layoffs, the employer is not required to implement that alternative. Even this loophole did not prevent an outcry from many corporate officers and business associations against the 1988 WARN Act—ample testimony to the degree of opposition management has historically taken to advance notice.[5]

Management has justified this reluctance to notify workers in advance about plant closings and layoffs in several ways. Many managers oppose advance notice because they fear that laid-off workers will lower their productivity, engage in work slowdowns, or commit industrial sabotage.[6] Other managers fear that laid-off workers will seek employment elsewhere before the organization is ready to terminate them, leaving the closing facility shorthanded at a time it will be most difficult to replace labor.[7] A third reason management is opposed to advance notice is that it fears competitors will be able to take advantage of such information to make further inroads on their business.[8] Finally, managers do not like restrictions that might reduce their discretion in business decision making; they do not want to be locked into a course of action any sooner than they have to be.[9]

Despite these fears, the evidence is that advance notice has very few adverse consequences for corporations. The announcement of an impending plant shutdown does create an initial shock, but employee reactions do not generally result in any perceptible decreases in productivity.[10] Indeed, in some cases productivity has actually increased after the announcement, as employees work even harder in an attempt to persuade management to reverse its decision and to keep the plant open.[11] Research also suggests that quit rates after announcements of impending layoffs are actually quite low,[12] especially when the layoffs threaten plants located in small or depressed labor markets where alternative job opportunities are generally limited. Under these circumstances workers see quitting early as probably increasing the length of their layoff. Moreover, there is little evidence that advance notification causes large losses in market share; rather, it is the loss of market share that created the necessity for the layoff in the first place.

There is, however, substantial evidence that advance notification has positive consequences for workers faced with a layoff. They have more time to search for jobs before they become unemployed, decreasing the length of time they will be without work. They have some advance warning to cut back current spending and defer major purchases, decreasing the likelihood of financial disaster.[13] They have time to get over the initial shock of job loss before going out on the job market, increasing their chances of successfully obtaining reemployment. In some cases, failure to provide advance notification can cause extreme and unnecessary hardships for laid-off workers, as the participants in our studies noted:

> I feel top management did not keep us informed enough about current conditions that might end up with a layoff. In my case, I had just

turned down a job two weeks before my layoff. I had no indication it was coming.

I'm very bitter about the manner in which the mills were closed. No warning, no one cared. There should be a better way than the way they went about it. It was a very traumatic experience.

The company should have done more to prepare the workers prior to the shutdown of the mills. Enough was not done in these areas.

Since purchasing a new home . . . before the plant was shut down without warning, I was forced to go bankrupt. Now it is hard to start all over again.

I was not informed about maybe moving to another plant. I knew nothing of the (training) program and I lost the chance to go to school again.

Advance notification may benefit the company as well. It permits more time for manpower planning under reduced employment, or more time for phasing out operations in cases of plant shutdowns. Also, employees may respond less negatively to layoffs if they feel that the company is attempting to buffer them from the adverse consequences of job loss.[14]

There may also be some positive goodwill advantages to giving advance layoff notification. For example, at Atari, laid-off employees complained about abrupt terminations, claiming that they made it more difficult to secure other jobs. These workers felt longer advance notice would have made it possible for them to secure new jobs without the stigma of unemployment.[15] In response, Atari's vice-president commented: "Frankly, I can't see anything out of the ordinary about asking a person to leave in two days in the world of big business. Most people can pack up an office in five minutes. I don't have much sympathy for anyone complaining about the time to get out." Such posturing gained substantial ill-will in the business community.[16] Stock brokerage firms received similarly bad press when they laid off thousands of employees after the stock crash of October 1987; many of these employees were asked to leave by 5 P.M. of the day they were notified.

In contrast, Brown and Williamson gave eighteen months' advance notice and phased out plant closings over a three-year period. Union Carbide, Ford, and Electrolux all gave six months to a year's advance notice, as well as other types of assistance (e.g., training, outplacement, and counseling).[17] In some locations, IBM and American Hospital Supply were able to use carefully scheduled layoffs that kept jobs open for "skeleton crews" at other facilities, hired laid-off workers on a contract basis, and significantly compensated the last group of employees to leave with overtime pay for their efforts. In so doing, these corporations were respected for protecting and taking care of former employees.[18]

Severance Pay and Extended Benefits

Like advance notification, severance pay and extended benefits allow workers whose jobs have been eliminated to weather the financial difficulties of unemployment. Those who received such benefits frequently commented that the financial assistance reduced the need for their spouses to work full time, reduced the pressure to grab any job that came along simply to obtain cash, and provided some resources for the household while the worker went back for training for a new career.

Most important, many workers feel that the company owes them some restitution for their years of service. Our respondents had many bitter comments about being thrown out with very little to show for their efforts:

> I resent the fact that I was not paid my severance pay from USX, especially when the company was not going to call me back.

> My pension payments were drastically reduced because [the company] defaulted on their premium payments.

> I worked for [the company] for fourteen years and have never received one cent [of pension]. That was not fair and I still feel cheated.

> I had only two and a half years to go for retirement, and had to settle for a big cut in pension. Because of my age I could not find full-time work; I had to settle for part time. Because of shifting me from one department to another, I was not able to get training benefits.

> The last few years of my service with U.S. Steel, even though I had over twenty-five years with the company, I was frequently laid-off, so it was almost impossible to put away money into savings. Also, it affected my pension payment. Now whatever I had in savings is exhausted and my pension barely covers my utilities and taxes.

I could not get any severance pay because they said I didn't work long enough. . . . I thought when you work in a place that closes up you can get severance pay regardless of the time you put in. I didn't receive anything.

Another benefit of severance pay and extended benefits is that it reduces the need for the unemployed to seek additional governmental financial assistance—an activity that is distinctly unpleasant to most people, as our respondents noted.

The people in these government offices make you feel like you are the scum of the earth for trying to get help. They really knock your self-esteem down. The people in these agencies need to realize they, too, could be on the other side of the counter. All I want is to be treated with some respect. It is not my fault I was laid off and I'm tired of making excuses for it.

The main thing I learned is that for every good program like the Job Training Partnership Act, there is an office like the unemployment office working against you.

I had a great deal of trouble dealing with the state getting my training benefits . . . my checks are always three weeks late, or have been stopped. It is very hard to get someone to listen or help when you try to help yourself the honest way.

When blue-collar workers do not have a union contract, they generally fare least well in the area of severance pay and benefits. It is mainly at this level that employers have held the line. Unfortunately, these blue-collar workers are the ones most in need of such benefits.

Because many blue-collar workers cannot afford major pay cuts without falling below the poverty level, adequate severance pay and continuation of health and life insurance programs are essential. A major problem arises, however, when the layoffs are due to financial difficulties in the corporation; those employees who need such economic support do not receive it because the organization itself is bankrupt. To guard against this problem, it has been suggested that companies in particularly volatile sectors of the economy such as high-tech manufacturing and steel commit funds durings profitable quarters to fund severance pay and extended benefits during economic downturns.[19]

Traditionally, companies have been much more concerned with giving severance pay and extended benefits to managerial and professional employees than to blue-collar workers. After corporate restructuring, for instance, Exxon gave many executives up to six months' salary as severance pay. In other corporations, laid-off executives are also likely to be handsomely compensated, often very handsomely indeed.[20] Partly from guilt and partly in fear of an increasingly litigious executive work force, corporations shower many top-level managers with generous severance packages. The so-called employment-at-will doctrine (that companies can hire and fire at will) often does not seem to apply. Each year displaced executives are collecting in excess of $30 million in damage awards and settlements, and that does not include damages awarded for age discrimination. Thus, companies are very reluctant to lay off high-level managers, especially those over age fifty, without considerable benefits.[21]

Middle and lower-level managers have not been treated nearly as generously. The best deal that most middle managers can count on is a week's severance pay per year worked; this is the type of severance package given by Polaroid and AT&T, for instance.[22] Thus, if a middle manager is earning $50,000 a year and has worked twenty years, his or her severance pay would be $20,000—just enough to make it through the six months the typical middle-manager is unemployed.[23] Other companies are less generous. For example, International Harvester expected its laid-off managers to apply for unemployment benefits, and deducted the severance pay checks by the amount of those benefits (roughly $100 per week).[24]

Retraining Programs

Another kind of assistance firms can provide to laid-off employees is training. Particularly for firms in declining industries and occupations, simply encouraging workers to go out and find new jobs misses the mark. These individuals need considerable retraining in order to obtain satisfactory new employment. In our studies fewer than a quarter of the respondents had received any training from their companies after they were laid off. Many, however, undertook training or went back to school with government assistance or on their own—often with very positive results. Getting retrained can help unemployed workers reduce the amount of time between jobs.[25] Enrollment in training programs can also have psychological benefits. Training programs give unemployed workers some structure to the day, provide them with regular work-related activity, and allow them opportunities for increased social contact:

> In some ways, the layoff has been a blessing in disguise. I am now in a field which has always seemed interesting, though I had never imagined ever working in it. But having been forced into it, so to speak, things are looking up. It is not unreasonable to expect to double my former income or earn even more within two years.

> I feel that working is very important, not only to support myself, but also to keep busy. I am planning on taking some night classes soon.

Despite these positive accounts, many who could have benefited from retraining did not get it. There were two dominant reasons why. First, many were intimidated by the prospect of going back to school. Some had not been good students earlier in life and others were afraid that in the wake of a job loss, they could not withstand another failure. Still others, particularly older workers, felt that getting more education at their stage in life would be futile, especially since they perceived there were so few "good" jobs of any sort for people their age. Second, many employees couldn't afford to go back to school because of insufficient benefits or because they had to work two jobs and had no time left in the day for school as well. The comments of some of our study participants express many of these concerns:

> Although I was eligible for education benefits, I could not utilize them because I was employed full time. Even though I greatly desire more education, I could not afford not to work full time without losing my home.

> I started retraining, but before starting my classes I went to work part time and needed to be available all hours. I felt it was more important to my family to pick up any work available.

> I wasn't sure what field to pursue anyway and I am not very academic. I learn much easier by experience, not a blackboard.

> I feel I need further education to get anywhere in a job situation, but I'm very afraid of failing. That would be like the final crushing blow. I think I would just give up then. So I have not enrolled in any courses.

What these comments suggest is that for retraining programs to be effective, many must also be structured to take into account employees' anxieties about failure and intimidation with the classroom. Moreover, our research suggests that retraining programs are more effective when combined with severance pay and other financial assistance programs so employees will not be forced to forego or interrupt their education out of financial necessity. Finally, training should ideally be something that is ongoing throughout a person's career. Recent initiatives like the new Career Development Program jointly sponsored by the Steelworkers union and major companies in the steel industry provide ongoing educational and developmental opportunities for individuals while they are still employed.

Outplacement Programs

Within the business community, the company intervention which has received substantial attention has been outplacement—"a series of services to terminated employees to minimize any period of unemployment following termination."[26] As this definition suggests, outplacement is not a specific program or service, but instead encompasses a variety of services such as resume-writing workshops, career-counseling sessions, and direct-placement assistance. Because the content and length of these programs varies so greatly from corporation to corporation, hard empirical evidence on their effectiveness has lagged behind their favorable publicity.[27]

There have been several noteworthy outplacement programs. After its reorganization, AT&T did not implement layoffs until it had first asked for volunteers to leave the company with increased financial incentives. Then it attempted to relocate within the company those employees who didn't want to leave but whose positions were slated as surplus. Finally, for those employees who were forced out, AT&T paid for a full-service outplacement package that included programs from individual career counseling to the printing of business cards.[28] Wang likewise provided its laid-off employees with office space, telephones, personal computers, job search workshops, and other auxiliary services for up to six months after termination.

Brown and Williamson helped relocate employees and provided vocational training, in addition to providing very generous separation pay and continued life and medical insurance. Electrolux involved state and local agencies in finding workers new jobs, provided retirement planning, offered some of the laid-off workers transfers or moving assistance, and gave paid time-off for job interviewing.[29] When Stroh's Brewery closed its seventy-year-old facility in Detroit, it set up different transition centers for hourly and salaried employees. These centers provided skill testing and assessment, individualized counseling and job-search assistance, and computerized job banks. One year after the plant closing, all of the salaried employees and 98 percent of the hourly employees had found jobs.[30]

Cooperation between the private sector and public sector has resulted in some impressive outplacement services as well. For instance, Bethlehem Steel Corporation joined the state of Pennsylvania and the U.S. Department of Labor to establish the Career Continuation Center with offices in Johnstown and Bethlehem. These centers contained bulletin boards with job listings, twenty-five desks with telephones, and other secretarial services. Laid-off workers could also participate in two-day seminars on job-seeking techniques, as well as one-on-one counseling. At the Bethlehem Center, almost two-thirds of the employees obtained jobs within ninety days.[31] After the *Challenger* disaster, Brevard Community College set up a similar center with federal funds to assist laid-off aerospace workers.

When Ford laid off more than two thousand employees in Ontario, it set up two Manpower Adjustment Committees, one for salaried and one for hourly employees. Members of these committees came from Ford's corporate staff, the United Automobile Workers union, and Canada Manpower Consultative Services. After obtaining specific information from laid-off workers about job skills, experience, and job preferences, these Manpower Adjustment Committees contacted 130 firms by letter and 2,000 smaller companies by telephone. This innovative program found new employment for nearly 85 percent of the displaced workers.[36]

Not quite so impressive are those outplacement programs that are well-intentioned but too narrow in scope or poorly executed.[33] For instance, NBC ran resume-writing workshops for its laid-off employees; however, employees complained that these workshops were "conducted by a youngster in the personnel department who didn't realize that seasoned professionals don't get jobs by sending out resumes." Similarly, an institutional sales trader at Lehman Brothers (who was let go when Lehman Brothers was bought by Shearson/American Express) agreed that Lehman had set up a "base of operations" for him, but the office had only one phone for three people, so employees couldn't seriously make or take calls.[34]

Some of the weakest outplacement activities are programs that have the veneer of helpfulness but which are perceived as manipulative or punitive by workers. General Motors' "Mainstream" activities have received much attention in this regard. The Mainstream program was designed to help persuade managers to leave and to ease the process; however, several employees initiated litigation after their experiences in the program. One planner claims that he and seven other managers who didn't "volunteer" to leave were put in a specially created area that was bare except for desks and telephones, where they stayed for four months with no work assignments. A draftsman who also didn't volunteer to leave says that for this defiance, he has been put at a desk in front of his boss's office where he files product-description manuals in binders. An engineer who didn't volunteer to leave has been assigned to wiping down oil drums.[35]

Not having an outplacement program, or having a poorly designed one, can increase the likelihood that employees will sue over their job loss. Four hundred workers laid off by Atari subsequently filed a $13.6 million class-action suit for damages related to the layoff. Seven hundred former employees of Singer Company filed a class-action suit seeking $28 million, contending that Singer reneged on a previous agreement to invest $2 million in upgrading their New Jersey plant; Singer eventually settled out of court. Before Western Electric was permitted to close its plant in Kearny, New Jersey, a federal judge required the company to create a $7 million fund for the two thousand women who were to be displaced.[36]

Our own research suggests that outplacement activities can be quite beneficial. Several of our respondents noted that outplacement activities gave them the added stimulus to seek further education, get into a more suitable occupation, or to relocate to an area with a healthier economy. Moreover, outplacement activities can provide some of the same positive secondary consequences of training. Out-placement provides workers with a structure to their day, some companionship and social support, and a signal from the company that they support employee efforts to obtain reemployment. All of these may help to reduce the anxiety levels of laid-off workers sufficiently to allow them to cope with job loss effectively.[37]

Research on outplacement suggests two other points. First, one very valuable facet of an outplacement program is the temporary base of operations provided laid-off workers from which to job hunt, as well as some clerical and technical support for resume writing and contacting potential employers. Second, mainly anec-dotal evidence suggests that counseling and career planning activ-ities are better implemented after the layoffs are finalized, and on a one-to-one basis.

Availability and Utility of Corporate Assistance Programs

In our research on layoffs, we examined the impact of four corporate interventions—advance notification, severance pay and extended benefits, retraining programs, and outplacement programs—on laid-off workers' experiences with unemployment. As the previous research in this area suggests, there are two possible explanations for why these corporate interventions can have positive conse-quences for the unemployed. First, these corporate practices may help workers obtain satisfactory reemployment (or do so more quickly), and thus eliminate the financial and psychological distress associated with layoffs. Second, by providing individuals with some goals, structure, financial support, and career guidance, these pro-grams may help the unemployed sustain some semblance of normal routine during layoffs.

Table 5–1 shows the percentage of employees who received each type of corporate assistance; results are reported for the total sam-ple, and for the Florida and Homestead samples separately.

Availability of Assistance

On the average, respondents in the Florida sample reported signif-icantly more advance notification and a higher incidence of sever-

TABLE 5–1

Availability of Corporate Assistance Programs

Corporate assistance Program	Total (N=361)	Home-stead (N=198)	Florida (N=163)	t*
Advance notice	47%	26%	73%	6.34**
Outplacement	21	11	33	.70
Severance pay	38	16	64	3.62**
Extended benefits	33	42	23	3.02**

*Indicates whether there are statistically significant differences between Homestead and Florida samples.
**p<.01.

ance pay. They were also more likely to obtain outplacement assistance. The Homestead sample reported a significantly higher incidence of extended benefits, no doubt due to union contracts. Very few employees received any retraining benefits; most of those who did were located in Pittsburgh. (Since fewer than twenty-five participants received training from their employers, no further analyses on this corporate intervention are possible.)

Consistent with the discussion of advance notification practices and severance pay earlier in the chapter, the white-collar workers in Florida were generally better treated at the time of layoffs than were blue-collar workers. Most of the firms and institutions laying off white-collar workers in Florida were hoping that the layoffs would be only temporary, and therefore were motivated to treat their employees more gently and generously. In contrast, in Pittsburgh it was generally assumed these layoffs were permanent.

Outplacement services, theoretically available to all, seem to be provided more frequently to white-collar than to blue-collar workers. We saw nearly three times the number of workers who had received outplacement assistance in Florida than in Pittsburgh. One possible explanation for this is that companies assume (often incorrectly) that governmental unemployment offices are adequately equipped to find new jobs for most lower-level employees. Another possible explanation for this is the assumption (usually a misperception) that most blue-collar workers belong to unions whose stewards and business agents are responsible for finding displaced workers new jobs. In contrast, most companies realize white-collar workers are more or less on their own after layoffs.

In terms of extended benefits, again consistent with the previous discussion, blue-collar workers are more likely to have union contracts that specify the nature and duration of their extended benefits. As expected, this was true for the Pittsburgh steelworkers.

While few employees received any training at all from their companies, the blue-collar workers in Pittsburgh were more likely to obtain this benefit than their white-collar counterparts in Florida. Blue-collar workers being laid-off from the steel mills were losing not only their current employer but also, quite likely, their occupation or craft as well. Therefore, they needed some retraining to prepare them for new careers. The more highly educated engineers and technical workers in Florida were more in need of opportunities in the same occupation elsewhere, and were thus more likely to receive outplacement.

Utility of Corporate Assistance Programs

The corporate interventions we examined in this study are modestly related to laid-off workers' reemployment status and prospects for reemployment (see table 5–2). Advance notice, outplacement practices, severance pay, and training programs are all associated with

TABLE 5–2
Helpfulness of Corporate Assistance Programs[1]

| Outcomes | Advance notice | Total sample | | Extended benefits |
		Outplacement	Severance pay	
Reemployment status	*	*	*	
Reemployment prospects	*	*	*	*
Satisfaction		*	*	
Psychological distress				*

[1]An asterisk (*) indicates a statistically significant relationship (p<.05).

workers' becoming satisfactorily reemployed; extended benefits tended to boost employees' expectations of becoming reemployed. Subgroup analyses reveal that these results are stronger in the Florida sample than in the Pittsburgh sample, where fewer employees received any assistance at all. Corporate assistance programs are less strongly and consistently associated with increasing the satisfaction of laid-off workers or decreasing their psychological distress.

In general, we found that corporate interventions are more strongly related to reemployment status and prospects than to attitudes. One possible explanation for these results is that corporate assistance programs often raise workers' expectations of getting reemployed in the near future. If laid-off workers do not get reemployed soon after getting retraining or outplacement assistance, their moods often take a strong turn downward.[38]

There is a second possible way that corporate assistance programs can facilitate the reemployment of laid-off workers. These interventions might also energize laid-off workers to engage in more problem-focused coping. For example, although outplacement may not directly get the unemployed new jobs, it may motivate laid-off workers to keep searching and focus their efforts more effectively. Similarly, although extended benefits may not directly improve the attitudes and psychological well-being of the unemployed, they may ward off the type of deep depression or apathy that stops job hunting altogether.

Thus, we also looked at the relationships between these corporate interventions and the six coping strategies we examined in the last chapter: direct job search, seeking retraining, relocation, obtaining financial assistance, seeking social support, and community activism (see table 5–3). We found significant relationships between corporate interventions and coping strategies. Employees who received advance notice needed to job search less, required less retraining, applied for less financial assistance, and were not as likely to relocate. Clearly, employees who have advance notice are more likely to find new employment in their present communities and career fields.

Outplacement has the most positive effects on retraining and relocation; it motivated our respondents to consider major alternatives to their current lines of work and their local labor markets.

TABLE 5–3

Relationships of Corporate Interventions and Coping Strategies[1]

Coping strategies	Advance notice	Outplacement	Severance pay	Extended benefits
Job search	* (-)		*	
Retraining	* (-)	*		
Relocation	* (-)	*	*	
Financial assistance	* (-)			* (-)
Social support		*	*	
Community activism			*	

[1]An asterisk (*) indicates a statistically significant relationship ($p < .05$). A minus sign (-) indicates a negative relationship.

As we suggested earlier, outplacement programs also provide a useful forum for laid-off workers to seek social support.

Severance pay systematically leads to more active coping of all kinds, especially in terms of job search and geographical relocation. Severance pay provides workers with some buffer so they do not need to immediately jump into another job, and can look around more systematically for jobs even in other geographical locations.

Extended benefits was the corporate intervention with the fewest consequences for coping behavior. Essentially, their main impact seems to be relieving the laid-off employees from needing to seek additional financial assistance.

Overall, the results are similar for the Florida and Pittsburgh samples. However, there were some interesting differences between the two groups of laid-off workers. Advance notification was especially appreciated by the Pittsburgh sample. As we noted in Chapter 2, the Monongahela Valley was much more community-oriented and family-oriented than the Space Coast in Florida. Relocating was especially traumatic for these people, as was noted by the following comments of steelworkers:[39]

They gave me two weeks. As soon as I got home, I sold everything
I had left . . . and rented a car and came down [South]. I had to give
up a lot of family. . . . I had to give up everything I had. It was a
hard choice. A very hard choice. I cried all the way down. Every state
I got to I had to think: Should I turn around? I cried for three days
when I got here.

[At first] I kept things going by doing handy-man work. But then the
winter came and there wasn't anything. I spent the idle time drinking
and gambling. It was time to make my move. . . . We weren't able
to sell our home so we can't buy one down here. I don't really want
to, though. I'm not settled here. I don't feel comfortable. . . . One of
these days we'll be back.

Outplacement assistance had different effects on the Florida and
Pittsburgh workers. For the Florida workers, outplacement motivated them to relocate. For the Pittsburgh steelworkers, outplacement motivated them to get retrained and to become involved in
community initiatives to stop the layoffs. Some examples of outplacement programs in these areas suggests reasons for these results.

In Florida, for example, the federal government funded an outplacement center at Brevard Community College for workers laid
off by Space Coast companies. This program provided counseling
and job placement for laid-off workers along the Space Coast. At
the height of the layoffs, sixty people a night showed up for advice
on resume writing, interviewing, and changing careers.[40] Many of
the aerospace workers believed their skills were so specialized they
could not be transferred to any other field, or any other geographical
location. One of the major goals of the Brevard Community College
placement efforts was to help them focus on their "skill packages"
rather than on their job titles, and to give them confidence in their
abilities to find jobs in other fields and in other areas.

In Pittsburgh, there was much less hope that the laid-off steelworkers could find new employment without obtaining new training; jobs in the steel industry were becoming scarcer and scarcer,
as were jobs in allied industries. Therefore, outplacement assistance
focused much more on retraining. The Steelworkers union was opposed to Bethlehem Steel's efforts at setting up outplacement centers
focused on helping employees write resumes and practice interview-

ing. As one union official noted, union workers "have jobs, not careers." Workers in Pittsburgh who did receive outplacement services were made much more concretely aware of the low reemployment prospects in steel, and the need to get on with new occupations. Some workers were able to take their severance pay and extended benefits, and with the student loans they became eligible for, finance a technical or junior college education program.[41]

Also in Pittsburgh, because of the closeness of the community, outplacement centers became a social as well as a professional network for unemployed workers. It is not surprising, therefore, that workers attending outplacement programs became more involved in community efforts to stop further unemployment. For instance, many of the steelworkers involved in the Mon Valley Unemployed Committee (a political action group in the Pittsburgh area) first became aware of community activities through their contacts at outplacement centers.

In the Florida sample severance pay and extended benefits had little impact on efforts to cope. In general, the Florida workers experienced less financial distress than their Pittsburgh counterparts, and most were hoping to ride out what they hoped would be a short-term problem. In contrast, severance pay allowed the Pittsburgh workers to obtain the retraining they so desperately needed to get reemployed. One worker used his severance pay to take an eight-month course in industrial x-ray technology; another used the money to become a registered nurse. Others pursued training in electronics, management, sales, and engineering.[42]

In the Pittsburgh sample, extended benefits decreased the need for workers to seek out governmental financial assistance in terms of food stamps, utility payment assistance, or public welfare. For many workers, having extended benefits helped them ride out a virtually nonexistent housing market. Without extended benefits, some workers had to let their homes be foreclosed, and move to other locations at greatly reduced wages.[43] Those workers who were unemployed for an extended period of time also became less and less involved in community activities. As time went by, they became increasingly pessimistic about the impact of their efforts. Moreover, the closer workers came to the end of their extended benefits, the more willing they became to accept minimum-wage, part-time jobs as janitors and fast-food servers—and the less time they had to devote to community activities of any sort.

Company Interventions Reconsidered

The data in our studies point out several important issues about the role of corporate interventions in the lives of workers who have been laid off.

First, corporate interventions play a relatively small role in *directly* influencing whether former employees get satisfactorily reemployed elsewhere. Demographic factors (age, education) and labor market factors (level of unemployment, skill level of occupation) play a much greater role in whether workers get satisfactorily reemployed or have good prospects for doing so.

Second, corporate interventions play a larger role in influencing laid-off workers' coping strategies. Corporate interventions seem to energize workers to engage in more active coping, which in turn leads to a better reemployment picture.

Third, to the extent that corporate interventions do play a role in influencing adjustment to life without work, they do so by facilitating coping behavior that leads to reemployment. Corporate interventions do not, in and of themselves, lead to less psychological distress or more life satisfaction. This is largely because, as we noted in the last chapter, coping itself is stressful and often anxiety-arousing. Thus, although corporate interventions do provide workers with some structured activities and social interaction, they also energize workers to engage in activities that they find inherently unpleasant.

Fourth, different corporate interventions seem to be differentially effective with different jobs categories. Because unemployed white-collar workers are more likely to be searching only for new jobs, outplacement assistance tends to be more critical to them. Because unemployed blue-collar workers are more likely to be changing occupations, retraining tends to be more critical to them. Since unemployment is likely to be shorter-term for white-collar than blue-collar workers, extended benefits are more critical for blue-collar workers. Losing a job without notice is stressful for anyone, but it entails the greatest financial hardship for the lower-paid blue-collar worker.

Implementation of Layoffs

How the layoffs are implemented also plays a major role in how individual workers respond to becoming unemployed.[44] Repeatedly, our respondents commented on how angry they were about how they had been laid off:

> I feel betrayed. We were told about several contracts and work being transferred from subdivisions of this company only last year. Now there is nothing. I was lied to.

> In my opinion, it was all company politics.

> The process of reducing the work force at my company could have been handled more tactfully and with greater concern for the individual.

Management needs to address five issues when they implement a layoff: (1) explanations of criteria for layoffs; (2) the role of performance evaluations in the layoffs decisions; (3) treatment of laid-off workers with dignity and social support; (4) fair recommendations to potential new employers; and (5) attention to the stress and discomfort of the "survivors" who remain.

Explanations of Criteria for Layoffs

We found substantial evidence that laid-off employees found their terminations to be arbitrary or biased. As we have documented extensively, many employees attributed their layoffs to age bias.

Many workers also believe that top managment spares barely competent management personnel while greatly slashing the number of lower-level employees:

> The company did not exercise good judgment in laying off lower-paid employees while keeping an overabundance of much higher-paid management and supervisory personnel.

> It distressed me greatly to see people's lives being literally ruined career-wise by management personnel that had little or no contact with these individuals yet had complete control over their futures.

The same phenomenom can be seen even when layoffs are caused by mergers and acquisitions, or by corporate restructuring. At NBC, for instance, a female associate producer was laid off from her job—and then discovered that all but one of the people laid off in her unit were women. NBC countered that men and women were laid off in equal numbers in the network's total corporate layoff.[45] Independent of the legal issues of gender discrimination involved, however, the perception of bias remained.

To avoid these perceptions, it is important for management to make clear both in words and in behavior the criteria for terminations, regardless of whether they are seniority, merit, or job category. Otherwise, management leaves itself open to legal action from those who are laid off, ill-will from the public, and justified distrust from those who remain.

Role of Performance Evaluations.

Contributing greatly to the feeling of arbitrariness or bias in the layoff procedures are perceptions that employee performance evaluations ratings are not used at all, or are purposely downgraded to justify terminations. In our study, 75 percent of the survey respondents had received "outstanding" or "excellent" on their last performance appraisal, and still they had been let go. As one manager noted: "Inaccurate and untrue performance appraisals were used in support of company layoff goals—a very cavalier attitude toward dedicated long-term employees. The human aspects were gruesome . . ."

Recently, Longenecker, Gioia, and Sims detailed just how political the performance appraisal process can be.[46] They found that managers are greatly influenced by political considerations when completing performance appraisals; they inflate them to maximize merit increases, and deflate them to speed up a termination process. The executives in the Longenecker study were quite open about the political pressures they felt:

> There is really no getting around the fact that whenever I evaluate one of my people, I stop and think about the impact—the ramifications of my decisions of my relationship with the guy and his future here.

> When I rate my people it doesn't take place in a vacuum—so you

have to ask yourself what the purpose of the process is. . . . I use this thing to my advantage and I know my people and what it takes to keep them going and that is what this is all about.

When layoffs occur, all the political games used to justify the performance results become open for inspection. The negative spin-off effects for top management prove embarrassing; the adverse consequences for laid-off employees who were unaware of the political rating (or who chose to pretend they did not exist) are disastrous. Corporations need to make sure the performance evaluations accurately reflect employee abilities. Otherwise, they risk not only litigation but also losing their best talent and retaining marginally competent members of a "good-old-boy" network.[47]

Treatment of Employees With Dignity and Social Support

Schweiger, Ivancevich, and Power write that one of the most important executive actions for managing human resources during layoffs is the treatment of laid-off employees with dignity and social support. The effective managers in their study gave terminated employees accurate and honest information so that they could make better decisions about their future plans. Better managers also spent time talking to the laid-off employees, allowing them to vent some of their anger and frustration. Such actions on the part of executives helped laid-off employees cope more realistically with the choices ahead, and to face the job hunt with more self-confidence and self-esteem:[48]

> He (the boss) was firm, honest, and open. He didn't tolerate saboteurs and rabble rousers who really heat up rather than help the situation. I respected his fair but direct style of acting professional.

> He was easy to talk to. Made me feel comfortable. He just paid attention to my concerns and uncertainty.

> She set up a workshop on her own for resume preparation and interviewing skills. She paid for a friend of hers—a personnel director from another firm—to spend three hours on three different nights to help us get our act together.

In contrast, there have been some very unpleasant episodes involving laid-off employees being mistreated. Sutton, Eisenhardt, and

Jucker, for instance, document problems with Atari in 1982 and 1983, just before it was sold by Warner Communications:[49]

> The manager gave the production employees directions to Sunnyvale High School and told them to be there on Friday, February 25—He then collected their badges and the production workers were escorted off the premises.

> Top management went around and spoke to everybody. What they said was, "Now we've gotten rid of all the rummies and the company's strong and all the good people are left." And they never should have said that. They should have said, "Because of business problems, we have to let people go." But they said, "We've gotten rid of all the scum," and that wasn't the case at all. And everybody knew it and everybody resented it. So it just got worse and worse.

Sutton, Eisenhardt, and Jucker also suggest several strategies for treating employees with dignity during layoffs.[50] Employees should be able to say goodbye to co-workers and to express their anger and sorrow. They should be free from being denigrated to their peers after their departure. Laid-off employees should be given the bad news in person and by people they know, not through the mail from managers they've never heard of. Treating departing employees with dignity and compassion is better for the laid-off workers themselves, better for the employees who remain, and better for the public image of the company.

Fair Recommendations to Potential Employers

More and more lawsuits are being filed by terminated employees who feel that they are not being fairly recommended for employment in other corporations. In 1986 the suits filed by discharged employees against their former bosses accounted for about a third of all defamation actions.[51] In the aftermath of layoffs, it is particularly important for executives to be sensitive to the legal implications of negative recommendations for terminated employees.

A well-publicized instance of termination resulting in litigation is the case of Buck vs. Frank B. Hall & Co.[52] A Hall executive told a detective posing as a representative of a prospective employer that Buck was "a Jekyll and Hyde person, a classic sociopath." Buck sued his former employer for malicious slander and libel, and collected $605,000 for lost wages, as well as a $1.3 million penalty.

Indeed, counseling companies on both small- and large-scale lay-offs in order to avoid discrimination suits has recently become an important phase of employment law.[53] Because of the many legal ramifications of layoffs—not only in terms of recommendations, but in terms of renegotiating contracts and pension plans—many corporations are using the services of "undertaker" firms such as The Directorate. Companies like The Directorate advise clients on the legal technicalities of laying employees off, financial incentives for management personnel, and other human resource problems that occur during a reorganization.[54]

Handling "Survivors" of Layoffs

From the viewpoint of the laid-off workers, losing the social support of friends and colleagues at work is one of the most distressing aspects of job loss. Companies dealing with the human resource problems resulting from layoffs have more recently been paying attention to the other side of this issue: the employees who survive the layoff are often upset and angry as well.[55] Survivors, too, miss their departed colleagues and are frequently angry with management for having caused the layoff, for having mishandled the layoff process, or for speaking disparagingly about the departed workers. The productivity of survivors may also decrease. Workers lose time discussing their emotions, speculating on whether more layoffs will be forthcoming, and often looking for new jobs of their own.[56] Survivors are especially negatively affected when they identify closely with the layoff victims and feel the laid-off workers were inadequately compensated.[57]

Because of these problems, firms have taken some positive, concrete actions to lift the morale and instill trust in the survivors of layoffs. For instance, consulting firms such as Eclecon and Good-measure advise corporations to give employees relatively easy work the first week or so after the layoffs, and then give them new, challenging assignments after that to distract them. Companies like Wang and AT&T have followed these strategies with success.[58]

Other organizations undergoing layoffs have focused their efforts on directly boosting morale. General Motors hired a motivational speaker who urged GM'ers: "So what if morale is bad at GM!

Repeat after me: I am not waiting! Today is my day! I feel good! I feel great." Other companies have run parties where people can reminisce, or have given groups of employees pep talks.[59]

The survivor problem should sensitize management to two other issues. First, layoffs should not be intermittent or sporadic or extended over a long period of time. Second, the number of job changes for survivors after the layoffs should be kept to a minimum. These policies will help to stabilize employee concerns and reduce needless anxiety and apprehension. At Amax, unfortunately, a series of layoffs occurred over a four-year period, each accompanied by management's claim that the company was now "lean and mean." Such actions only served to further demoralize workers.[60]

Alternatives to Layoffs

There can be no disagreement that losing a job has a strong negative impact on an individual. Our results suggest that laid-off workers are much more likely to suffer psychological distress (e.g., depression, anxiety, nervousness, fear of the future), physiological distress (e.g., increased alcohol and cigarette use, eating and sleeping irregularities, increased drug usage), and financial distress (e.g., 10% of our sample had to relocate, 5% lost their homes due to mortgage foreclosure, and 7% had to move in with relatives outside of their immediate families).

There are long-term financial consequences of layoffs as well as short-term ones. Half of the respondents in our study indicated that they would accept a pay cut of at least 15 percent to secure a job within the next month. Even these presumed concessions, however, may have been optimistic. Of the people in our studies who had been fortunate enough to secure alternative employment, nearly two-fifths had to take a pay cut of at least 30 percent, and one-fifth were working for less than half of their former salaries. Clearly, layoffs have an adverse impact on the long-term earnings of workers.[61]

Firms suffer adverse consequences as a result of layoffs, too. Valuable talent is lost. As we noted earlier, there can be both morale and productivity problems for survivors. There are public relations and community goodwill issues to consider as well. Even if laid-off employees are recalled, it is unlikely that they will ever have the same commitment and loyalty to the corporation now that the employment "contract" has been broken.

Because of all of the problems associated with layoffs, several researchers have urged corporations to consider alternatives to lay-offs when faced with adverse business conditions.[62] Instead of mass layoffs, they argue that corporations should make major changes in internal human resource planning practices, compensation practices, labor-management relationships, and company-community relationships to manage the downsizing.

Human Resource Planning Practices

From their case study of how IBM handled a workforce reduction, Greenhalgh, McKersie, and Gilkey point out several alternatives that organizations can use instead of layoffs. The IBM case is particularly instructive because IBM traditionally has had a high commitment to preserving job security, yet still was forced to redeploy personnel.[63]

IBM immediately reduced the rate of new hiring. Temporary employment was stopped, as were overtime assignments. Limited employment programs (e.g., co-op programs and summer internships) were discontinued as well. Transfers into the facilities with excess personnel were not approved.

Next, IBM exercised care and concern as it tried to increase the outflow of employees. It allowed normal attrition, but did not replace many of the departed workers. It encouraged voluntary relocations to other plants. It tried to divert those employees returning from leaves of absence to other plants. IBM also set up salary incentives to encourage relatively older workers to take early retirement.

IBM was also conscious of the need to communicate the reasoning and logic of their decisions. Although IBM has traditionally been perceived as very successful—and generally is—the semiconductor industry is very volatile. IBM rented a theater in the city where the plant retrenchment was occurring, and explained the dynamics and economics of the semiconductor industry. It also established an open-door policy and a hotline for employees so that they could get quick and accurate information about IBM's plans. IBM's activities illustrate that corporate staffing strategies can redeploy personnel and provide viable alternatives to massive layoffs during business downturns.

In a recent article, Greenhalgh, Lawrence, and Sutton suggest that corporations use a hierarchy of workforce reduction strategies. In order of increasing severity, those strategies are: (1) natural attrition; (2) voluntary redeployment incentives; (3) forced redeployment; (4) layoffs with outplacement assistance; and (5) layoffs with no assistance. In addition, they note that the decision to lay off workers is also influenced by important "context" factors. They note that corporations are most likely to use layoffs with largely unskilled, nonunionized workers, because these workers are the easiest to replace with the least training. These authors also note that publicly held firms are more likely to use severe layoffs than public-sector firms because of the pressure to return profits, while diversified firms are more capable of redeploying personnel than one-product-category firms.[64]

Compensation Practices

A variety of innovative compensation practices have also been attempted to reduce personnel costs. One that has received considerable attention is "short-time pay." Instead of laying off employees, companies are encouraged to voluntarily split reduced work among existing staffers by cutting the working hours and paychecks of all.[65]

The advantages of short-time pay are straightforward. Employees who would be laid off get to keep their jobs and fringe benefits. Firms are able to hold on to experienced employees, avoiding the expense of hiring and training new workers when business picks up. Some employees actually welcome a stretch of short weeks with only partial loss of pay. However, there are several drawbacks to short-time pay. The burden is greatest for employees with seniority, who must sacrifice part of their pay to keep colleagues working. It is also more costly than it may first appear, since companies still continue to pay for complete benefits for short-time work weeks.[66]

There have been some notable examples of short-time programs working effectively. Motorola and Signetics have used short-time pay with considerable success. Currently, the Department of Labor has not heavily marketed the idea, and some union leaders are wary of advocating a program for "sharing the misery" of unemployment. Nevertheless, surveys conducted by Mathematica Policy Research suggest that employers using short-time compensation were generally satisfied and that it may be a viable alternative to massive layoffs.[67]

Perry suggests several other compensation alternatives. Polaroid experimented with job-sharing, where two employees cut back their hours to half-time to share a job. Pacific Northwest Bell implemented a leave-of-absence policy, where workers could take unpaid leaves of absence but were guaranteed jobs on return. Mountain Bell saved substantial money by reducing paid vacation time and decreasing the number of long weekends. At Natomas, top executives took a 10 percent pay cut.[68]

Of course, forcing some of these compensation plans on workers will have negative spin-off effects; however, research suggests that innovative compensation plans seem to elicit more volunteers than originally expected. Moreover, these volunteers, when considered all together, really allow corporations to make less drastic staffing cuts than they would have to otherwise. When faced with large-scale layoffs, it makes sense to allow workers to reassess their priorities about work, money, and leisure before making across-the-board reductions in force.

Labor-Management Relationships

As their members have become increasingly hard-hit by plant closings, unions have increasingly engaged in cooperative ventures with management to stem layoffs. The areas for possible cooperation and innovation in labor-management relationships include collective bargaining agreements as well as political action activities.[69]

In the area of collective bargaining, unions have been willing to give concessions in wages, benefits, and work rules in an attempt to help the company become more profitable and survive. They have also been willing to exchange wage demands for increased job security, more advance notice of layoffs, and increased severance pay for workers.[70]

In the area of political action, some unions and employers have joined forces to seek legislation aimed at protecting their industry from foreign competition and to oppose environmental regulations that may have a negative effect on profitability. For example, the Glass, Pattern, Plastics, and Allied Workers in the glass-bottle industry joined employer associations to prevent passage of laws that would reduce demand by requiring deposits for glass beverage containers. The United Automobile Workers, on several occasions, have supported industry efforts to weaken or postpone implementation of emissions standards.

There have even been cases where unions have worked with management to develop new uses for plants faced with declining product demand or burdened with obsolete technology. For example, the Auto Workers and Machinists have been working with the management of McDonnell Douglas to develop alternative products (to defense components) to stabilize production and employment levels.[71]

Traditionally hostile labor-management relationships are unlikely to take a positive turn overnight, and there are complex public policy issues involved. Yet, in some cases, management's willingness to work more cooperatively with unions can reduce the number of employees who are laid off, or can ameliorate the negative consequences for the unemployed. Especially when large-scale layoffs involve blue-collar production facilities, management should consider more cooperation with the affected unions.

Company-Community Relationships

Carroll suggests that corporations consider their social responsibilities in the layoff process, not only for humanitarian reasons but also to avoid the costs of losing community goodwill. Carroll suggests a series of steps socially responsible organizations can take to avert layoffs, reduce their sizes, or mitigate their effects.[72]

Before shutting down a plant or a division, he urges companies to consider selling off the unit as an ongoing enterprise, an option likely to reduce the need for layoffs. For instance, when Viner Brothers (Bangor, Maine) was going out of business, it sold its three plants to Wolverine Manufacturing; almost 90 percent of the nine-hundred workers were eventually hired by Wolverine. Other companies have sold plants or divisions to the employees themselves; this has been the case at dozens of sites such as National Steel's Weirton (West Virginia) mill. Although employee ownership has not been without costs to employees (i.e., employees often have to take pay cuts of up to 33%), jobs can be saved, and the National Center for Employee Ownership reports that most employee-owned firms have a good chance for survival.[73]

After the decision to close a plant or division has been made, there are a variety of actions that corporations can take to mitigate the social and economic impact of its action on employees and their communities. Some of these we have discussed earlier, such as providing advance notice to employees. Another action corporations can take to help their communities is to find replacement industries. For example, when Tate and Lyle (United Kingdom) closed its sugar refineries, it acted as an investment banker to other firms in the area; it invested capital in firms willing to expand their work forces by offering jobs to former Tate and Lyle workers. Both Olin (when it left Saltville, Virginia) and R.J. Reynolds (when it left Winston-Salem, North Carolina) made substantial gifts to their communities. Olin gave Saltville 3,500 acres of property, mineral rights, the plant, and all remaining tangible property as well as over a half-million dollars in cash subsidies; R.J. Reynolds donated its corporate headquarters to Wake Forest University in Winston-Salem.[74]

All of these actions suggest that corporations are responsible to other stakeholders in their firms besides the shareholders. When layoffs occur, these social responsibilities are not suspended. Corporations need to anticipate actions that might have adverse consequences to stakeholders, and minimize the negative effects that do result from forced job terminations.[75]

However, as these last two sections point out, even well-intentioned corporations operate in environments that are not without constraints. For corporations to effectively handle layoffs, they also need the cooperation and support of other important institutions and constituencies. In the next chapter, we examine the role unions and community groups play in ameliorating the factors contributory to, and the adverse consequences of, large-scale layoffs.

Notes

1. A. Kinicki, J. Bracker, R. Kreitner, C. Lockwood, and D. Lemak, "Socially Responsible Plant Closings," *Personnel Administrator*, 1987, no. 6 (June): 116–28.

2. H.G. Kaufman, *Professionals in Search of Work: Coping with the Stress of Job Loss and Unemployment* (New York: John Wiley and Sons, 1982).

3. C.R. Leana and J.M. Ivancevich, "Involuntary Job Loss: Institutional Interventions and a Research Agenda," *Academy of Management Review* 12 (1987): 301–12.

4. Kaufman, *Professionals in Search of Work*.

5. J.T. Addison, "The Controversy over Advance Notice Legislation in the United States," *British Journal of Industrial Relations* 27 (1989): 235–63.

6. B. Harrison, "Plant Closures: Efforts to Cushion the Blow," *Monthly Labor Review* 107 (1984): 41–43.

7. A.R. Weber and D.P. Taylor, "Procedures for Employee Displacement: Advance Notice of a Plant Shutdown," *Journal of Business* 36 (1963): 312–15.

8. Harrison, "Plant Closures"; Weber and Taylor, "Procedures for Employee Displacement."

9. J.J. Chrisman, A.B. Carroll, and E.J. Gatewood, "What's Wrong with Plant Closing Legislation and Industrial Policy," *Business Horizons* 28 (1985): 28–37.

10. R.G. Ehrenberg, and G.H. Jakubson, "Advance Notification of Plant Closings: Does It Matter?" *Industrial Relations* 28 (1989): 60–71; J.T. Addison and P. Portugal, "The Effect of Advance Notification of Plant Closings on Unemployment," *Industrial and Labor Relations Review* 41 (1987): 3–16, 43–45, 49.

11. Weber and Taylor, "Procedures for Employee Displacement."

12. J. Fedrau, "Easing the Worker's Transition from Job Loss to Employment," *Monthly Labor Review* 107 (1984): 38–40; B. Harrison, "Plant Closures: Efforts to Cushion the Blow," *Monthly Labor Review* 107 (1984): 41–43; M.L. Sweet, *Industrial Location Policy for Economic Revitalization: National and International Perspectives* (New York: Praeger, 1981); R. Hershey, "Effects of Anticipated Job Loss on Employee Behavior," *Journal of Applied Psychology* 56 (1972): 273–75.

13. Ehrenberg and Jakubson, "Advance Notification"; Addison and Portugal, "The Effect of Advance Notification."

14. Leana and Ivancevich, "Involuntary Job Loss."

15. M. Langley, "Many Middle Managers Fight Back as More Firms Trim Work Forces," *Wall Street Journal*, 29 November 1984, p. 55.

16. R.I. Sutton, K.M. Eisenhardt, and J.V. Jucker, "Managing Organizational Decline: Lessons from Atari," *Organizational Dynamics* 14 (1986): 17–29.

17. Kinicki et al., "Socially Responsible Plant Closings."

18. Langley, "Many Middle Managers Fight Back."

19. J.C. Latack and J.B. Dozier, "After the Ax Falls: Job Loss as a Career Transition," *Academy of Management Review* 11 (1986): 375–92.

20. A. Bennett, "After the Merger, More CEO's Left in Uneasy Spot: Looking for Work," *Wall Street Journal*, 3 February 1987, p. 35.

21. C.H. Deutsch, "Why Being Fired Is Losing Its Taint," *New York Times*, 24 January 1988, pp. 3–1, 3–11.

22. F. Kessler, "Managers without a Company," *Fortune*, 28 October 1985, pp. 51–56.
23. Ibid.
24. Ibid.
25. Kaufman, *Professionals in Search of Work*.
26. J. Scherba, "Outplacement as a Personnel Responsibility," *Personnel* 50 (1973): 40–44.
27. C.R. Leana and D.C. Feldman, "Individual Responses to Job Loss: Perceptions, Reactions, and Coping Behaviors," *Journal of Management* 14 (1988): 5–19.
28. Langley, "Many Middle Managers Fight Back."
29. Kinicki et al., "Socially Responsible Plant Closings."
30. J. Jannotta, "Stroh's Outplacement Success," *Management Review* 76 (1987): 52–53.
31. J.S. DeMott, "After the Mills Shut Down," *Time*, 15 August, 1983, p. 46.
32. Kinicki et al., "Socially Responsible Plant Closings."
33. C.R. Leana and D.C. Feldman, "When Mergers Force Layoffs: Some Lessons about Managing the Human Resource Problems," *Human Resource Planning* 12 (1989): 123–40.
34. Langley, "Many Middle Managers Fight Back."
35. A.K. Naj, "GM Now is Plagued with Drop in Morale as Payrolls Are Cut," *Wall Street Journal*, 26 May 1987, pp. 1, 18.
36. Kinicki et all., "Socially Responsible Plant Closings."
37. Leana and Ivancevich, "Involuntary Job Loss"; Leana and Feldman, "Individual Responses to Job Loss."
38. Kaufman, *Professionals in Search of Work*.
39. J. Blotzer and E. Bergholz, "Moving On When Hope Runs Out," *Pittsburgh Post Gazette*, 30 December 1985, pp. 39–40.
40. J. Kelley, "Jobless Workers Feel Lost in Space," *USA Today*, 2 October 1986, p. 1.
41. J.S. DeMott, "After the Mills Shut Down," *Time*, 15 August 1983, p. 46.
42. E. Bergholz, "Some Retrain for New Careers," *Pittsburgh Post Gazette*, 30 December 1985, p. 37.
43. J. Blotzer, "Jobless Adrift, Cling to Hope," *Pittsburgh Post Gazette*, 30 December 1985, pp. 33–36.
44. Leana and Feldman, "Individual Responses to Job Loss"; Leana and Feldman, "When Mergers Force Layoffs."
45. Langley, "Many Middle Managers Fight Back."
46. C.O. Longenecker, D.A. Gioia, and H.P. Sims, "Behind the Mask: The Politics of Employee Appraisal," *Academy of Management Executive* 1 (1987): 183–94.
47. Leana and Feldman, "Individual Responses to Job Loss"; and "When Mergers Force Layoffs."
48. D.M. Schweiger, J.M. Ivancevich, and F.R. Power, "Executive Actions for

Managing Human Resources Before and After Acquisition," *Academy of Management Executive* 1 (1987): 127–38.

49. R.I. Sutton, K.M. Eisenhardt, and J.V. Jucker, "Managing Organizational Decline: Lessons from Atari," *Organizational Dynamics* 14 (1986): 17–29.

50. Ibid.

51. G. Stricharchuk, "Fired Employees Turn the Reason for Dismissal into a Legal Weapon," *Wall Street Journal*, 2 October 1986, p. 33.

52. J.B. Copeland, "The Revenge of the Fired," *Newsweek*, 16 February 1987, pp. 46–47.

53. Langley, "Many Middle Managers Fight Back."

54. W.C. Putnam, "Undertaker Helps Businesses Close Down," *Gainesville Sun*, 27 April 1987, p. 8C.

55. J. Brockner, S. Grover, T. Reed, R. DeWitt, and M. O'Malley, "Survivors' Reactions to Layoffs: We Get By with a Little Help from Our Friends," *Administrative Science Quarterly* 32 (1987): 526–41; L. Greenhalgh and Z. Rosenblatt, "Job Insecurity: Toward Conceptual Clarity," *Academy of Management Review* 9 (1984): 438–48.

56. Naj, "GM Now Is Plagued."

57. L. Reibstein, "Survivors of Layoffs Receive Help to Lift Morale and Reinstill Trust," *Wall Street Journal*, 5 December 1985, p. 33.

58. Ibid.

59. S.G. Harris and R.I. Sutton, "Functions of Parting Ceremonies in Dying Organizations," *Academy of Management Journal* 29 (1986): 5–30.

60. Reibstein, "Survivors of Layoffs."

61. P.O. Flaim and E. Sehgal, "Displaced Workers of 1979–1983: How Well Have They Fared?" *Monthly Labor Review* 108 (1985): 3–16; D.O. Love and W.D. Torrence, "The Value of Advance Notice of Worker Displacement," *Southern Economic Journal*, 56 (1989): 626–43.

62. L. Greenhalgh, A.T. Lawrence, and R.I. Sutton, "Determinants of Work Force Reduction Strategies in Declining Organizations," *Academy of Management Review* 13 (1988): 241–54; L. Greenhalgh, R.B. McKersie, and R.W. Gilkey, "Rebalancing the Work Force at IBM: A Case Study of Redeployment and Revitalization," *Organizational Dynamics* 14, (1986): 30–47; L.T. Perry, "Least-Cost Alternatives to Layoffs in Declining Industries," *Organizational Dynamics* 14 (1986): 48–61; A.T. Lawrence, "Union Responses to Plant Closure," in P.D. Staudohar and H.E. Brown, eds., *Deindustrialization and Plant Closure*, 201–15 (Lexington, Mass.: Lexington Books, 1987); and *Plant Closing and Technological Change Provisions in California Collective Bargaining Agreements*. (Sacramento: Division of Labor Statistics and Research, California Department of Industrial Relations, 1985).

63. Greenhalgh, McKersie, and Gilkey, "Rebalancing the Work Force."

64. Greehalgh, Lawrence, and Sutton, "Determinants."

65. S. Feinstein, "Short-Time Pay Fails to Catch On as a Way to Hold Down Layoffs," *Wall Street Journal*, 3 February 1987, p. 35.

66. Ibid.

67. Ibid.
68. Perry, "Least-Cost Alternatives."
69. Lawrence, *Plant Closing*; and "Union Responses."
70. R.B. McKersie and W.S. McKersie, *Plant Closings: What Can Be Learned from Best Practice?* (Washington, D.C.: U.S. Department of Labor, 1982).
71. Lawrence, "Union Responses."
72. A.B. Carroll, "When Business Closes Down: Social Responsibilities and Management Action," *California Management Review* 26 (1985): 125–39.
73. Ibid.
74. Ibid.
75. S.P. Sethi, "Dimensions of Corporate Social Performance: An Analytical Framework," *California Management Review*, 17 (1975): 55–64; R.H. Miles, *Managing the Corporate Social Environment* (Englewood Cliffs, N.J.: Prentice-Hall, 1987).

Union and Community Responses
to Job Loss

While the company interventions described in Chapter 5 have attenuated some of the ill effects of corporate downsizing and plant closings, when compared to the problems created by large scale unemployment, these efforts are generally inadequate in both size and scope. To more thoroughly address the problems, many unions and community groups have become directly involved in efforts to retain or create jobs and industries or help dislocated workers to adjust to their new circumstances.

The erosion of U.S. manufacturing in traditional industries has been accompanied by a decline in union membership. The first half of this chapter examines how unions increasingly have become involved in trying to find solutions to the problems of plant closings and dislocated workers. Unions have utilized a variety of strategies based upon and guided by diverse philosophies and perspectives on the role of organized labor in decisions and practices traditionally reserved for management. In this chapter we focus on two unions in particular—both headquartered in Pittsburgh—which offer contrasting approaches to dealing with these problems. These are the United Steelworkers of America (USW) and the United Electrical, Radio and Machine Workers (UE).

Essentially, the USW has adopted programs to retain or create jobs through working with management and assisting businesses to stay open through labor cost reductions, employee buyouts, and joint lobbying for trade restrictions. The UE, conversely, has adopted a stance antagonistic to management and has concentrated its efforts on creating public pressure campaigns and exit barriers to induce corporations to stay in businesses or industries they might otherwise abandon or, at a minimum, provide assistance to dislocated workers beyond that required by the labor contract. The markedly different approaches these two unions take to the same set of problems provide a context in which to discuss the role of organized labor in declining industries.

The second part of this chapter discusses community responses to plant closings and job eliminations. Many of the communities in which large-scale production facilities were located have been devastated economically by shuttered mills and long unemployment lines. With the departure of corporate taxpayers, municipal revenues have been depleted. At the same time, the swelling ranks of the unemployed have placed increased demands on public services, severely straining the weakened resources of their communities. Several federal initiatives and a variety of state programs have been established or proposed in an attempt to assist the unemployed and to attract jobs and industry to the areas and to retain what jobs and industry might have remained. In addition to these larger initiatives, local communities that have been most directly affected by a plant closing or other large-scale job loss have also gotten into the act of business attraction and retention. As with the union programs, some of these community initiatives have been characterized by cooperation with the corporations involved, while others have been confrontational. Examples of each of these perspectives will be discussed along with their implications for larger-scale public policy. Again, because the layoffs were more widespread in the Pittsburgh area than at the Space Coast, and because of the stronger community cohesiveness and tradition of union activism, we found more examples of community initiatives in our Pittsburgh studies.

Union Initiatives

The past decade has been a particularly difficult one for the American labor movement. Many unions, particularly those concentrated in the manufacturing sector, have suffered substantial declines in membership. The 1980s were also characterized by a federal government administration distinctly unsympathetic to the goals of organized labor. Moreover, public opinion had grown markedly less favorable toward unions. Heckscher, for example, cites public opinion surveys conducted in the 1980s that indicated that less than 10 percent of the American public had "a great deal of confidence" in organized labor and its leaders; less than 17 percent felt that the country would be better off with more labor influence.[1]

Many writers have documented the decline in American manufacturing, the traditional base of organized labor. Terms ranging from "postindustrialism" to "deindustrialization" to a "second industrial divide" have been popularized to describe the erosion of U.S. manufacturing and the corresponding industrial union base.[2] This decline has been attributed to a variety of causes ranging from bad management to union representation, with the primary culprit being international competition in traditional U.S. markets. Whatever the cause, however, the effect has been a decline in traditional manufacturing jobs, an erosion of real average wages, an increasing disparity between the economic "haves" and "have nots"; in short, the creation of what Harrison and Bluestone have termed, a "great U-turn in the American standard of living."[3] Accompanying this has been a decline in both union membership and acceptance of the traditional goals of organized labor.

The United Steelworkers of America

The United Steelworkers of America (USW) has seen a dramatic decrease in its traditional membership base over the past ten years. In 1979, there were close to 1,200,000 active members; by 1987 that number had been reduced by almost half to a little over 600,000. Much of this decline was in the steel industry. In 1976, the USW represented over 337,000 workers in the steel industry alone; by 1988 that figure had been reduced to just over a third of its former level, or 129,000 workers. Moreover, although much of the U.S. steel industry was again profitable in the latter part of the 1980s, employment in steel was still down dramatically; USW membership stabilized at approximately 170,000 members in 1990.[4]

This rapid erosion of the membership base has affected the union financially as well as politically. In 1990, the General Fund—which supports the ongoing activities of the union—had a balance of a little over $26 million, or nearly 40 percent less than the $43 million fund balance in 1979. The union has also lost some measure of its former power both in collective bargaining and in legislative lobbying.[5] These declines have been described in a recent USW policy report as a "crisis"—one that requires "broad-ranging changes rather than temporary, band-aid solutions."[6]

Some of these changes have been structural in the form of more decentralization of both decision-making authority and responsibility within the union. Others have more directly addressed plant closings and job loss and reflect a change of position in terms of the issues the union involves itself with. Traditionally, for example, the USW had deliberately avoided direct involvement in member pension plans. Recent bankruptcies by major steel producers such as LTV, however, have caused the USW to monitor more closely companies' administration of pension funds.

To promote the retention of jobs the USW has also made several changes in bargaining and has taken a much more active role in the management and, in some cases, ownership of production. They have also stepped up efforts to involve government in the management of the steel industry. Finally, recognizing that much of the decline in the industry is permanent, the USW has become involved in programs to assist displaced workers. Nearly all of these efforts are characterized by cooperation between the union and its traditional adversary, the owners and managers of the firms that employ its members.

BARGAINING STRATEGIES AND JOB RETENTION EFFORTS. Much of organized labor's ability to promote the financial interests of its members has traditionally depended on its ability to take wages out of competition; that is, to ensure that companies do not continually seek competitive advantage over other firms by reducing labor costs. Within large industrial unions like the USW, this has been accomplished primarily through "pattern bargaining"—establishing a consistent pattern of wages, benefits, and work rules across major firms within an industry. The success of this strategy depends not only on the union's ability to organize and represent a substantial number of workers within an industry, but also on a certain level of growth and profitability among major employers. After decades of predictable levels of prosperity within the steel industry, the 1980s made clear that this latter condition could no longer be assumed.

In an attempt to slow the precipitous decline in the domestic steel

industry through the late 1970s and early 1980s, the USW negotiated a new labor agreement with the major producers in 1983
that cut wages, vacation time, benefits, and cost-of-living allocations
for members. This was thought to be a stopgap measure that would
help the major producers lower labor costs and maintain employment levels. Labor costs were certainly reduced by these measures,
but plants continued to close and workers continued to lose jobs
through the next several years. In 1986, the companies abandoned
a long tradition of industry-wide bargaining and instead negotiated
separate contracts between the union and the six major producers
that required some further wage and benefit concessions and created
discrepancies in wages and benefits among workers in different
facilities. Both of these major departures from traditional union
practices, concession bargaining and the break with industry-wide
contracts, represented attempts to assist struggling steel producers
in order to preserve jobs.[7]

EMPLOYEE OWNERSHIP. USW efforts to keep the steel industry afloat
have not stopped with bargaining. Perhaps the issue that best reflects
the USW's changing position on the traditional roles of management
and labor is that of employee ownership. Traditionally, the USW,
like most unions, rejected the concept of employee ownership of
business. The interests of workers were considered to be inherently
in conflict with those of owners and managers. Growing employer
interest in Employee Stock Ownership Plans (ESOPs) during the
1970s was thought to be largely a matter of corporate opportunism
designed to avail themselves of tax breaks, or an attempt to displace
more costly pension plans.

With the decline in U.S. manufacturing and the corresponding
erosion of union membership in the early 1980s, however, the USW
has become more receptive to ESOPs and has, in fact, been the
catalyst in the formation of many of them. As early as 1982, the
USW initiated a policy of exchanging company stock for wage
concessions at smaller firms. In 1985, the USW negotiated its first
ESOP with a major producer—Bethlehem Steel—in exchange for
wage concessions. Since that time, the USW has been an active
participant in arranging a number of ESOPs; Pittsburgh Forging
Co., Northwestern Steel and Wire Co., McLouth Steel Co., Chester
Roofing Products, Republic Storage, Republic Container, Copper

Range Co., Oremet, and Bliss-Salem are all USW plants that are at least partially, and in some cases wholly, owned by workers.

The union has also been active in providing technical assistance and in arranging financing for employee buyouts. In exchange, it has instituted policies for structuring ESOPs in USW plants. It requires that participating employees be immediately vested in stock owned through the ESOP, that employees have full voting rights for their shares, and that the ESOP not be used to replace a fully funded pension plan. In addition, the ESOPs are typically structured so that participating employees are not required to pay cash for the stock they receive. The establishment of formal cooperative arrangements between workers and managers such as Labor-Management Participation Teams is also recommended and indeed has been described as "the most crucial element" in the success of ESOP-financed firms.[8]

TRADE RESTRICTIONS. Another way that the USW has worked cooperatively with domestic steel producers to maintain jobs is in legislative lobbying for the creation and maintenance of trade restrictions on the import of finished and semifinished steel. Clearly, the protection of U.S. markets from the dumping of foreign steel serves the interests of both the steel producers and the union. In 1984 the parties convinced the Reagan administration to enact "voluntary" quota provisions with major steel exporters to the United States. The goal of the Voluntary Restraint Agreements (VRA) program was to restrict imports to under 19 percent of the finished steel market; in 1988 imports had constituted approximately 21 percent of the domestic market, down from a high of over 26 percent in 1984. Combined with the weakened U.S. dollar, the VRAs were successful in curbing imports. They did not, however, cover all countries exporting to the United States and U.S. producers have complained that enforcement of the VRAs has often been weak.[9]

As the dollar weakened through the late-1980s and early 1990s, foreign imports became a less significant concern for U.S. producers. In the 1990s, in fact, the United States once again became a net exporter of structural steel. The Bush administration nonetheless chose to maintain the VRAs in their previous form and extend them for an additional thirty months past their September 1989 expiration date. Both the USW and major steel producers had hoped for a five-year (rather than thirty-month) extension and stronger enforcement measures. However, manufacturers who rely on steel products for raw materials complained that the restraints artificially inflate their production costs and, although they boost employment and profit margins in the steel industry, contribute to unemployment and lower profits in other industries. Apparently the Bush administration was attempting to accommodate both these positions with the thirty-month compromise.[10]

DISLOCATED WORKER PROGRAMS. Although the USW has been active in efforts to create and maintain jobs for members, it has also been realistic in its assessment that many of the laid-off steelworkers will never return to their former jobs. Consequently, it has been actively involved in the creation and maintenance of assistance programs to help dislocated workers find new employment and make the financial, social, and psychological adjustments required by unemployment. At the USW's impetus, the 1983 Steel Basic Labor Agreement represented the first industry-wide contract to address issues of retraining and reemployment assistance for dislocated workers. By 1990, over seventy worker assistance centers had been established jointly by the USW and major steel employers. These have been jointly funded by the union, the involved companies, and federal money from Title III of the Job Training Partnership Act (JTPA). By 1988 company and union financial contributions to these programs totaled $11 million with an additional $50 million in JTPA allocations. Moreover, the major steel employers were committed to provide $11 million in additional funding through 1991.

The primary vehicle for assisting terminated workers has been the dislocated worker centers set up in nearly all of the USW's twenty-three districts. Joint labor-management committees oversee the development of programs for the centers that include reemployment counseling, retraining, basic educational programs such as literacy, and some psychological counseling. Since their establishment, over 35,000 dislocated USW members have used the centers. According to USW publications, over 20,000—or two-thirds of those using the centers—have found new employment or have entered training programs that have led to reemployment. Only sporadic data have been reported, however, on wage retention levels in these new jobs.[11]

UNEMPLOYMENT COMPENSATION AND PENSION BENEFITS. Two other USW programs for dislocated workers warrant attention. Both concern financial benefits rather than retraining or job placement activities. Each has had a profound effect on employers in terms of their costs in closing a plant, and on employees in terms of the quality of their lives after their jobs are terminated.

Borrowing from the Japanese, in the late-1970s the USW began to discuss the concept of "lifetime job security" and how it might be introduced in the steel industry. Although jobs could not be guaranteed, some level of income could in the form of generous unemployment compensation. This was introduced in 1977 contract negotiations and eventually took the form of two programs: "Supplemental Unemployment Benefits" (SUB) and the "Rule of 65" pension plans.

Under the SUB plan, employees with at least twenty years service qualified for benefits for up to two years after their layoffs. Moreover, this money was "guaranteed" in that employers were required to cover SUB benefits even if their SUB fund was exhausted. After two years, an employee who was still laid off and could not be permanently employed at another facility could qualify for a full pension if his age and years of service totaled 65 ("Rule of 65"). In addition, employees who were unable to find new employment were also entitled to a $400 per month supplemental benefit until they became eligible for social security benefits at age sixty-two. Any employee who qualified for a pension was guaranteed health insurance benefits as well.

The Rule of 65 program made it possible for people who were still in their early forties to collect full pension benefits. While relatively few workers received benefits from the plan in the late 1970s when it was first introduced, within five years thousands of dislocated steelworkers availed themselves of the plan. Hoerr cites studies that estimate that in 1985 alone, one company—U.S. Steel—paid out nearly $165 million to early pensioners. Tens of thousands of dislocated workers received benefits under this program in 1990.[12]

These benefit programs represent one of the most significant ways in which the USW has addressed the issue of job loss for its members. The programs are significant not only for the benefits they provide to dislocated workers, but, equally important, for the deterrent effect they may have on companies which are considering closing a facility. Because of their substantial costs, the pension and health benefit obligations may act to block a corporation's exit from a community or industry.

United Electrical, Radio, and Machine Workers

If the USW's efforts to address plant closings and job loss can be characterized as largely cooperative, the efforts of the United Electrical, Radio, and Machine Workers (UE) must be seen as distinctly confrontational. The UE has focused its efforts on erecting penalties or exit barriers on plant closings in the form of public campaigns, government intervention, and escalating severance payments and other closing costs. The UE is fundamentally opposed to employee ownership and generally will not engage in concession bargaining to bolster a firm's profitability. The first is seen as an inevitable failure and the second as means of financing a company's inevitable exit. The union considers neither course to be in the best interests of the union as an institution or of its individual members.[13]

Like the USW, the UE has seen a sharp decline in its membership over the past ten years. Dozens of UE plants have been closed, and membership has dropped from a high of about 160,000 in the mid-1970s to a reported 80,000 members in 1990. Much of this loss is due to the export of industry abroad by major employers such as the General Electric Corporation, or the abandonment of basic manufacturing by domestic producers in the face of stiff international competition.

As a smaller union, the UE does not have the resources of the USW to pursue similar strategies for job retention—even if it did consider those strategies desirable. More to the point, however, the UE does not agree with the strategies and overall philosophy of cooperation between labor and management in solving problems they view as largely of management's creation. The UE has, however, engaged in other types of activities both to retain jobs and to assist dislocated workers.

JOB RETENTION EFFORTS. The UE's overall strategy for job retention is to move as quickly as possible to avert closings or to place as large a penalty as possible on exiting firms. Unlike the USW, of this activity occurs at the local level with relatively little intervention by the national union. Consequently, there has been a great deal of variety in how the campaigns have been conducted. Most, however, are characterized by some combination of four tactics: membership mobilization, coalition building with other stakeholders such as community groups and churches, early campaigns to publicize management intentions and practices, and the enlistment of government assistance.

To date the model UE campaign for job retention has been the UE's experience at the Morse Cutting Tool plant in New Bedford, Massachusetts. Although the plant was shut down in 1990, it is nonetheless often cited as the most successful example of the UE's approach to building labor and community coalitions.[14] The campaign is instructive in understanding the responses of both the union representing the affected employees and the community in which the plant is located.

Morse Cutting Tool had been in operation for 125 years manufacturing drill bits and cutting tools. Workers had been unionized at Morse for nearly fifty years and were represented by Local 277 of the UE. Gulf + Western bought the plant in 1968 but by 1981 were laying off employees, moving large pieces of machinery to other plants, and demanding wage and benefit concessions. Local 277 countered these actions with an analysis that showed G + W's systematic undercapitalization of the plant and by simultaneously mobilizing a community campaign to publicize G + W's apparent strategy to "milk" the facility. The UE would not give in to concessionary demands, and when the labor contract expired in May 1982, members voted to strike.

The strike lasted three months and, consistent with UE's policies, was resolved without significant wage or benefit concessions. By 1983, however, G + W announced plans to sell off the facility. All offers by city and state officials to help locate a suitable buyer were rejected by G + W. When no buyer was found by 1984, G + W threatened to liquidate the facility. In response, the UE organized a "Citizens Committee to Support the Morse Workers" and galvanized the city of New Bedford to threaten to exercise its power of eminent domain to seize the plant and equipment from G + W in the public interest. In August 1984 the plant was sold to James Lambert, who pledged not to cut wages or benefits but to instead invest in the facility to make it competitive within the industry.[15]

Within a year Lambert faced cash flow problems. Despite philosophical opposition to concessions, Local 277 agreed to forego vacations and wage increases, and was instrumental in getting a $1.5 million loan for the company through the state-funded Massachusetts Industrial Services Program, the largest such loan ever granted by the agency. Despite these measures, Lambert declared bankruptcy early in 1987, and the plant was closed in May. With the local union's assistance and appeals to the bankruptcy court, a new buyer was found for the facility. Through these efforts, the plant maintained operations for several more years and three hundred jobs were temporarily saved. The new owners were unable to sustain the facility, however, and by 1990 the plant was again closed.

Despite the ultimate failure to save the facility, the Morse experience remains a model for the UE on how to organize community and political support to retain industry without resorting to large-scale wage and benefit concessions. Other UE locals have mounted similar public pressure campaigns. In a campaign to save 850 jobs in a housewares plant bought by Black & Decker from GE in Allentown, Pennsylvania, UE Local 128 organized a picket of Black & Decker's advertising agency in charge of promoting the company's new line of houseware products. This same local brought busloads of workers to the Black & Decker stockholders' meeting and picketed Black & Decker products at national housewares shows. In response to the announced closing of a Westinghouse plant in Chicago, the UE local there challenged the cable licenses of Group W, a Westinghouse subsidiary.[16]

A somewhat different strategy was used by UE Local 1202 when General Electric notified 450 workers that it would be closing its Charleston, South Carolina, steam turbine plant. There the local compiled a list of eleven alternative products that could be produced in the facility—such as pollution control equipment—and included a detailed strategic marketing plan to show the viability of each.[17] Although the plant was subsequently closed, these alternative-use tactics represented a new response to plant closings for the UE. At the same time, however, they further illustrate the differences between the UE and USW strategies. At first glance, it would seem that in conducting feasibility studies and developing marketing plans, the UE is entering the traditional domain of management, much as the USW has done. These tactics, however, are more accurately viewed as the UE doing management's work *for* them rather than working *with* them, an important distinction to the UE.

DISLOCATED WORKER PROGRAMS. When it becomes clear that a plant cannot be saved, the UE concentrates on assisting dislocated workers to secure increased severance payments. These are often larger than what is specified in the labor contract and can be linked to the UE public campaigns described above. In the Black & Decker case, for example, the company offered workers an average of $19,000 each in severance pay along with close to $2,000 in retraining benefits. In Chicago, Westinghouse offered terminated employees an additional $1,200 each in retraining money and made construction jobs available to them on the Group W studio. When it was announced that the 102-year-old Stone Safety plant in Wallingford, Connecticut, would be moving to the South, the UE mounted a strong public campaign to retain the facility. It became increasingly clear that the company would not reverse its decision to relocate; the UE then pushed for a generous severance package, including an average of over $7,000 per worker in cash payments, full vesting in the pension plan, and $1,000 in retraining money.

USW vs. UE Strategies

The USW and the UE provide two very different models of union response—cooperation vs. confrontation—in dealing with plant closings and unemployment. Clearly, the USW strategy is the more common one and is employed in various forms by other large unions, including the Communication Workers (CWA) and the United Automobile Workers (UAW).

Both the cooperative and the confrontational approaches have their problems. On the one hand, by refusing to accept concession agreements or enter into ESOP or other corporate arrangements, the UE is maintaining the traditional—and, they would argue, most essential—role of labor: It has refused to support programs that place labor in competition and does not view its role as that of helping companies to be efficient at the expense of its members' wages and working conditions. On the other hand, the union has lost numerous plants, and there is little likelihood that these facilities or industries will be revived. Consequently, the UE must concentrate its energies on organizing, primarily in new industries, and accept the decline in its traditional membership base.

The USW has taken the cooperative path in an attempt to shore up the domestic steel industry. To date this seems to have been the more successful strategy—although many would argue that without factors such as the weakened dollar or programs such as the VRAs, the domestic steel industry would continue its decline, regardless of the USW's posture. Even legislative initiatives such as the VRAs, however, reflect a willingness on the part of the USW to work cooperatively with employers in pursuit of common goals.

Others have voiced concern about the USW's embrace of labor-management participation programs and ESOPs, noting that these strategies put the union in the business of assisting the domestic steel industry to stay in business. While this has the obvious benefit of preserving jobs, it is accompanied by the less obvious threat of promoting labor efficiency at the expense of labor's traditional agenda. Efficiency and maximized profitability are the traditional goals of management; these are balanced by the goals of organized labor—reasonable wages, good benefits, specified work rules— through the collective bargaining process. Whether labor works with management (as in cooperation programs) or *becomes* management (as in ESOP arrangements), the ability of the union to promote its own goals, while at the same time promoting those of management, is a very difficult balancing act indeed.

Recent negotiations in the steel industry, however, suggest that, despite the "new industrial relations,"[18] the USW has come nowhere close to abandoning its traditional role. In 1989, Bethlehem Steel signed an agreement with the USW that stipulated an immediate 8 percent increase to restore wages conceded in the 1983 and 1986 contracts, as well as substantial hikes in the subsequent two years for a total estimated increase of $4.15 an hour. Also included were a $1,000 per worker "signing bonus," profit-sharing arrangements, and "inflation recognition payments"—a return to cost-of-living adjustments. The 1991 contract with USX similarly restored past wage concessions along with provisions for cost-of-living bonuses, profit sharing, graduated wage increases, and signing bonuses. As summarized by USW president, Lynn Williams, the Bethlehem contract, like the one with USX, "is an agreement that puts the past behind us."[19]

These recent agreements signal a return to traditional "bread and butter" issues. In the process, however, the lessons of the 1980s have not been lost. In recent contract negotiations the USW continued to stress job security issues as well as compensation concerns. Most recently, job security provisions have taken the form of innovative restrictions on corporate activities and management prerogatives. For example, some recent contracts have restricted dividend disbursements if capital investment is below agreed-upon levels. Another recent contract guarantees employees the right of first refusal on the sale of a plant, and the union veto rights over proposed new owners. In the 1991 USX contract, job—or at least benefits—security issues were addressed through successorship protections in the event that the U.S. Steel division is divested by the parent company. The contract also called for a joint study on the feasibility of reopening the USX South Works in Chicago.

As these programs, contracts, and provisions illustrate, over the past decade the USW has demonstrated its willingness to work cooperatively with management during industry downturns. Equally clear, however, is that a concessionary posture does not extend to the industry's more prosperous times. A lasting effect of the hard times of the 1980s may be a stronger recognition of the mutual concerns of management and labor within the steel industry. How this will develop through the 1990s will partially determine the answer to questions asked earlier concerning the long-term implications of the cooperative path.[20]

Other Union Activity

The USW and the UE are not, of course, the only unions faced with the problems of plant closings and an eroded membership base. The percentage of American workers represented by unions has been declining for quite some time, and unions now claim less than 17 percent of the U.S. work force. The UAW has faced problems at least as severe as those of the USW and has followed similar programs in an attempt to resurrect the U.S. auto industry. Major concessions were granted on wages, benefits, and work rules, labor-management cooperation efforts are prevalent, and lobbying jointly with the major automakers for trade restrictions has occupied much of the UAW's efforts in the political arena. Wage and benefit concessions have also been made by other large unions such as the United Food and Commercial Workers, the United Rubber Workers, and the United Mine Workers, to name a few.

In addition to these concessionary gestures, unions have also worked to enhance assistance programs and severance packages for their laid-off members. In this regard, the UAW has performed remarkably well. As a result of the 1990 labor contract, over 100,000 UAW members employed by the "Big Three" producers (GM, Ford, and Chrysler) are covered by a severance package that guarantees dislocated workers up to 85 percent of take-home pay for up to three years after their terminations. This is the most generous package ever negotiated by an American union. As noted in the *Wall Street Journal*, these benefits have the effect of essentially making labor a fixed cost since employers will be paying employees regardless of whether they are working.[21]

Cooperation between labor and management to streamline production and reduce labor costs has also been adopted by many unions that have traditionally viewed these types of programs as antithetical to the role of labor. The UAW's "Jointness" programs at plants such as NUMMI in California have received substantial attention—both positive and negative.[22] Other labor leaders such as Morton Bahr, president of the Communication Workers of America, have enthusiastically endorsed cooperation programs and have embraced such efforts as a means of restoring U.S. industry. As he stated in a recent address, "Employee participation works! There's no question about it."[23]

The question that is asked by those—such as the UE—who mistrust such a partnership concerns the eventual outcome of such programs. The history of employee involvement in the United States is not long enough to resolve labor's doubts. What is clear, however, is that unions and management may have substantially different ideas about the purposes of such programs and the means for implementing them.

In endorsing labor-management cooperation, Lynn Williams, president of the USW, has often described corporate decision making as too important to be left in the hands of management; moreover, like many industrial unions, the USW views worker involvement in corporate decisions as not only desirable, but a "matter of right" and a necessary step toward industrial democracy.[24] Management practitioners and consultants, on the other hand, are more likely to favor employee participation in decision making that is limited to shop-floor issues for the purpose of productivity or product improvements, rather than as encompassing questions of corporate strategy for the purpose of enhancing workers' rights.[25] It is not clear that these two positions are mutually exclusive. At the same time, it is also not clear that they are entirely compatible. Our understanding of these and other issues regarding the role of organized labor in industrial restructuring will no doubt grow during the 1990s as major unions continue down their chosen, largely cooperative, paths.

Community Initiatives

The experiences of, and responses to, plant shutdowns and unemployment by communities have been even more diverse than those of unions. When plants are closed, it not only affects employees, their families, and their unions, but also the communities in which the plants were located. Citizen groups and local governments become involved in trying to remedy and prevent the inevitable social problems that accompany large-scale dislocation. Over the past ten years there have also been numerous instances of communities challenging corporations in their right to exit.

Although many plant closings and large-scale job losses have occurred in urban areas, the stories from smaller communities are perhaps more poignant. Unlike larger urban areas, these communities have often come to rely on a single corporation to provide much of their economic vitality and thus have no portfolio of alternate employers to offset the loss of a major plant or corporation. The small communities outside Pittsburgh, in the Monongahela Valley, were highly dependent on "Big Steel," and were hurt badly when the steel industry began its drastic decline.

Portz Typology of Community Responses

In his book on local government initiatives on plant closings, John Portz describes a typology of community responses based on who decides to shut down a plant and who must provide the resources needed to deal with the problems accompanying the shutdown.[25] He identifies three prototypes of community responses.

The first, the "bystander" response, is characterized by passivity on the part of local government and community leaders. As noted by Portz, "[i]n cases where the [plant] closing is subject to debate, local officials may be present at community or labor-management meetings, but they do not take part in negotiations and discussions. If a plant closes, local policymakers play little role in the transition" (p. 6). In short, the local government observes, rather than participates in, decision making concerning nearly all aspects of the plant closing. The general effect of this bystander posture is that the costs and benefits of the plant closing are dictated largely by private market forces and, in the absence of a labor union, the principal player will be the company pulling out of the area.

Portz's second approach, the "offset" response, is characterized by local government not attempting to take a primary decision-making role; this is still largely reserved for the corporation. It does, however, attempt to influence both the process and the types of decisions made. Thus, local government pursuing an offset response would join in the discussion of whether and/or how the plant should close, and how resources should be allocated to ease the transition for those affected. Local government purchases its place at the discussion table by offering financial inducements ranging from tax abatements to keep a company from relocating to financing worker retraining or other assistance programs.

The third response, the "player role," is described by Portz as follows:

> There are times when officials cross the line and use policy tools and resources to reshape and redirect the adjustment process, when they assume a player role by asserting public voice in the decision-making process. Policymakers assume an active part not only in defining the problem but, most important, in implementing a solution. In essence the government policy is meant to do more than just create an equal playing field; government officials are to be players on the field. (p.10)

Examples of player responses range from local legislation that restricts corporate decision making on plant closings, to the active participation of local officials in areas such as identifying a new buyer for a plant, a new president for a business, or a new product line to replace an obsolete one. The player approach differs from the bystander and offset responses in that local government is involved in all aspects of decision making and takes an active, rather than reactive, stance.

Like the labor unions just described, the orientation of the local government can be cooperative in its dealings with the exiting corporation (Portz calls this a "corporate" player role), or it can form its alliances with labor and community groups rather than the exiting business (a "populist" player in Portz's terminology). Regardless of the posture chosen, the important difference between the player role and the others is that players are—or at least attempt to be—full participants in economic decision making.

Community Responses from the Mon Valley

During the 1980s, the Monongahela Valley outside of Pittsburgh offered examples of each type of community response. Before describing some of these approaches, it is useful to first review the historical structure for collaborations between the Pittsburgh region's public and private sectors in dealing with issues of economic or social change. Using Portz's classification, city and county government had traditionally played a comfortable "corporate player role" over the course of several decades preceding the 1980s, cooperating if not collaborating with the region's private sector.

THE ALLEGHENY CONFERENCE. For close to forty years in Pittsburgh, economic development planning and decision making outside of the public sector was largely carried out by the Allegheny Conference on Community Development, a civic organization supported and controlled by powerful corporate executives in the region. As described by Ahlbrandt,[27] the Allegheny Conference was founded in the 1940s by industrialist Richard King Mellon with the full cooperation of the city's mayor and other elected officials in the county and state. Over many years the Conference worked with public officials and agencies on projects ranging from air and water pollution clean-ups, to flood control, to highway and other infrastructure constructions and improvements.

For several decades this arrangement worked to the mutual advantage of the public and private sectors. State and local government received support and assistance from powerful business interests. In exchange, powerful business interests were able to affect the communities in ways that served the interests of corporations, while at the same time serving as citizens who worked for the public good. The assumption implicit in this arrangement, of course, is that the public and private interests were largely mutual and that development efforts would benefit both groups. Moreover, because the Conference was a collection of executives representing many different corporations, the projects undertaken by the Conference were also ones that could serve the interest of a diverse business community.

As Ahlbrandt describes, because the otherwise-diverse parties' interests were largely in alignment, decision making by the Conference was consensual. The problems brought on by the large-scale deindustrialization in the region in the 1980s, however, challenged and eventually rendered ineffectual the consensus model, and, to a large extent, the Conference itself, as the major player in the region's economic development. As Ahlbrandt notes:

> In the early 1980s, foreign competition and two back-to-back recessions forced the region's manufacturers to significantly restructure their operations. This created a new set of problems to which the region's consensual decision-making structure of top corporate and political leaders was not capable of responding. The business community had little experience in dealing with the social and economic problems that arose in the mill towns; and while some companies were directly responsible for the loss of jobs there, others never had any direct involvement in these communities. As a result, top corporate leadership, through the Conference, could not agree on appropriate courses of action. (p. 33)

Thus, consensus within the Conference broke down. More important to our discussion, however, is the fact that corporate and community interests also moved further apart, leaving city and county officials with little direction on how to deal with the growing economic and social problems in the region. Eventually, a new model of sorts was developed; this has largely taken the form of a patchwork quilt of various partnerships between business, government, and private foundations. In the mill towns outside Pittsburgh, however, the old model of cooperation and reliance on corporate initiative and action died harder and, with far less in the way of resources, local government often waited passively for news of the next shutdown and signals of its effects.

BYSTANDERS AND OFFSETTERS. While officials in the city of Pittsburgh and Allegheny County struggled to develop new private-public alliances, elected officials in the majority of the Mon Valley mill towns affected by plant closings during the 1980s assumed "bystander" and "offset" postures. Some elected officials were extremely passive. They seemed to be doing little more than closing their eyes and waiting for the dust to settle after each plant closing. Although each shutdown was viewed as extremely serious and greeted with genuine expressions of deep concern for the future of the community, local officials did not get involved in the process largely because they saw the closings as events beyond the ability of public policy to influence.

Others did get involved in the process, joining in the discussion only to the extent of devising schemes for how the community could work with the company to assist in the adjustment of dislocated workers and a financially weakened local government. By avoiding discussions about whether—rather than how—the plant should close and thus presenting no real obstruction to the exiting corporation, some officials hoped that the corporation would be more generous in terms of the potential resources it left behind (e.g., land, plant, revenues) after severing its relationship with the municipality.

The mayor of one community, for example, did not attempt to interfere when the American Standard Company announced in 1986 that it would relocate its Westinghouse Air Brake plant to the South. The UE, which represented the employees of the plant, predictably waged an extensive public campaign against the company but without the cooperation of the mayor or local government. Similarly, public officials in Duquesne would not get involved in a highly charged labor-community challenge to USX's closing of a steel blast furnace located there.[28] These responses were typical of local government through most of the 1980s. The communities crumbled while city, county, and local government floundered without traditional corporate leadership.

THE NEW "PLAYERS." Despite the passivity of many local officials, the Mon Valley was not without a high level of activity and, in many instances, resistance to the plant closings in the region. One of the first organizations to challenge corporate decision making on plant closings in the region was the Tri-State Conference on Steel. The Tri-State Conference drew much of its early leadership from local union activists in the United Steelworkers union. Although initially focused on internal union governance issues, these activists quickly turned their attention to plant closings, beginning in 1979 with the shutdown of several steel facilities in Youngstown, Ohio. The movement quickly moved east as plant closings began to plague the Pittsburgh region in the early 1980s.

The Tri-State Conference describes itself as a labor-religious-community coalition made up of activists from all three domains. Although its current agenda encompasses a wide range of issues and projects under the general headings of economic justice and community control, its initial focus was on plant closings and, more specifically, on obstructing corporations from moving or closing steel facilities in the region.[29] During the 1980s, Tri-State's most highly publicized campaign involved the Dorothy Six blast furnace in U.S. Steel's Duquesne plant.

In October, 1984, U.S. Steel announced plans to demolish much of its steel-making facility located in Duquesne, a small mill town outside of Pittsburgh. The plant had stopped most of its operations and laid off the majority of the work force earlier in the year. The announcement of the Dorothy demolition, however, seemed to galvanize a community that had already witnessed and, for many of its citizens, directly experienced the shutdown of much of the steel-making capacity in the region. In mill towns like Duquesne, unemployment estimates ran as high as 25 percent; stopping U.S. Steel from demolishing the blast furnace became, for many, the point of resistance to the economic collapse of their hometowns.[30]

The campaign to save Dorothy was spearheaded by the Tri-State Conference. The campaign consisted not only of rallies and plant gate vigils, but also of feasibility studies and coalition formation with the United Steelworkers and city, county, and state government officials. By 1986, various feasibility studies supported by public and USW financing had eventually shown the blast furnace not worth salvaging.[31] The Dorothy campaign did, however, spur the creation of the Steel Valley Authority (SVA), a state-chartered industrial jobs authority vested with the state's power of eminent domain. Through the creation of the SVA, Tri-State hoped to establish a permanent state-sanctioned entity capable of legally stopping the closure of or removal of equipment from facilities such as Dorothy that might be abandoned in future corporate exits.[32]

The SVA's early activity concentrated on obstructing corporate exits. The previously mentioned American Standard plant located in Wilmerding was the focus of an extensive campaign that eventually ended in federal court. In the meantime, however, elected officials from municipal council members to U.S. senators joined this campaign to hinder corporate mobility. Later, the SVA oversaw the completion of numerous feasibility studies to examine the possibility of an ESOP-financed restart of a local steel facility abandoned by the LTV Corporation. Other recent projects have included the completion of a business plan for an employee-owned commercial bakery in place of a facility closed by the Continental Baking Company. The SVA has also implemented an "Early Warnings Network" set up to anticipate plant closings well before the sixty-day notification period required by the federal Worker Adjustment and Retraining Notification (WARN) Act.[33]

As these examples demonstrate, the Tri-State Conference and, in particular, the Steel Valley Authority, testify to the existence of a "populist player role" fostered by community activists and assumed by several government officials. These are not the only examples of player responses. Through the 1980s, other organizations also sprang up in the Mon Valley to address the problems of deindustrialization and economic restructuring. Some more closely resembled Portz's corporate player role such as the recently established Mon Valley Initiative, an organization supported by private foundations and set up to assist local Community Development Corporations (CDCs) initiate and fund small economic development projects.[34] Others were, like the Tri-State Conference, clearly "populist" in orientation such as the Mon Valley Unemployed Committee and the Rainbow Kitchen, organizations that not only provide direct assistance to the unemployed but also foster community and individual political empowerment.

Responses from Other Communities

The Mon Valley was not, of course, the only area of the country hit by plant closings and large-scale layoffs during the eighties. Nor was it the only area where citizens and their elected representatives took an active role in dealing with, questioning, and in some instances attempting to stop corporations from closing plants or eliminating jobs. Groups aimed at fostering a "populist player response" range from the New Jersey–based "Hometowns Against Shutdowns" organization and Connecticut's "Naugatuck Valley Project" in the Northeast, to California's "Oakland Plant Closing Project" in the West, to the "Tennessee Industrial Renewal Network" in the South. An example of a larger organization financed by both state and federal funding is the Machine Action Project (MAP) in Massachusetts. Organized in response to numerous layoffs and plant closings in the state's metalworking industry, MAP's projects concern technology transfer, retraining efforts, and job retention and creation.

All of the organizations cited attempt to foster Portz's player response and are "populist" in orientation. Many were formed in response to a particular plant closing or industry decline in a region and, like the Tri-State Conference and the Steel Valley Authority, have expanded to incorporate a broader set of issues and a more inclusive set of organizations and individuals. Most have also moved away from finger-pointing and primarily protest or confrontational tactics to stress instead cooperative relationships among community activists, union officials, clergy, politicians, and academics.

In 1988, a national umbrella organization, the Federation for Industrial Retention and Renewal (FIRR), was created to facilitate the transfer of expertise and ideas among the local plant closing groups and to work toward facilitating an industrial policy at the national level. In its literature, FIRR describes itself as:

> a national coalition of community and regionally based organizations which are working to preserve basic industry and protect the economic and social welfare of workers and communities. We support the concept that economic development should be guided by deliberate planning, not left solely to market forces, and that satisfaction of people's social needs—in addition to the economic demands of business—should be a primary goal. We also believe there should be

maximum feasible participation in economic policy development; that is, everyone who is affected by economic change should be directly represented in the decision making that shapes that change.[35]

In 1991, FIRR had several dozen member organizations. Through its statements, it is clear that FIRR hopes to foster at the national level what the previously-described community groups are attempting to accomplish at the local level.

Cooperation and Confrontation Revisited

If the Tri-State Conference began with rallies and protests against corporations, it has moved to planned feasibility studies and institutional networking as its primary responses to the economic problems in the region. In this regard, the group has certainly maintained its posture of active player; at the same time, however, it has shed its former confrontational tactics. Indeed, a recent Tri-State project involving the construction of a magnetic levitation train in the region is being spearheaded not by community activists but by the corporate executives once vilified by Tri-State.

Many other populist-oriented community groups have also approached, if not embraced, partnerships with their former adversaries, much as the USW and other industrial unions are experimenting with cooperative efforts with the major employers of their members. As with the unions, it is unclear where these cooperative ventures will lead or the extent to which they will be pursued as the 1990s bring new forms, affected occupational categories, and geographic areas of economic restructuring.

Notes

1. See C. Heckscher, *The New Industrial Relations* (New York: Basic Books, 1988).
2. See M.J. Piore and C.P. Sabel, *The Second Industrial Divide: Possibilities for Prosperity* (New York: Basic Books, 1984); B. Bluestone and B. Harrison, *The Deindustrialization of America* (New York: Basic Books, 1982); D. Bell, *The Coming of Post-Industrial Society* (New York: Basic Books, 1976).
3. A detailed discussion of both the causes and effects of the erosion of the U.S. standard of living is presented in B. Harrison and B. Bluestone, *The Great U-Turn: Corporate Restructuring and the Polarizing of America* (New York: Basic Books, 1988).

4. United Steelworkers of America (USWA), "Report of the Committee on Future Directions of the Union," August 1988; and "Serving Steelworkers in Times of Change," August 1990.
5. J. Hoerr's book, *And the Wolf Finally Came: The Decline of the American Steel Industry* (Pittsburgh: University of Pittsburgh Press, 1988), discusses in detail the changes in both the USWA and the industry. The 1990 figures are taken from USWA, "Officer's Report," August 1990.
6. USWA, "Report of the Committee," p. 6.
7. See Hoerr, *And the Wolf Finally Came.*
8. A special report in *Steelabor*, July 1988, pp. 7–13, entitled "Employee Stock Ownership Plans: USWA Workers Become Owners," describes current USWA ESOP programs.
9. Detailed in USWA, "Basic Steel Industry Conference, United Steelworkers of America, Policy Statement," December 1988.
10. See H. Stoffer, "Bush Plan Gives Steel Industry Half the Pie," *Pittsburgh Post-Gazette*, 26 July 1989, pp. 1, 18; and C. Farnsworth, "Steel Import Quota Extended While U.S. Seeks Subsidy Curbs," *New York Times*, 26 July 1989, pp. 1, 24.
11. USWA, "Responding to Steelworkers' Needs in a Changing Economic Environment: The International Headquarters Task Force for Dislocated Workers Program Development," August 1988; and "Serving Steelworkers." Also see "Job Assistance Enters New Fields," *Steelabor*, January 1988, p. 19.
12. See Hoerr, *And the Wolf Finally Came.*
13. This position is argued in M. Slott, "The Case against Worker Ownership," *Labor Research Review* (1988): 83–97. Also see United Electrical, Radio & Machine Workers of America (UE), "Policy Resolutions and Reports adopted by the 53rd UE Convention," August 1988, for UE policy statements.
14. Conversations with Rick Peduzzi, educational director, UE, January 1991.
15. See B. Doherty, "The Struggle to Save Morse Cutting Tool: A Successful Community Campaign," Arnold M. Dubin Labor Education Center, South eastern Massachusetts University; and P. Gilmore, "Union-Community Campaign Reopens Morse Tool," *UE News*, 20 July 1987, pp. 6–7.
16. Described in L. Bedsie, "Unions, Firms, Congress Struggle with Problem of Plant Closings," *Christian Science Monitor*, 2 April 1985; and W. Serrin, "Ruling Saves Jobs at New Bedford Tool Plant," *New York Times*, 14 July 1987.
17. Reported in "A Bold Tactic to Hold On to Jobs," *Business Week*, 29 October 1984, pp. 70–71.
18. See Heckscher, *The New Industrial Relations.*
19. The Bethlehem contract is described in C. Ansberry and P. Pae, "Bethlehem Steel Accord Signals Higher Costs," *Wall Street Journal*, 8 May 1989; J. Hicks, "Bethlehem Steel in Pact with Union," *New York Times*, 6 May 1989; T. Buell, "USW Presidents Approve Contract with Bethlehem," *Pittsburgh Press*, 6 May 1989; and J. McKay, "USW Approves Pact with Bethlehem Steel," *Pittsburgh Post-Gazette*, 6 May 1989. The USX contract is described in USWA

"Summary of Proposed Agreement between the United Steelworkers of America and USX Corporation," February 1991.

20. See Hoerr, *And the Wolf Finally Came.*
21. G. Patterson, "Blue-Collar Boon: Hourly Auto Workers Now on Layoff Have a Sturdy Safety Net," *Wall Street Journal*, 19 January 1991, pp. 1, A6.
22. See, for example, the views expressed in M. Parker and J. Slaughter, "Behind the Scenes at NUMMI Motors," *New York Times*, 4 December 1988, versus those in B. Lee, "Worker Harmony Makes NUMMI Work," *New York Times*, 25 December 1988.
23. From M. Bahr, "The Union Makes Us Strong; Participation Makes Us Stronger," *Workplace Democracy*, Fall 1988, pp. 12–15.
24. USWA, "Report of the Committee."
25. See C. Leana and G. Florkowski, "Employee Involvement Programs: Integrating Psychological Theory and Management Practice," in G. Ferris, ed., *Research in Personnel and Human Resources Management*, 10 (Greenwich, Conn.: JAI, 1992).
26. J. Portz, *The Politics of Plant Closings* (Lawrence: University of Kansas Press, 1990).
27. R. Ahlbrandt, "The Revival of Pittsburgh: A Partnership between Business and Government," *Long Range Planning* 23, no. 5 (1990): 31–40.
28. Interviews with Geraldine Homitz, mayor of Wilmerding, July 1986, and Mike Carbo, president, UE Local 610, June, July, 1986; Also see Portz's description of Duquesne's response in *Politics of Plant Closings*, chap. 5.
29. For a history of the Tri-State Conference, see C. McCollester and M. Stout, "Tri-State Conference on Steel: Ten Years of Labor-Community Alliances," in J. Brecker and T. Costello, eds., *Building Bridges: The Emerging Grassroots Coalition of Labor and Community*, 106–12 (New York: Monthly Review Press, 1990).
30. For descriptions of the Dorothy Six campaign, see W. Serrin, "Pittsburgh Area Rallies to Save Blast Furnace," *New York Times*, 30 January 1985; J. Hoerr and W. Symonds, "A Brash Bid to Keep Steel in the Mon Valley," *Business Week*, 11 February 1985; M. Hoyt, "Steelworkers Propose Viable Plan to Revive Dying Plant," *In These Times*, 20 February 1985; and P. Perl, "Dorothy Six Is Hope of Pennsylvania Steelworkers," *Washington Post*, 26 April 1985.
31. See D. Hopey, "USW Report Says Dorothy 6 Can't Earn Profit," *Pittsburgh Press*, 8 January 1985.
32. The Steel Valley Authority is described in various pamphlets and publications produced by the Tri-State Conference on Steel and the Steel Valley Authority. For positive editorials on the SVA from the local papers, see "A Good Neighbor Response," *Pittsburgh Post Gazette*, 3 June 1985; and "Steel Valley Glimmers," *Pittsburgh Press*, 25 November 1986.
33. From Steel Valley Authority Quarterly Reports, 1989, 1990, 1991.
34. See Ahlbrandt, "The Revival of Pittsburgh."
35. From pamphlets produced by the Federation for Industrial Retention and Renewal; also see *FIRR News* 1, no. 1 (1989).

7

Future Issues and Considerations

In studying the experiences of laid-off employees at the Pittsburgh steel mills and the Challenger disaster site, we learned a great deal about the meaning of job loss for individuals and how they respond to their unemployment. Many of our expectations were confirmed; some were disconfirmed; in other cases, the results were much more complex than we had originally anticipated. As with other major empirical research projects, we end this study with many new questions. In this final chapter, we suggest several ways to expand and extend our research.

We begin by discussing the theoretical issues about job loss that demand future study: the differences between large-scale and small-scale layoffs, the role of stress in job loss, employee attribution processes, the nature of employee coping, and the role of individual differences. We also discuss some of the differences between the experiences of laid-off workers and of those who have lost their jobs in other ways—firing and retirement, for instance. In addition, we suggest ways the findings from this study can be used to explore other related phenomena, such as the reactions of family, friends, and co-workers of the unemployed.

In the second portion of the chapter we examine ways in which the methodologies used to research job loss can be improved and expanded upon. Here we explore issues of research design, sampling, instrumentation, and data analysis. We also focus here on ways in which the psychologically-based research on job loss can be integrated with research from other relevant disciplines such as economics.

In the third, and final, section of the chapter we look at future issues and considerations in the management of job loss from an institutional perspective. From the perspective of corporations, we explore some of the implications of our findings for policies on advance notification, termination compensation, retraining and out-placement programs, and the implementation of layoffs. From a public policy perspective, we examine the implications of our findings for the termination-at-will doctrine, plant-closing legislation, and age and sex discrimination issues. We also explore here the policy issues that confront unions in terms of strategies for preventing layoffs, for stemming their adverse impact, and for cooperating with management. As we have come to discover, collaboration among major institutions in the face of layoffs is necessary for effectively handling this complex economic and behavioral problem.

Theoretical Issues

Long-Term vs. Short-Term Layoffs

As we noted in Chapter 1, the nature of layoffs in the United States changed around the middle of the 1980s. Before 1986, most of the layoffs involved thousands of employees at a time, and the further decline of generally unprofitable firms; after 1986, most of the layoffs were smaller, involving only hundreds of employees, and the downsizing, but not closing, of historically profitable firms.

After seeing the differences between the Pittsburgh and Florida samples, we speculate that the size and kind of layoff might be important factors in understanding reactions to job loss.

First, consider the case of widespread layoffs affecting large numbers of employees in an industry in sharp decline. Although this scenario is more frequently associated with blue-collar industries like steel, there have been similar occurrences in white-collar industries. For example, in the aftermath of the stock market crash of 1987, 45,000 stockbrokers lost their jobs, and many are just beginning to reenter the investment banking market.[1]

The reactions that workers experience after large-scale layoffs will likely be consistently negative. Because the whole industry is going downhill, workers will see their job loss as very severe, irreversible, and externally caused. Their emotional reactions are more likely to be deenergizing rather than stimulating, and they are likely to have more adverse physiological reactions as well.

Under these circumstances, we suspect that people will engage in very little problem-focused coping outside of some local job hunting, and will direct most of their energy into seeking social support. Consequently, most of those laid off will remain unemployed or underemployed and will experience high levels of distress.

Because the situation is so consistently bleak, personality differences will not play much of a role in how people cope with job loss; the powerful impact of the situation will probably overwhelm the modest influence of individual differences. In terms of demographic factors, we would predict that age and education will have the greatest impact on reemployment prospects. Older, less educated workers will have much more difficulty becoming reemployed; they will also be the most reluctant to pick up and move to get new jobs or to go back to school for training. Those who are younger and better educated will have somewhat more flexibility in what jobs they can perform and where they live.

In cases of large-scale layoffs, the companies themselves are often in financial distress and are dealing with hundreds or thousands of workers. Helpful though it might be, we doubt corporations will provide these laid-off workers with more training. The best realistic case we envision is corporations giving workers sufficient advance notice to allow them to start lining up new jobs as quickly as possible, and giving them sufficient financial assistance to help them through a period of unemployment or get retraining on their own.

For people involved in these large-scale layoffs, then, federal and state government play a vital role. These dislocated workers must rely on the government for aid to get retrained and for extended financial benefits. Because whole towns may be adversely affected by mass layoffs in their midst, federal and state support may also be needed to provide extra help for mortgage holders and for attracting new employers to affected municipalities.

Second, consider the case of smaller-scale layoffs occurring periodically in generally profitable industries or companies. The process here, we expect, will differ from our first scenairo in several ways.

The reactions to the layoff will be negative, but not so intensely as with large-scale reductions in force. The workers will view the layoff as somewhat less severe and somewhat more easily reversible. Although people may still be depressed and subdued, they should also be more optimistic about obtaining new employment and more energized to job hunt.

In terms of coping behavior, we would expect people in these circumstances to seek new jobs or explore relocation possibilities more frequently. These workers are less likely to see their previous occupations as dead ends and therefore will either try to find another job in the same location or the same job in a different location. Retraining would be a distant third choice.

In cases of widespread layoffs, it is clear that the layoffs are externally caused; however depressed these employees might feel, they do not feel personally to blame for losing their jobs. Laid-off employees can easily get together and commiserate without personal shame. Small-scale layoffs are somewhat more ambiguous. Certainly the layoffs are externally caused, but without a seniority system, it is often the marginal performers who are let go first.[2] Indeed, rather than seeking additional social support, these individuals (especially if they are professional workers) are liable to isolate themselves from friends and former work colleagues because of the negative stigma they attach to the job loss.[3] Thus, we would expect that in smaller-scale layoffs, employees will be less likely to seek extensive social support—and there would be fewer colleagues available to provide it.

Unlike the case of large-scale layoffs, in our second scenario we would expect personality factors to play a more important role in how employees cope. Two personality charactertistics, in particular, should help individuals weather their period of unemployment successfully. High self-esteem should help employees sustain their sense of self-worth and project a nondefensive sense of self-confidence in the job search process.[4] Hardiness should help employees bounce back from their initial disappointment and sustain a sense of equilibrium during the ups and downs of the job hunt.[5]

In the case of large-scale layoffs, we do not expect corporate interventions to significantly and directly help employees to get new jobs; the extent of the unemployment problem is usually too great for that. However, in the case of small-scale layoffs, we suspect corporate interventions (especially outplacement) could directly assist in getting a more manageable number of employees placed. Also, advance notice and severance pay would help laid-off employees get a head start on job hunting and give them some capital to relocate if necessary. Particularly with white-collar workers, there is a definite stigma to being unemployed when searching for a new job; advance notice might make it possible for them to line up new positions without that handicap.

At least in contrast to widespread layoffs, we would expect reemployment prospects in the case of smaller-scale layoffs to be more positive for two reasons. First, there are fewer people out searching for new jobs, and the number of positions has not yet declined dramatically; objectively, the labor market has not completely soured. Second, in the case of smaller-scale layoffs, individuals are more likely to engage in the problem-focused coping that directly facilitates reemployment.

The models we have presented in our two scenarios are certainly speculative, and much more research is needed to confirm or disconfirm our ideas. However, these models do suggest that the magnitude of the layoff is a major factor in understanding reactions to job loss, and that various individual coping strategies, corporate interventions, and government policies are differentially useful in facilitating reemployment.

Job Loss and Stress

Our research projects at the Pittsburgh steel mills and on the Space Coast suggest that concepts from the stress literature help explain employees' responses to job loss. The threat and uncertainty evoked by unemployment seem to drive many of the psychological and physiological reactions to job loss and to determine in some ways how employees choose to cope.

There remain at least three important theoretical questions concerning job loss and stress. The first concerns the differences between temporary job layoffs and permanent layoffs. Temporary layoffs create more uncertainty in employees' minds (for instance, about how long the layoff will last and about whether they should seek new employment) but are likely to be perceived as less threatening in the long run. On the other hand, permanent layoffs generate less uncertainty (at least in the sense that employees know there is no likelihood of reemployment at the same firm) but are seen as much more threatening. Our own best guess is that temporary layoffs, because they cause less financial distress, would be less stress inducing. However, looking more systematically at these differences may help us discover the relative importance of threat vis-à-vis uncertainty in employee reactions to job loss.

A second issue pertaining to stress and job loss concerns the frequency of layoffs. Viewed from one perspective, the first time an employee loses a job should be the most stressful; it would create the most uncertainty, and the employee would have no ready coping routines to deal with the crisis. Viewed from a different perspective, however, subsequent layoffs should be more stressful than the first; employees would typically have fewer financial reserves to absorb the job loss, and less psychological energy after multiple job searches. Given the despairing comments from workers who have suffered multiple layoffs, we are inclined toward the second position. Exploring this issue more closely, too, may help researchers get a better sense of the role of threat and uncertainty in motivating coping behavior.

A third important research question concerns the *patterns* of attributions and reactions that laid-off workers experience after job loss. In terms of cognitive appraisal, for instance, not all job losses will be seen as severe, irreversible, and externally caused. A person may be permanently laid off from a job, but may have found the job neither lucrative nor enjoyable. Conversely, an employee may be temporarily laid off from a job, but the stigma of the layoff, the loss of enjoyable work, and the loss of significant income may create a great deal of stress. We need to know much more about how these attributions work in combination with one another in motivating (or deenergizing) efforts to cope.

Along the same lines, much more research is needed on the relationships among cognitive appraisal, emotional arousal, and physiological reactions.[6] Indeed, some of the "mood swings" after a job loss noted in the research might be explained by the interactions of these factors. The initial shock of the job loss might evoke deenergizing emotions and, consequently, a particularly negative cognitive appraisal of the event. After the negative emotions have subsided somewhat, the individual may appraise the job loss as more controllable and reversible, and emotional reactions may become more positive or optimistic. A prolonged, unsuccessful job search, however, might trigger a mutually reinforcing downturn of both perceptions and emotions.[7]

Coping Behavior

As our studies suggest, the unemployed do engage in active coping behavior in order to deal with their joblessness; they are not merely passive observers of their fates. Our research opens several new directions of inquiry in this area.

One area of research that needs further study is the timing of coping efforts. With our research design, we were unable to determine how quickly (or slowly) employees started to cope with job loss. Previous research suggests that the timing of coping behavior is critical to its effectiveness.[8] If a person starts to try to exert control over the unemployment problem while he or she is still highly agitated, it is likely he or she will not only fail, but will also be discouraged from trying again. On the other hand, if employees wait too long to cope actively, the number of job options may be very small and their financial resources will have all but dried up. For practical purposes as well as theoretical ones, it is important to discover the most effective timing for coping behavior.

Another important research topic concerns motivating employees to engage in active coping even though coping itself is stressful. As we discussed earlier, the common assumption about coping behavior is that it reduces stress by eliminating the source of threat and uncertainty in the environment. However, our data suggest coping can actually increase psychological distress. We need much more research on how to motivate the unemployed to engage in active job search despite the unpleasantness of that activity.

A third research topic that needs further investigation is that of "palliative coping,"[9] those activities which deaden the negative reactions to job loss but do not change the situation itself. Psychologically, the unemployed can use defense mechanisms to repress their feelings about job loss or distort its reality. Physiologically, they can use alcohol or drugs to calm their nerves or deaden their responses to stress. Unfortunately, all too often people use palliativ coping to deal with job loss even though it does not help them en unemployment—and, moreover, often lessens their energy and de sire for job hunting. The conditions under which individuals tur to palliative coping, and the interventions that are most successfu in turning individuals away from it, need much more careful atter tion.

Individual Differences

In our research, we found that demographic factors (such as edu cation) can play an important role in whether laid-off workers secur new employment, and that personality factors generally played much less central role. At least three important issues in the arer of individual differences need further investigation.

First, our sample did not include sufficient numbers of raci. minorities to explore in depth how large a part race plays in re actions to job loss (or choice of coping strategies). Although previou research suggests that racial minorities have more difficulty obtair ing new jobs, more research on this issue in the context of layof is needed.[10] As lawsuits about discrimination in layoffs proliferat this area will have increased practical implications as well.

Second, more careful attention should be paid to the role c marital status as an individual difference. Most research has ex amined the impact of job loss on the marriage, rather than th impact of marital status on coping with job loss. Implicitly, marriag has been seen as a buffer to reactions to job loss; the married persc will have another wage earner to rely on and built-in social suppor However, as two-career couples become more and more commoi it is also possible that being married will make the job search proce: even more stressful and complicated. Geographical relocation fc one partner can mean displacement for the other; retraining for or partner can mean increased financial pressure on the other. Parti ularly as layoffs of more mobile white-collar professional and ma) agerial workers increase, this issue becomes increasingly importan

Third, the role of age in the unemployment picture needs to k reconceptualized. Much of the research on age has produced mode results; the bulk of the research suggests age is an impediment 1 reemployment, but empirical results are sometimes not as strong as one might expect from anecdotal accounts.

We have an alternative hypothesis that seems to explain our qualitative data. The employees caught in the middle—in terms of age and career stage—seem to have the most difficulties in adjusting to life without work. Younger employees are less likely to own homes or have spouses and children to support; they can more readily start over in a career or a new location. Workers over fifty-five are also adversely affected by job loss, of course, but they are also closer to retirement. The biggest expenses of mortgage payments and child support are behind them. With more severance pay and pension benefits than their middle-aged colleagues, they might be able to survive on part-time or lower-paying jobs until they are eligible for retirement.

In contrast, middle-aged, mid-career workers seem to have the worst of all worlds. They are often the most rooted in their communities and the most unwilling to leave. Even if they were willing to relocate, they would have the most difficulty in breaking even on heavily-mortgaged homes in a bad real estate market.[11] They are more intimidated about going back to school and with spouses and children to support are often less able to afford to do so. As we saw in many cases, workers with ten to nineteen years of service got significantly less severance pay and retirement benefits from their employers than did their more senior colleagues. However, unlike their older co-workers, they have too many years ahead to slide by on lower-paying or part-time jobs.

Thus, in future studies of job loss, the special problems of the middle-aged mid-career employee need much more detailed investigation. Statistical tests of linear relationships between age and reemployment problems may be overlooking an important curvilinear pattern.

Differences in Types of Job Loss

A critical direction for future research is understanding the differences in reactions among people who lose their jobs because of plant closings and downsizing, those who are fired, those who retire, and those who lose their jobs through mergers and acquisitions. Comparing or contrasting differences among these groups of workers might well provide a richer view of the ways individuals experience the loss of work.

For employees who are discharged for cause (poor performance), job loss should be the most stressful. The job loss has to be attributed at least partially internally; there is likely to be a loss of self-esteem as well. Not only will the employee lose income, but he or she is unlikely to get enthusiastic recommendations or leads for new jobs from the previous employer. Moreover, if the employee is the only person terminated from the organization, there are no opportunities for receiving social support from people in the same situation.[12]

For employees who retire, job loss can negatively affect their social support network, their sense of structure to the day, and their feelings of power and control.[13] On the other hand, retirement can mean an escape from a frustrating job, a chance to pursue hobbies, or an opportunity to take life a little more slowly. Many people retire, move away from their previous residences, and never look back with regret.[14] For retirees, the meaning of job loss will largely be determined by their perceptions of financial security, the availability of stimulating alternative activities, and their assessment of their physical health.[15] People who are financially secure, have activities they enjoy outside of work, and feel healthy view retirement as a pleasurable alternative. People who are nervous about money or fear inflation, genuinely like their job activities, and are anxious about their own health or that of their spouses see retirement much more negatively.

For those who lose their jobs through mergers and acquisitions, there may be little financial loss, since these tend to be white-collar employees who are more likely to be given generous severance packages. However, these employees are forced to rethink their career plans and are often forced to relocate to obtain new employment. Moreover, for many members of the "baby boom" generation, there are too many middle managers chasing a decreasing supply of middle-management jobs. There is increased pressure to sustain an upwardly-mobile career path with fewer and fewer opportunities.[16] By exploring the differences among these various groups of people who are not working, we should be able to get a better sense of what types of deprivations motivate different types of coping behavior and which aspects of the job loss experience create the most stress.

Job Loss as Financial Distress or Job Loss as Unemployment

It is certainly the case that most people do feel a sense of loss and distress after their layoffs, but we discovered there are some individuals who view their job loss as a new challenge or as an opportunity to make long-overdue changes in their careers. In reviewing our results, we believe one overlooked area of research on why this occurs is the variability in how central people view work in their lives.

Prototypical middle-class values suggest that work is central to most people's self-concept and loss of work represents, in some sense, a disintegration of self-concept. In studying layoffs, however, we noticed quite frequently that what most troubled the unemployed was not the loss of self-actualization, but the loss of income. Job loss was most distressing not because it deprived workers of valued activities, but because it created financial hardship.[17]

In future research on the psychology of job loss, increased attention should be paid to the financial conditions of the unemployed— their accumulated savings, the amount of severance pay and extended benefits they receive, and the percentage of household income the job loser contributed to the family's total income. To understand how the unemployed react to job loss, we also need to understand the ways it is distressing in *their* eyes. In some cases, corporate and governmental interventions miss the mark because they misread what job loss means to individuals. For instance, providing resume writing workshops to steelworkers rather than extending their benefits may be misguided. Many of these workers may be most concerned with having lost a pay check, not a vocation; they need more money and a new job (quickly), not an exercise in introspection.

Job Loss and the Family

Not since the Depression has the impact of job loss on the nuclear family been such a focus of concern. The popular press, in particular, has reported the high rates of divorce and child abuse that occur in families where the major wage earner has lost his or her job.

Our research suggests that layoffs stress marriages, but do not necessarily break them. In our studies, only 7 percent of the participants attributed their separations or divorces to the layoff. Perhaps the national divorce rate is already so high that even the stress of unemployment cannot raise it; perhaps the unemployed simply can't afford divorce.

Much more research is needed on how layoffs change marriage relationships, both in the short run and in the long run. Certainly, in the short term, the job loser's spouse is often forced to work longer hours and cut household expenditures, creating a situation in which the spouse may be working harder and enjoying a lower standard of living. In the long run, preliminary research suggests that spouses who reenter the work force after a job loss tend to stay reemployed even after the layoff ends. This has implications for the independence of the spouse and the power balance in the marriage relationship.

In addition, the major research focus on spouses has been on changes in their employment situation (e.g., whether they start a job, work longer hours, etc.). We know much less than we should about the emotional, perceptual, and physiological reactions of spouses to their partners' job loss: whether they become depressed or not; whether they mirror their spouses' hopelessness or not; whether they encourage active coping behavior or not; whether they are sources of social support or not. In order to understand how the unemployed bear up under job loss, we need to understand much more about whether spouses reinforce feelings of despondency, or counteract them.

Previous research suggests that job loss may place minor children under increased risk of abuse.[18] While certainly a severe outcome of layoffs, child abuse is still, fortunately, a relatively rare one. Of more widespread interest are the lessons children might learn from their parents' layoffs and how they cope with it. Do children whose parents lose their jobs carry negative attitudes towards management into adulthood? Do they value corporate loyalty less? Do they come to view important events in their lives as out of their control? When they watch their parents react to a layoff, do they see examples of perserverance or self-pity and hopelessness? All of these questions need much further research.

Layoffs and Survivors

A research issue coming increasingly to the forefront is what happens to "survivors," those employees who are not laid off but retained. One topic that certainly needs more investigation is that of survivor productivity. Laboratory studies suggest that survivors are likely to work harder in order to escape the next round of layoffs;[19] anecdotal evidence from the field suggests that survivors lose time discussing their own reactions, speculating on whether more layoffs will be forthcoming, and often looking for new jobs of their own.[20] Empirical research in organizations where layoffs are actually occurring is sorely needed on this issue.

A more subtle set of research questions concerns the types of social, or vicarious, learning that survivors engage in. What sorts of attributions do survivors make about the organization from its layoff procedures? What types of attributions do survivors make about their own performance levels from the fact they were not laid off? Do survivors become more attached to the organization because they were spared, or less attached because they fear future layoffs? How do survivors cope with increased work loads, or loss of friends, or both? As layoffs among nonunionized white-collar workers with no seniority tradition become more and more common, corporations and academics alike need to investigate much more carefully the organizational dynamics of the workers who remain.

Long-Term Consequences of Job Loss

Lastly, much more research is needed on the long-term consequences of job loss. Most of the research on layoffs takes as its starting point the notification of layoff, and as its ending point the day of reemployment. We know very little about what happens to laid-off workers once they go back to work.

Our qualitative data suggest that although the loss of income is important to nearly all laid-off workers, layoffs may also represent much more to employees than simply a financial loss. In many ways, the layoffs represent a violation of an unstated employment contract and thus a violation of employee trust. We suspect that when laid-off workers return to work, they no longer have the same levels of organizational commitment or job involvement. It is also quite possible that layoffs have similar effects on survivors as well. Having seen the layoffs of colleagues, they, too, might conclude it is wiser to take the next good offer that comes along, since they no longer see their security with the current employer as guaranteed.

Indeed, the layoffs of middle managers over the past twenty years may have fundamentally changed commonly-held assumptions about the wisdom and utility of job involvement and organizational commitment. If organizations are no longer responsible for seeing to their employee's best interests, then employees have to learn to help themselves. If the future within an organization is uncertain, then it follows that individuals should get the most out of organizations that they can and move on. If organizations can be arbitrary or biased in letting their employees go, then employees can be cavalier in leaving their employers. The popular saying, "Let's do it to them before they do it to us," may become the appropriate credo.[21]

Methodological Issues

Our research projects, while larger in scope than many other studies of layoffs, still had some design limitations that temper the definitiveness of our results. Below we discuss several methodological issues that should receive special attention when conducting research on job loss.

Longitudinal Research

There is a critical need for more longitudinal research in the area of job loss. Not only do we need to know more about the changes that occur in individuals as they go through the experience of unemployment, but we also need to know more about the changes that occur in individuals as a consequence of unemployment (and reemployment).

Unfortunately, as we discovered, it is very difficult to obtain research sites where this type of pre-test, post-test research can be done. Management does not want to notify employees any sooner than it has to about layoffs—and it typically does not want to notify researchers early about those layoffs, either. In one case, we contacted a company whose impending layoffs had already been announced in the local press, only to have the management categorically deny any layoffs would occur; four hundred people received their pink slips that week.

Nevertheless, longitudinal research is vital in understanding many of the phenomena associated with layoffs. For examining issues such as the optimal timing of coping behavior, the nature of "mood swings" after job loss, and the long-term consequences of job loss for organizational involvement and attachment, longitudinal research is absolutely necessary.

In addition, future reseach should try to collect data from laid-off workers, their spouses and children, and "survivors" on the job simultaneously. Previous research has examined the plights of these groups of individuals separately without considering their joint interactions. A much richer picture of the consequences of layoffs could be obtained by studying all of these affected individuals together. This would be particularly useful, for instance, in exploring how the unemployed, their families, and their former co-workers influence each others' coping strategies over time.

Sampling

Even in the 1930s Depression, researchers focused most of their attention on job loss among blue-collar workers in heavy manufacturing industries. In several ways, this attention was duly warranted. Heavy manufacturing was much more central to the economy than it is today, and blue-collar workers were far and away the most likely to be laid off.

As our research suggests, however, many of the research findings with blue-collar workers are not completely generalizable to white-collar workers. There have been very few studies that have examined the differences between blue-collar and white-collar layoffs, and our research suggests that some of these differences may be substantive and substantial. Future research should include much broader samples in terms of occupational titles and geographical locations. In particular, more attention must be paid to the increasingly frequent phenomenon of white-collar layoffs. From 1980 to 1985, close to one million middle-level executives with annual salaries of over

$40,000 lost their jobs;[22] another quarter million are estimated to have been laid off between 1985 and 1990. The lessons that we take for granted from blue-collar workers should not automatically be assumed to be applicable to their white-collar counterparts.

Along similar lines, in order to determine the impact of demographic factors on reactions to job loss, much more heterogeneous samples in terms of age, gender, race, and marital status are needed. Researchers need to move away from almost exclusive reliance on white male subjects.

Measurement Issues

In our research projects, our main focus was on examining broad concepts and factors, and the relationships among them. For instance, we looked at the relationships between employee reactions and individual coping behaviors, and at the impact of corporate interventions on employee coping strategies and reemployment status. Sometimes our measures of these variables were quite broad. For coping, we measured the frequency with which employees engaged in various coping strategies, but did not obtain more detailed information about the intensity of those coping efforts. Similarly, we asked laid-off workers whether they had received any corporate assistance during unemployment, but did not collect any data about the design or the effectiveness of the interventions.

In future research on job loss, more detailed specification of variables should be employed. Now that the general theory presented here has established relationships among broad classes of variables, more careful attention should be paid to the nuances of those relationships. In particular, in terms of coping behaviors, it is important to track how employees change coping strategies over time, whether employees change where they seek social support or job leads, and whether the effectiveness of coping strategies change as unemployment lengthens. In terms of corporate interventions, much more careful analysis of outplacement programs and retraining programs is needed in particular, as there appears to be a great deal of variance in terms of their quality and their effectiveness.

Integrating Behavioral Research with Other Disciplines

Finally, much more research is needed to integrate psychologically based research on job loss with the findings of other relevant disciplines. Economic research, for example, has looked at the relationship between rapid changes in the economy and levels of mental-health disorders, but has not looked at the intervening processes—such as stress—that might explain that relationship. Conversely, behavioral research on job loss has not attended carefully to labor market conditions that make people vulnerable to layoffs, nor their impact on employee coping strategies and the availability of corporate assistance programs.

Another area where increased collaboration could be used is between behavioral research and medical research on psychosomatic illness. Job loss presents an important context in which to study the impact of acute stress on physical well-being; collaborative medical research would certainly improve the validity of research on physiological well-being beyond mere self-reports. Similar arguments could be made for integrating research on job loss with clinical research on depression and anxiety. Job loss research would be well-served by collaborative research among disciplines, and layoffs provide a particularly rich context in which to study important interdisciplinary research questions about stress.

Implications for Institutional Interventions

Although our studies focused mainly on individual reactions to job loss, some of our findings suggest additional avenues for research on the role of institutional interventions in ameliorating the effects of layoffs. Below we briefly consider the kinds of further research needed on corporate, governmental, and union initiatives.

Corporate Practices

In the past few years, corporations have engaged in a great deal of rhetoric about how much assistance they have provided laid-off workers, and how valuable that assistance has been. Our research suggests that corporate interventions have been much less available than generally claimed, that they vary a great deal in terms of quality, and that they may have much less direct impact on individuals' reemployment prospects than might be expected.

Future research in the area of corporate interventions should move beyond determining whether any assistance was provided to more detailed explorations of the type, quality, and utility of various corporate assistance practices. For instance, we need to know much more about the amount of severance pay or extended benefits (in terms of percentages of wages) needed to keep employees afloat after layoffs and how long extended benefits are typically required. We need to know much more about the types of retraining and outplacement assistance that can most benefit different groups of employees, and how those services are best delivered. We need to know much more, too, about how to manage survivors in the wake of job loss so that productivity and morale do not drop dramatically.

Another area in which further research is warranted is the process of notifying employees and implementing layoffs. From the comments of our study participants, it is clear that how the layoffs are handled has a strong influence on their feelings of anger and self-worth. There have been some interesting case studies done on how layoffs have been implemented, but much more comparative, empirical research is required. Moreover, research on these issues needs to move out of the lab and into real-life settings.

Lastly, in our research we examined corporate interventions from the perspective of how they focus the coping strategies of the unemployed and faciliate their reemployment. Our earlier comments suggest that future research should also explore how the ways layoffs are announced and implemented exacerbate or alleviate stress, and the kinds of attributions employees draw about the severity, reversibility, and externality of the layoffs from these announcement procedures.

Governmental Policies

As the debates in the late-1980s made clear, there is considerable disagreement about the role the federal government should play in layoff policies and procedures. Some people are firmly in favor of extensive governmental regulations and intervention; others are firmly opposed to any governmental regulation on the basis of principle; still others feel governmental regulation will hurt America's competitive stance in the world economy. Although our research projects did not directly address these issues, our findings do provide some relevant insights and suggest some future avenues for research.

In terms of advance notification, our research suggests that this is clearly of benefit to laid-off employees, not only in terms of their psychological well-being but also in terms of their ability to find new jobs. It is surprising that there has been very little empirical research on the impact of advance notice on management. Prior to the passage of the WARN Act, management advocates claimed that advance notice would decrease productivity, increase employee sabotage, and lead to mass resignations. The small amount of empirical research on this issue simply does not support these fears. Much more systematic investigation is needed on these issues. With the passage of time since the WARN Act, this research question should become easier to address.

Another area for future research is the termination-at-will doctrine. Where once termination of employment was clearly a management prerogative, recent court rulings suggest that the termination-at-will doctrine is eroding. These rulings will have a substantial impact on how management decides which employees, and how many employees, to lay off, and what level of justification and documentation will be needed. Because layoffs appear to have a particularly adverse impact on historically disadvantaged groups, management will also need to be much more careful about layoffs that adversely affect work groups with large numbers of women and racial minorities. Thoughtful, empirical research will be needed on these labor law issues as well.

Another fruitful area for research is the collaboration of governmental and private sector institutions in providing layoff assistance, particularly in the area of retraining activities. Anecdotal accounts and case study evidence suggest such cooperation leads to impressive results, but once again, this is a research domain where there has been little comparative work. The whole question of what local and state governments can do to help laid-off employees—either in terms of slowing down the rate of layoffs, requiring organizational restitutions, attracting new industries, or providing training—needs much more detailed investigation as well.

Last, the area of "punitive" plant closings should be subjected to careful analysis by those interested in industrial-relations issues. Like the question of advance notification, many of the participants in the debate on plant closings are largely guided by their philosophical biases rather than empirical data. Management feels plant closings are their prerogative absolutely, while employees may feel quite the opposite. Even more basic issues—such as how to determine whether a plant closing is punitive and how to determine its net potential damage—certainly deserve future study.

Union Strategies

Unions, as institutions, have received the least amount of research attention in terms of layoffs. Unions have also been portrayed by some as passive agents in layoffs. Layoffs typically result in lower union membership levels and less job security, and what research there has been on unions has focused on how unions react to these adverse conditions.

Future research needs to investigate at least five issues much more analytically: (1) how unions develop strategies for preventing layoffs; (2) how unions decide on how much to cooperate with management to avoid layoffs; (3) how unions sustain their institutional identity with an eroded membership base; (4) whether union cooperation with and concessions to management will permanently weaken the role of unions in protecting workers' rights; and (5) how union handling of layoffs builds or decreases commitment to unions in future employment contracts. Although these issues were largely outside the scope of our own research, they are nonetheless critical in examining the role of labor unions in the 1990s and beyond.

Concluding Note

We can expect the problem of layoffs to continue to be at the forefront of major economic policy debates as deindustrialization and corporate restructuring proceed apace. Our experience suggests that there are very few policymakers without strong opinions on the issues we raise here, but that careful, analytic research has not caught up with people's assumptions and philosophical biases. We hope that further research on the question of layoffs will shed as much light as heat on this important policy problem.

Notes

1. R. Lowenstein, "Still Disbelieving, A High-Flying Yuppie Tastes Unemployment," *Wall Street Journal*, 17 July 1990, pp. A1, A5.
2. Ibid.
3. H. G. Kaufman, *Professionals in Search of Work* (New York: John Wiley and Sons, 1982); S. Fineman, *White Collar Unemployment* (Chichester, England: John Wiley and Sons, 1983).
4. R. M. Cohn, "The Effect of Employment Status Change on Self-Attitudes," *Social Psychology* 41 (1978): 81–93.
5. S. C. Kobasa, "Stressful Life Events, Personality, and Health: An Inquiry into Hardiness," *Journal of Personality and Social Psychology* 37 (1979): 1–11.
6. B. S. Dohrenwend and B. P. Dohrenwend, "Some Issues in Research on Stressful Life Events," *Journal of Nervous and Mental Disease* 166 (1978): 7–15.
7. C. R. Leana and D. C. Feldman, "Individual Responses to Job Loss: Perceptions, Reactions, and Coping Behaviors," *Journal of Management* 14 (1988): 375–89.
8. R. W. White, "Strategies of Adaptation: An Attempt at Systematic Descriptions," in G. V. Coelho, D. A. Hamburg, and J. E. Adams, eds., *Coping and Adaptation*, 47–68 (New York: Basic Books, 1974); J. M. Brett, D. C. Feldman, and L. R. Weingart, "Feedback-Seeking Behavior of New Hires and Job Changers," *Journal of Management* 16 (1990): 737–749.
9. D. C. Feldman and J. M. Brett, "Coping with New Jobs: A Comparative Study of New Hires and Job Changers," *Academy of Management Journal* 26 (1983): 258–72; L. I. Pearlin and C. Schooler, "The Structure of Coping," *Journal of Health and Social Behavior* 19 (1978): 2–21.
10. R. S. DeFrank and J. M. Ivancevich, "Job Loss: An Individual Level Review and Model," *Journal of Vocational Behavior* 28 (1986): 1–20.
11. L. F. Dunn, "Measuring the Value of Community," *Journal of Urban Economics* 6 (1979): 371–82; L. D. Dyer, "Job Search Success of Middle-Aged Managers and Engineers," *Industrial and Labor Relations Review* 26 (1973): 969–79.
12. T. Jick, "As the Ax Falls: Budget Cuts and the Experience of Stress in Organizations," in T. Beehr and R. Bhagat, eds., *Human Stress and Cognition in Organizations*, 83–114 (New York: John Wiley and Sons, 1985); P. B. Warr, "A Study of Psychological Well-Being," *British Journal of Psychology* 69 (1978): 111–21; A. Zaleznick, G. W. Dalton, and L. B. Barnes, *Orientation and Conflict in Careers* (Boston: Harvard Business School Division of Research, 1970).
13. D. C. Feldman, *Managing Careers in Organizations* (Glenview, Ill.: Scott Foresman, 1988); L. P. Bradford, "Can You Survive Your Retirement?" *Harvard Business Review* 57 (1979): 103–9.

14. U. V. Manion, "Retiring Early?" *Personnel Administration* 17 (1972): 20; R. E. Barfield, *The Automobile Worker and Retirement: A Second Look* (Ann Arbor: University of Michigan Institute for Social Research, 1970); A. W. Pollman and A. C. Johnson, "Resistance to Change, Early Retirement, and Managerial Decisions," *Industrial Gerontology* 1 (1979): 33–41.

15. N. Schmitt and J. T. McCune, "The Relationship between Job Attitudes and the Decision to Retire," *Academy of Management Journal* 24 (1981): 795–802; J. W. Walker and K. F. Price, "Retirement Policy Formulation: A Systems Perspective," *Personnel Review* 5 (1976): 39–43.

16. Lowenstein, "Still Disbelieving."

17. M. Jahoda, "Economic Recession and Mental Health: Some Conceptual Issues," *Journal of Social Issues* 44 (1988): 13–23.

18. B. Justice and R. Justice, *The Abusing Family* (New York: Human Services Press, 1976).

19. J. Brockner, J. Davy, and C. Carter, "Layoffs, Self-Esteem, and Survivor Guilt: Motivational, Affective, and Attitudinal Consequences," *Organizational Behavior and Human Decision Processes* 36 (1985): 229–44.

20. A. K. Naj, "GM Now Is Plagued with Drop in Morale as Payrolls Are Cut," *Wall Street Journal*, 26 May 1987, pp. 1, 18.

21. D. C. Feldman, "The New Careerism: Origins, Tenets, and Consequences," *The Industrial Psychologist* 22 (1985): 39–44.

22. G. Russell, "Rebuilding to Survive," *Time*, 16 February 1987, pp. 44–45.

Appendix

Methodologies for Studies

Research Sites

Studies in the Monongahela Valley

The data for our studies were collected from two geographic regions. The first research site was the Monongahela Valley outside of Pittsburgh, Pennsylvania. The Monongahela Valley was home to several major steel-making facilities as well as to other heavy industrial manufacturing plants. Through the 1980s it became an area hard hit by unemployment; between 1979 and 1985 alone, the Pittsburgh–Beaver County metropolitan area lost 113,200 manufacturing jobs, 58,700 of them in basic steel. Despite the rebound in the steel industry in the early 1990s, there is widespread agreement that the vast majority of the Mon Valley layoffs are permanent and that recalls are unlikely. By 1991, many of the major steel-making facilities in the area, including the U. S. Steel Homestead works, have been, or are in the process of being, razed. The Monongahela Valley is largely made up of blue-collar communities where, prior to the steel mill closings, residents had traditionally worked for one employer most of their work lives and had been geographically stable.

Two different studies were conducted in the Monongahela Valley. The first study ("The Homestead Study") was conducted in 1986 and centered on steelworkers formerly employed in the U.S. Steel Homestead works who lost their jobs in 1985 and 1986 when that facility closed. The second study ("The Economic Development Study") was conducted in 1989 and included former steelworkers from six different steel plants in the region that had either completely closed or severely cut back operations through the early and mid-1980s.

Florida Study

The second research site was the Space Coast of Florida, which encompasses most of Brevard and Palm Bay Counties, including Titusville, Cape Canaveral, Melbourne, and Palm Bay. Brevard County, Florida, is home of the Kennedy Space Center (KSC), as well as numerous defense contractors' production facilities. After the space shuttle *Challenger* disaster in January 1986, over 2,500 technical, managerial, and clerical employees lost their jobs (1,100 in February and 1,400 in September). The local Florida economy was more robust than that of the Monongahela Valley and there was greater hope for recall, but the Space Coast workers faced a different set of challenges. In past layoffs at the Kennedy Space Center, for example, as soon as the space program became reenergized, employees left their new jobs to return to KSC; after the *Challenger*-related layoffs, employers were reluctant to hire laid-off space workers for that reason.

Samples

Homestead Study

Respondents in the Homestead Study were 198 former steelworkers who had lost their jobs over a twelve-month period because of the plant's closing. At the time of the study, 88 percent had been unemployed for a mean period of nine months. These employees were the last to be let go from the plant and thus had enjoyed substantial seniority and job stability. Their mean age was forty-seven. On the average, they had spent over twenty-five years working full time, twenty-three of those years with the same company—U.S. Steel.

Ninety-seven percent of the respondents were male; 94 percent were Caucasian. Eighty-eight percent had completed high school, with one-third reporting some post-secondary education. Eighty percent were married, and 64 percent had at least one dependent child.

Florida Study

Respondents in the Florida sample were 163 laid-off employees of the Kennedy Space Center itself or related defense contractors. Approximately 25 percent of these employees were engineers or engineering managers, 60 percent were technical support workers, and 15 percent were clerical workers. Eighty percent were still unemployed at the time of the study and had been for a mean period of four months.

The mean age of the Florida sample was thirty-eight; the sample was 59 percent male and 90 percent Caucasian. Besides being younger and having a larger representation of women, the Florida sample was also somewhat better educated than the Pittsburgh group. All respondents, except one, had graduated from high school, and two-thirds had either some college or college degrees. Seventy-four percent of the sample were married; 46 percent had children.

Economic Development Study

The study of former steelworkers conducted in 1989 consisted of a total of 2,192 participants. The average age of respondents in this study was fifty. Like the Homestead study, nearly all of the participants were male (94%), Caucasian (90%), married (75%), high school graduates (91%). Most of the respondents were long-term residents of the region (average length of residence was 34 years) and owned their own homes (69%).

Since the study was conducted several years after the closing of many of the steel facilities, most (60%) of the respondents had, by the time of the study, gained some form of new employment. Of the total respondents who were employed, two-third were employed full time. Wages and benefits in the new jobs were generally reported as being substantially lower than those in the former steel job, paying on average 40 to 60 percent less. Employed respondents also rated their new jobs as worse than their old ones on issues such as health and life insurance benefits (76%), career opportunities (69%), health and safety at work (47%), and job security (46%). Fewer than one quarter (23%) of the employed respondents were represented by a union in their new jobs; over 82 percent reported that they would like to find different jobs from the ones they currently held.

Most (79%) of the respondents who were unemployed at the time of the study were also interested in finding new jobs although many reported age (60%) and occupational (60%) discrimination in their job searches.

Procedures

In all three of the studies that provided the basis for this book, much of the data were collected through mail surveys.

Homestead Study

In the Homestead Mill sample, names and addresses of workers laid off over an eighteen-month period were obtained from a local chapter of the United Steelworkers of America union. Questionnaire packets were mailed to all individuals on this list. Each packet contained a questionnaire, a cover letter from a union officer encouraging them to complete the questionnaire, and a postage-paid envelope for returning the completed questionnaire directly to the researchers. The response rate was 40 percent. Efforts were made to gather demographic data on nonrespondents but, because the union local had recently been put into receivership, these efforts were unsuccessful. However, interviews with the local president and union officers indicated that the demographic profile of respondents was representative of remaining membership.

Florida Study

In the aftermath of the *Challenger* disaster, a placement service was set up at a local Florida community college to assist laid-off aerospace workers. The Kennedy Space Center itself and major defense contractors sent the names and addresses of employees recently laid off to the community college center. For the Florida study, the same packets used in the Pittsburgh study were mailed to the employees on these layoff lists. Instead of a letter from a union officer, the Florida packet contained a letter from a community college administrator encouraging them to participate. The response rate was 36 percent.

Economic Development Study

The third study again involved former steelworkers in the Monongahela Valley. The population lists were provided by the Steelworkers union. Questionnaire packets contained a survey, a cover letter signed by representatives from the USW, the Tri-State Conference on Steel, and the research team. The response rate was 25 percent.

Instrumentation: Homestead and Florida Studies

The Homestead Mill study and the Florida study were both conducted at approximately the same time (1986). The questionnaires in both studies were largely similar and measured the same variables in the same ways.

Job Loss Characteristics

Several characteristics of the job loss were assessed. Through questionnaire items, respondents in both studies were asked to indicate: (1) the number of months they had been out of work; (2) whether they had been laid off before; (3) whether they perceived the job loss to be temporary or permanent; (4) whether the job loss created substantial financial problems for them; (5) their perceptions of the level of unemployment in their communities; and (6) their perceptions of the level of unemployment in their jobs or professions. The last two items were measured on five-point scales with anchors ranging from (1) "very low" to (5) "very high."

Career Attachment

In the Homestead and Florida studies, two aspects of job attachment were assessed: (1) the total length of time spent in full-time employment with the company that let them go; and (2) work involvement. Work involvement was measured using Lodahl and Kejner's (1965) five-item measure with respondents indicating their level of agreement on five-point scales.[1] The internal consistency estimate (Cronbach's alpha) of the five items was .74.

Cognitive Appraisal (Perceptual Changes)

Homestead and Florida respondents' cognitive appraisal of the job loss was measured on three dimensions: (1) the degree to which the job loss was perceived as externally caused, i.e., due to circumstances outside of the individual's control; (2) the degree to which the job loss was perceived as reversible; and (3) the degree to which the job loss was perceived as mild in intensity. Two items were used to measure each dimension. Respondents were asked to indicate their level of agreement with each item on five-point scales with anchors ranging from (1) "strongly disagree" to (5) "strongly agree." Mean responses for each dimension were used to indicate respondents' perceptual reactions to the layoff.

Depressed Affect (Emotional Distress)

Many previous studies of job loss have found decreased levels of emotional arousal to be common among job losers. Symptoms include feelings such as apathy and depression.[2] Decreased arousal was measured in the Homestead and Florida studies by asking respondents to indicate the frequency with which they experienced feelings of passivity, depression, apathy, and tiredness. These were measured on four-point scales with anchors ranging from (1) "not at all" to (4) "a lot." Mean responses to the four items were used to indicate decreased arousal. The internal consistency estimate (Cronbach's alpha) for the four items was .78.

Physiological Distress

Physiological response in the form of distress was measured using Brett and Werbel's (1980) scale of psycho-physiological disorders.[3] Respondents were asked to report on the frequency with which they experienced a variety of problems, including sleeping irregularities, headaches, stomachaches, changes in weight, dizziness, rashes, coughing and colds, shortness of breath, and pounding heart. Altogether there were sixteen items, which were scored on four-point scales with anchors ranging from (1) "never" to (4) "all the time." The internal consistency estimate (Cronbach's alpha) of the sixteen items was .90.

Coping Strategies

Coping strategies were assessed by asking respondents in both the Homestead and Florida studies to indicate on four-point scales the frequency with which they had engaged in twenty types of coping behavior since becoming unemployed. The scale points ranged from (1) "not at all" to (4) "a lot." A factor analysis with varimax rotation indicated that eighteen of the twenty items loaded on six distinct types of behavior: (1) self-initiated job search activities (e.g., going to employment agencies; following up on "help wanted" notices); (2) seeking education and/or training (e.g., college courses; technical retraining); (3) investigating geographical relocation (e.g., making moving plans; looking for jobs in new locations); (4) applying for financial assistance beyond unemployment insurance (e.g., food stamps; AFDC); (5) community activism (e.g., becoming active in community efforts to assist the unemployed); and (6) seeking social support (e.g., talking to family and friends; counseling). The first three categories of coping behaviors were problem-focused or aimed at finding alternate employment (i.e., job search activities, retraining, relocation); the last three were symptom-focused or aimed at ameliorating the adverse effects of job loss (i.e., seeking financial assistance, social support, community activism). Mean responses within each category of coping strategies were used in subsequent analyses.

Life Satisfaction

Overall feelings of satisfaction were assessed using Warr's (1978) fifteen-item measure.[4] Respondents were asked to indicate on five-point scales their level of satisfaction with aspects such as family and social relationships, activities, financial standing, and accomplishments. Anchors on the scales ranged from (1) "very dissatisfied" to (5) "very satisfied." Cronbach's alpha for the fifteen items was .83.

Psychological Distress

Psychological distress was measured using the twelve-item version of Goldberg's (1972) General Health Questionnaire.[5] The GHQ is commonly used in studies of reactions to job loss. In it, respondents are asked to report on the frequency of their feelings on factors such as self-confidence, happiness, self-efficacy, and worry. Items are measured on four-point scales with anchors ranging from (1) "not at all" to (4) "much more than usual." In our studies, Cronbach's alpha for the scale was .87.

Job Reattainment

Reemployment status was measured by asking respondents to indicate whether they were currently (1) employed in a job at least as good as the one they lost, (2) employed in a job worse than the one they lost, or (3) unemployed. Approximately 85 percent of respondents were unemployed at the time they completed the surveys. They were asked to indicate their perceived prospects for future employment. Possible responses were (1) "In the near future I will obtain a job as good as the one I lost," (2) "I will obtain a job as good as the one I lost, but it will take some time," (3) "I will obtain another job but it won't be as good and it may take some time," and (4) "There is no end in sight to my unemployment."

Personality Measures

Self-esteem, internal locus of control, and Type-A behavior pattern were assessed in both the Homestead and the Florida studies. Self-esteem was measured using Rosenberg's (1965) ten-item scale.[6] Cronbach's alpha was .82 for the ten items. Internal/external locus of control was measured using Rotter's (1966) eleven-item scale with Cronbach's alpha at .66.[7] Type-A behavior pattern was measured using Friedman and Rosenman's (1974) six-item scale with Cronbach's alpha at .90.[8]

Demographic Variables and Corporate Assistance

Respondents were asked to provide demographic information on age, gender, marital status, educational level, etc. In addition, respondents were asked to report on the corporate assistance they had received prior to, or after, their layoffs. Respondents were asked to indicate the amount of advance notification given and the availability of company-sponsored outplacement programs, retraining, financial severance benefits, and extended health-care benefits.

Qualitative Data

Respondents were provided an extra sheet of paper on which to report any aspects of their job loss or their current situations they felt were not adequately addressed in the questionnaire. The number of narratives provided was rather small, constituting less than 25 percent of the total sample for both the Homestead and Florida groups. These narratives are used throughout the book to provide anecdotal accounts of the experience and effects of job loss.

Instrumentation: Economic Development Study

Quantitative Data

The primary purpose of the Economic Development Study was to compile a computerized data bank of skilled workers in the Pittsburgh region who could be employed in new jobs being created through public and private economic development projects. As such, much of the questionnaire focused on issues such as training, employment history, education, and demographics. Data were also collected on some variables more compatible with the central interests of our study, however, such as current employment status, company assistance, retraining efforts, and financial situation. These were asked in standard checklist formats for which responses could be easily quantified and compared.

Qualitative Data

In addition to this quantitative analysis, respondents were also asked to provide qualitative data. In the questionnaires, respondents were asked to write a narrative describing their layoffs, their current situation, how they coped with the job loss and/or their feelings about the job loss, and their new situation. Respondents were instructed to write about as many of these aspects as they wished and were given no limitations on the length of their responses. Nearly 70 percent provided some form of written narrative. These were content analyzed and coded according to their subject matter. They form the basis of much of the anecdotal evidence presented in this book.

Differences among the Samples

The Homestead and Florida samples differed in demographic characteristics, job loss characteristics, perceptions, attitudes and personality measures, the use of coping strategies, the level of company assistance, and adjustment measures (see Table A–1). The questions and measures in the Economic Development study were generally quite different from those of the other two. For this reason, although some demographic data from the Economic Development study has been included, comparisons presented in the table have been limited to those between the Homestead and Florida groups.

There were significant demographic differences between the Homestead and Florida samples. Specifically, the Homestead sample was significantly older, had a higher percentage of males, a lower frequency of working spouses, more children, and longer tenure in the community. Moreover, they had significantly more work experience, tenure with the company that laid them off, and time spent unemployed.

A significantly higher percentage of the Homestead sample also reported their layoffs as permanent although the Florida sample had a significantly higher percentage indicating a previous layoff. This is to be expected. In Pittsburgh there was little likelihood that the steel industry would rebound substantially; in Florida, aerospace workers had experienced layoffs in the space industry in the past. There were also significant differences between the samples in com-

TABLE A-1
Characteristics of the Samples

	Home-stead N=198	Florida N=163	t	Eco-nomic Develop-ment
Demographics				
Age	47	38	7.18[b]	50
Male %	95	59	10.20[b]	94
Caucasian %	91	90	0.79	91
Married %	80	75	1.10	75
Spouse working full time %	49	77	3.68[b]	34
Mean number of children	1.31	0.71	3.53[h]	—
Mean years in community	30	13	12.19[b]	34
Mean work experience (years)	25.68	16.08	8.68[b]	—
Job loss characteristics				
Mean time unemployed (months)	9.36	4.19	14.27[b]	—
Reporting layoff as permanent (%)	80	53	5.26[b]	—
Laid off before (%)	31	52	3.68[h]	—
Reporting "severe" financial problems (%)	30	22	1.84[a]	—
Unemployment rates				
Perceived unemployment level in community as "high" or "very high" (%)	92	59	7.39[b]	—
Perceived unemployment level in job/profession as "high" or "very high" (%)	85	49	8.13[b]	—
Job attachment				
Mean level of job involvement (7-point scale)	4.05	4.08	0.34	—
Mean experience with company (years)	23.06	4.01	21.89[b]	—
Cognitive appraisal				
$\bar{X}$ External attribution of job loss (5-point scale)	4.52	4.51	0.03	—
$\bar{X}$ Feeling of low intensity of job loss (5-point scale)	2.37	2.98	4.97[b]	—
$\bar{X}$ Feeling of reversibility of job loss (5-point scale)	2.36	3.46	8.94[b]	—

(*continued*)

	Home-stead N=198	Florida N=163	t	Economic Development
Emotional and psychological responses				
$\bar{X}$ Level of decreased arousal (4-point scale)	2.09	2.22	1.61	—
$\bar{X}$ Level of physiological distress (4-point scale)	1.57	1.61	0.85	—
Personality				
$\bar{X}$ Level of self-esteem (7-point scale)	5.46	5.54	0.83	—
$\bar{X}$ Internal locus of control (7-point scale)	4.41	4.58	1.83	—
$\bar{X}$ Level of Type-A behavior pattern (5-point scales)	2.11	2.12	0.20	—
Coping strategies (4-point scales)				
$\bar{X}$ Job search activity	2.27	2.76	5.34[b]	—
$\bar{X}$ Seeking training	1.65	1.47	2.10[a]	—
$\bar{X}$ Seeking relocation	1.27	1.65	5.93[b]	—
$\bar{X}$ Seeking social support	2.59	2.69	1.17	—
$\bar{X}$ Seeking financial assistance	1.17	1.08	2.43[a]	—
$\bar{X}$ Community activism	1.44	1.44	0.01	—
Company interventions				
Receiving ≤ 1-week notice (%)	74	27	6.34[b]	—
Receiving company outplacement assistance (%)	11	33	0.70	—
Receiving severance pay (%)	16	64	3.62[b]	—
Receiving extended benefits (%)	42	23	3.02[b]	—
Adjustment				
$\bar{X}$ Level of satisfaction (5-point scale)	3.37	3.42	0.58	—
Still unemployed (%)	88	80	3.27[b]	40
Felt they would find comparable new job (%)	14	70	11.09[b]	—

[a] $p < .05$.
[b] $p < .01$.

pany practices regarding layoffs. The Florida sample reported significantly more advance notification and a higher incidence of severance pay. The Homestead sample reported a significantly higher incidence of extended benefits, probably due to union contractual agreements with the company.

The Florida sample reported significantly greater optimism in prospects for finding comparable new jobs and lower perceptions of unemployment rates in their communities and professions. The Florida respondents also reported perceptions of the job loss as significantly less intense and more reversible than the Pittsburgh sample did. This again is to be expected given their expectations regarding the probability of being called back to work.

Concerning coping, respondents in the Homestead sample reported higher mean levels of effort directed toward seeking retraining and financial assistance. The Florida sample reported significantly more effort directed toward job search and relocation activities.

Quantitative Analyses of Data From Homestead and Florida Samples

Table A–2 shows the results of analyses of variance of the effects of job loss characteristics, financial distress, attachment to the previous job, and unemployment levels on respondents' perceptual, emotional, and psychological reactions to job loss. The analyses split the Homestead and Florida samples. The results of these analyses are discussed and displayed graphically in chapter 3.

Table A–3 shows the results of multiple regression analyses of predictors of individual coping strategies in both the Homestead and Florida samples. Perceptions of the job loss (external attribution, low intensity, reversibility), emotional reactions (depressed affect), physiological reactions (distress), personality measures (Type-A behavior pattern, locus of control, self-esteem), and company interventions (advance notice, outplacement, severance pay, extended benefits) were simultaneously entered in the analysis for each sample as predictors of the six coping strategies described in chapter 4. The results of these analyses are discussed in chapters 3, 4, and 5.

Table A–4 shows the results of multiple regression analyses of

TABLE A-2.
Reactions to Job Loss

	n	External attribution			Perceptual reactions low intensity			Reversibility			Emotional reaction			Physiological reaction		
		$\bar{x}$	SD	F	$\bar{x}$	SD	F	$\bar{x}$	SD	F	$\bar{x}$	SD	F	$\bar{x}$	SD	F
Homestead sample																
Job loss characteristics																
Months out of work																
1–3	31	4.26	.92	2.40	2.13	.93	1.19	2.81	1.08	2.99*	2.31	.67	3.26*	1.72	.61	2.19
4–6	52	4.41	.77		2.42	.93		2.75	1.01		2.24	.70		1.67	.49	
7–9	63	4.69	.67		2.34	1.07		2.43	1.00		1.90	.75		1.49	.42	
10–12	52	4.45	.88		2.55	1.03		2.26	.96		2.17	.79		1.56	.47	
Laid off before																
No	127	4.49	.80	1.09	2.46	1.00	1.04	2.52	1.01	1.10	2.07	.73	1.23	1.52	.45	1.40
Yes	69	4.48	.83		2.25	1.02		2.55	1.06		2.21	.79		1.71	.54	
Status of layoff																
Temporary	37	4.59	.67	1.31	2.61	1.11	1.24	2.53	1.04	1.11	1.81	.58	3.08**	1.49	.44	1.23
Permanent	133	4.52	.76		2.39	.99		2.47	.99		2.15	.75		1.59	.49	
Financial problems																
No	123	4.55	.70	1.43	2.77	.91	1.57*	2.46	1.01	1.08	2.00	.73	3.45**	1.49	.42	1.69**
Yes	66	4.46	.84		1.61	.73		2.70	1.05		2.37	.74		1.81	.54	
Job attachment																
Job involvement:																
Moderate	66	4.30	.88	3.06*	2.73	1.03	8.06**	2.67	1.01	3.66*	1.97	.63	3.41*	1.54	.46	3.62*
Somewhat high	55	4.51	.81		2.40	1.00		2.71	.95		2.07	.66		1.50	.41	
High	73	4.63	.72		2.07	.91		2.28	1.06		2.30	.89		1.72	.57	
Years in job																
Under 5	31	4.11	1.17	3.08*	2.21	1.07	0.78	2.84	1.05	2.58*	2.41	.81	3.47*	1.74	.55	2.15
5–10	47	4.46	.72		2.28	.90		2.72	.89		2.18	.64		1.64	.46	
10–20	54	4.59	.65		2.47	.98		2.43	1.03		2.17	.71		1.60	.47	
Over 20	66	4.60	.72		2.47	1.07		2.33	1.05		1.92	.79		1.49	.49	
Perceptions of unemployment rate																
In community																
Low to moderate	20	4.28	.92	0.99	2.90	1.03	4.79**	3.15	1.04	5.54**	2.30	.66	0.61	1.55	.41	0.75
High	62	4.54	.67		2.51	.94		2.62	.95		2.09	.74		1.54	.47	
Very High	111	4.52	.79		2.22	.99		2.37	1.01		2.15	.77		1.63	.52	
In occupation																
Low to moderate	52	4.35	.95	1.10	2.30	1.02	0.25	2.90	1.05	5.43**	2.47	.78	12.35**	1.76	.61	4.96**
High	46	4.52	.64		2.40	.96		2.51	.83		2.28	.61		1.61	.42	
Very high	97	4.55	.79		2.24	1.02		2.34	1.04		1.91	.72		1.50	.44	

Florida sample

Job loss characteristics	n	M	SD	F	M	SD	F	M	SD	F	M	SD	F	M	SD	F
Months out of work				0.45			.63			0.19			0.39			0.49
1–3	56	4.55	.91		2.92	1.03		3.45	1.10		2.16	.66		1.59	.45	
4–6	74	4.49	.85		2.98	1.23		3.52	1.23		2.25	.76		1.58	.44	
7–9	7	4.14	1.49		2.36	1.10		3.33	1.25		2.39	.85		1.72	.53	
10–12	11	4.46	.91		2.91	1.32		3.27	1.10		2.14	.66		1.72	.62	
Laid off before				1.47			1.10			1.17			1.04			1.26
No	76	4.59	.81		2.95	1.12		3.45	1.21		2.20	.72		1.56	.43	
Yes	82	4.42	.98		2.90	1.17		3.48	1.12		2.22	.71		1.63	.49	
Status of layoff				1.38			1.58*			1.11			1.06			1.13
Temporary	64	4.66	.79		3.03	1.31		3.54	1.19		2.19	.72		1.57	.47	
Permanent	80	4.41	.93		2.91	1.04		3.44	1.13		2.27	.69		1.64	.44	
Financial problems				1.29			2.69**			1.36			1.12			1.98**
No	119	4.51	.87		3.30	1.02		3.55	1.10		2.08	.67		1.49	.39	
Yes	35	4.54	.98		1.71	.62		3.09	1.28		2.55	.71		1.91	.54	
Job attachment																
Job involvement				11.57**			5.49**			4.93**			0.34			1.70
Moderate	56	4.33	1.02		3.24	1.00		3.61	1.19		2.14	.62		1.51	.38	
Somewhat high	39	4.63	.79		3.03	1.19		3.78	1.02		2.25	.71		1.63	.49	
High	62	4.57	.86		2.57	1.16		3.11	1.04		2.23	.80		1.66	.51	
Years in job				0.58			0.15			1.14			2.83*			1.50
Under 5	69	4.53	.88		2.97	1.15		3.65	1.06		2.30	.68		1.64	.45	
5–10	43	4.37	1.09		2.94	1.06		3.28	1.11		2.29	.70		1.66	.47	
10–20	25	4.64	.70		2.80	1.42		3.38	1.34		2.10	.65		1.56	.51	
Over 20	17	4.38	.86		2.91	1.03		3.29	1.34		1.81	.81		1.41	.44	
Perceptions of unemployment rates																
In community				0.09			6.10**			4.29*			2.37			6.65**
Low to moderate	63	4.48	.83		3.22	1.11		3.79	1.04		2.13	.69		1.49	.40	
High	54	4.49	.99		3.01	1.06		3.32	1.11		2.13	.71		1.58	.46	
Very high	37	4.55	.93		2.42	1.15		3.16	1.36		2.42	.76		1.82	.52	
In occupation				4.48**			1.13			1.35			1.36			3.27*
Low to moderate	83	4.33	1.02		3.02	1.10		3.56	1.05		2.13	.71		1.52	.44	
High	43	4.70	.60		2.95	1.24		3.47	1.18		2.34	.77		1.69	.50	
Very high	28	4.79	.55		2.55	1.06		3.14	1.41		2.26	.69		1.73	.45	

* $p < .05$.
** $p < .01$.

Multiple Regression Analyses of the Effects of Individual Characteristics and Company Interventions on the Use of Coping Strategies

| | Problem-focused coping | | | | | | | | |
| | Job search | | | Retraining | | | Relocation | | |
	Beta	$R^2\Delta$	F	Beta	$R^2\Delta$	F	Beta	$R^2\Delta$	F
Homestead sample									
Cognitive appraisal									
External attribution	.07	.00	0.78	−.09	.01	1.45	−.05	.00	0.35
Low intensity	−.29	.06	10.87**	−.12	.01	1.75	.03	.00	0.09
Reversible	.21	.04	7.24**	.23	.05	8.95**	.05	.00	0.36
Depressed affect	−.11	.00	0.91	.11	.00	0.75	−.13	.01	0.99
Physiological distress	.16	.01	2.19	.05	.00	0.22	.09	.00	0.60
Personality									
Type A	−.08	.00	0.37	−.17	.01	1.61	.09	.00	0.40
Self-esteem	−.07	.00	0.62	−.01	.00	0.01	−.01	.00	0.01
Internal locus of control	.01	.00	0.01	−.04	.00	0.25	−.06	.00	0.47
Company interventions									
Advance notice	−.01	.00	0.04	−.01	.00	0.01	−.19	.03	5.40*
Outplacement	.22	.00	0.92	.81	.07	11.51**	−.46	.02	3.43
Severance pay	.05	.00	0.06	−.64	.05	8.99**	.32	.01	2.02
Extended benefits	−.11	.00	0.56	−.19	.01	1.50	.12	.00	0.54
Florida sample									
Cognitive appraisal									
External attribution	−.10	.00	1.27	.13	.01	1.91	.04	.00	0.26
Low intensity	−.14	.01	1.95	−.02	.00	0.03	−.24	.04	6.57*
Reversible	.07	.00	0.53	.05	.00	0.30	.20	.03	5.07*
Depressed affect	−.01	.00	0.00	−.24	.02	3.39	−.09	.00	0.55
Physiological distress	−.11	.00	0.57	.16	.00	1.04	−.25	.02	3.08
Personality									
Type A	.19	.01	1.49	.19	.01	1.61	.48	.07	11.64**
Self-esteem	−.14	.01	1.63	−.02	.00	0.03	.02	.00	0.06
Internal locus of control	−.03	.00	0.10	.05	.00	0.29	−.05	.00	0.00
Company interventions									
Advance notice	−.02	.00	0.07	−.05	.00	0.39	.08	.01	0.84
Outplacement	.05	.00	0.32	.41	.01	2.36	.27	.06	9.86**
Severance pay	.11	.01	1.49	−.14	.01	2.74	.05	.00	0.40
Extended benefits	−.04	.00	0.15	.08	.00	0.83	−.12	.01	1.87

| Symptom-focused coping | | | | | | | | |
| Financial assistance | | | Social support | | | Community activism | | |
Beta	$R^2\Delta$	F	Beta	$R^2\Delta$	F	Beta	$R^2\Delta$	F
−.15	.02	4.16*	−.12	.01	2.23	−.09	.01	1.47
.08	.02	3.18	−.23	.04	6.52**	−.07	.00	0.65
−.16	.00	1.11	−.07	.01	0.84	.07	.00	0.83
.06	.00	0.22	−.03	.00	0.05	−.11	.00	0.76
.01	.00	0.00	.09	.00	0.67	.02	.00	0.04
.27	.02	4.46*	−.03	.00	0.04	.17	.01	1.61
.06	.00	0.48	.06	.00	0.38	−.05	.00	0.38
−.11	.01	1.81	−.04	.00	0.27	−.06	.00	0.46
−.02	.00	0.04	.12	.01	1.99	.07	.00	0.65
.36	.01	2.38	.07	.00	0.07	.73	.05	9.27**
.11	.00	0.26	−.16	.00	0.53	−.29	.01	1.83
−.37	.03	6.06*	.14	.00	0.71	−.45	.05	8.43**
−.09	.01	1.01	.08	.01	0.83	−.03	.00	0.10
−.19	.03	4.06*	.19	.03	3.78*	.15	.00	0.49
−.17	.02	3.38	−.09	.01	0.88	.15	.00	2.36
−.15	.01	1.56	.05	.00	0.16	−.27	.03	1.23*
.14	.01	0.91	.11	.00	0.49	−.03	.00	0.03
.16	.01	1.14	−.02	.00	0.02	.28	.02	3.55
.07	.00	0.41	.20	.02	3.43	−.21	.03	4.06*
.07	.00	0.70	−.21	.03	5.04*	−.04	.00	0.15
.02	.00	0.06	−.13	.02	2.29	−.04	.00	0.22
−.09	.01	1.18	.09	.01	1.08	−.08	.01	0.75
.01	.00	0.00	.08	.01	0.90	−.06	.00	0.45
.01	.00	0.00	.11	.00	0.02	−.08	.00	0.72

*p < .05
**p < .01

Multiple Regression Analyses of the Effects of Coping Strategies, Demographic Characteristics, and Company Interventions on Attitudinal and Behavioral Adjustment to Job Loss

	Satisfaction		
	Beta	$R^2\Delta$	F
Homestead sample			
Coping strategies			
Job search	−.10	.00	1.31
Retraining	.19	.03	4.25*
Relocation	−.11	.01	1.43
Financial assistance	−.14	.02	2.57
Social support	.01	.00	0.02
Community activism	−.02	.00	0.02
Demographics			
Age	.05	.00	0.26
Education	−.12	.01	1.91
Gender[a]	—	—	—
Company intervention			
Advance notice	.03	.00	0.11
Outplacement	−.14	.00	0.28
Severance pay	.14	.00	0.33
Extended benefits	.01	.00	0.00
Florida sample			
Coping strategies			
Job search	−.26	.05	8.35**
Retraining	.00	.00	0.00
Relocation	.12	.01	1.63
Financial assistance	−.19	.03	5.69*
Social support	.15	.02	3.69*
Community activism	−.27	.06	10.90**
Demographics			
Age	.08	.00	0.86
Education	.14	.02	2.74
Gender	−.06	.00	0.44
Company interventions			
Advance notice	.03	.00	0.11
Outplacement	−.12	.00	1.29
Severance pay	.10	.01	2.00
Extended benefits	−.15	.02	3.31

Re-employment status			Prospects for re-employment		
Beta	$R^2\Delta$	F	Beta	$R^2\Delta$	F
−.08	.01	0.81	−.12	.01	2.54
−.03	.00	0.75	.33	.07	15.43**
.02	.00	0.82	−.14	.02	3.27
.06	.00	0.54	.04	.00	0.17
−.17	.02	3.64*	−.02	.00	0.09
.11	.00	1.20	.04	.00	0.13
.06	.00	0.33	−.35	.07	15.49**
.00	.00	0.08	.08	.00	0.75
—	—	—	—	—	—
.00	.00	0.00	−.06	.00	0.48
.07	.00	0.07	−.03	.00	0.03
−.33	.01	1.73	−.04	.00	0.05
.26	.01	2.14	.16	.00	1.06
−.19	.02	3.60	−.12	.01	0.95
.06	.00	0.46	.08	.00	0.58
.29	.06	8.84**	.12	.01	0.96
−.03	.00	0.15	.04	.00	0.12
.11	.01	1.62	.08	.01	0.72
−.23	.05	7.28*	.05	.00	0.16
−.07	.00	0.71	−.13	.01	1.34
.11	.01	1.51	−.05	.00	0.21
−.03	.00	0.08	−.10	.00	0.74
−.10	.01	1.24	.02	.00	0.03
.00	.00	0.00	−.04	.00	0.10
.12	.01	1.77	−.08	.00	0.50
−.03	.00	0.09	.10	.01	0.78

[a]97% male.
* $p < .05$
** $p < .01$

the effects of coping strategies, demographic characteristics, and company interventions on respondents' satisfaction, re-employment status, and perceived prospects for re-employment. Again, the Homestead and Florida samples are split. These results are discussed in chapters 4 and 5.

Notes

1. T. M. Lodahl and M. Kejner, "The Definition and Measurement of Job Involement," *Journal of Applied Psychology* 49 (1965): 24–33.
2. P. B. Warr, *Work, Unemployment, and Mental Health* (London: Oxford University Press, 1987).
3. J. M. Brett and J. Werbel, *The Effect of Job Transfer on Employees and Their Families* (Washington, D.C.: Employee Relocation Council, 1980).
4. P. B. Warr, "A Study of Psychological Well-Being," *British Journal of Psychology* 69 (1978): 111–12.
5. P. Goldberg, *The Detection of Psychiatric Illness by Questionnaire* (London: Oxford University Press, 1972).
6. M. Rosenberg, *Society and Adolescent Self-Image* (Princeton: Princeton University Press, 1966).
7. J. B. Rotter, "Some problems and misconceptions related to the construct of internal vs. external control of reinforcement." *Journal of Consulting and Clinical Psychology* 43 (1975): 56–67.
8. M. Friedman, and R. H. Rosenman, *Type A Behavior and Your Heart* (New York: Knopf, 1974).

Acknowledgments

This book, and the research studies that comprise it, truly represent a collaborative project. We began the research studies of job loss when we were both on the faculty of the University of Florida. There we received financial support to begin what was to become a long term research partnership. Since that time, the University of Pittsburgh and the University of South Carolina have also provided release time and financial assistance to enable us to complete our studies.

We could not have carried out the research without the help of many people from the unions, government agencies, and community groups that deal with the daily problems of the unemployed. In Florida, Anita Moore of Brevard County Community College provided us with a way to reach people on the "Space Coast" who lost their jobs after the explosion of the *Challenger*.

In Pittsburgh, we worked with many different organizations. The United Steelworkers of America provided partial funding for one of our research studies and helped us contact former members who lost their jobs. Andrew "Lefty" Palm, Gary Hubbard, and J. T. Smith were particularly helpful in conducting the Economic Development Employment Survey. Chuck Martoni and Kevin Smay of the Community College of Allegheny County also assisted in data collection. Officers of the former 1397 USWA Local helped us get the Homestead study underway. We are also indebted to the United Electrical, Radio and Machine Workers Union, especially to Amy Newell and to the officers of the 610 Local. We have worked for many years with the Tri-State Conference On Steel and the Steel Valley Authority. There, Jay Weinberg, Judy Ruszkowski, Tom Croft, Jim Benn, and Annemarie Draham were especially helpful and generous with their time and effort.

We would also like to acknowledge the many people at Lexington

Books and the Free Press who assisted us. Beth Anderson at Lexington was especially helpful. As editors of the series, Ben Schneider and Art Brief read every page of the manuscript and pushed us to make it more accessible and polished.

David Goldman also read the manuscript carefully and critically. We benefited from his insights, as well as from his encouragement and good cheer.

Finally, we wish to thank the many, many people who participated in our research studies. Our survey instruments were often quite long and our interviews quite demanding. We asked people to reveal intimate aspects of their lives so that we might understand and document the consequences of job loss. They did so generously, and we thank them for the insights they provided and enabled us to pass on through this book.

Carrie Leana
Pittsburgh, Pennsylvania

Daniel Feldman
Columbia, South Carolina

Index